RED APPLE

RED APPLE
COMMUNISM AND McCARTHYISM
IN COLD WAR NEW YORK

PHILLIP DEERY

Empire State Editions
An imprint of Fordham University Press
New York 2014

Library of Congress Cataloging-in-Publication Data

Deery, Phillip.
    Red apple : communism and McCarthyism in cold war New York / Phillip
Deery.
        pages cm
    Includes bibliographical references and index.
    ISBN 978-0-8232-5368-5 (hardback)
    1. Anti-communist movements—New York (State)—New York—History—
20th century.   2. Political persecution—New York (State)—New York—
History—20th century.   3. Anti-communist movements—United States—
History—20th century.   4. Political persecution—United States—History—
20th century.   5. Joint Anti-Fascist Refugee Committee.   6. United States.
Congress. House. Committee on Un-American Activities.   7. New York
(N.Y.)—History—20th century.   I. Title.
    E743.5.D374 2014
    974.7'043—dc23
                                                                              2013032064

Printed in the United States of America
16 15 14   5 4 3 2 1
First edition

For my sons, David and Michael

Contents

Abbreviations

AAUP	American Association of University Professors
AIF	Americans for Intellectual Freedom
ALP	American Labor Party
COINTELPRO	Counterintelligence Program
Cominform	Communist Information Bureau
CPSU	Communist Party of the Soviet Union
CPUSA	Communist Party of the United States of America
FBI	Federal Bureau of Investigation
FO	Foreign Office (Great Britain)
FOIA	Freedom of Information Act
HUAC	House Committee on Un-American Activities
IIA	International Information Administration
INS	Immigration and Naturalization Service
JAFRC	Joint Anti-Fascist Refugee Committee
MLA	Modern Language Association
NCASP	National Council of the Arts, Sciences and Professions
NYU	New York University
OWI	Office of War Information
PIC	Peace Information Center
SACB	Subversive Activities Control Board
TOPLEV	Top Level Informants Program
USIS	United States Information Service
VOA	Voice of America

Acknowledgments

This book would not have been possible without the generous assistance of numerous archivists and librarians in Australia, Great Britain, and the United States. I wish to pay special tribute to Mark Armstrong-Roper, Radical Collection, Victoria University; Donna Brandolisio, Manuscript Librarian, University of Pennsylvania; Nancy Cricco, University Archivist, New York University; and the wonderful staff at the Tamiment Library and Robert F. Wagner Labor Archives at New York University. In particular, I am especially indebted to the late Michael Nash, director of the Tamiment, for his knowledge, assistance, and friendship. I am also grateful to Victoria University, which granted me research leave, and the Frederick Ewen Academic Freedom Center at New York University, which granted me a Fellowship. I wish to thank Taylor & Francis for permission to reproduce some of the research that first appeared in issues of *American Communist History*. Fordham University Press has been a pleasure to work with, and I am indebted to Fredric Nachbaur, Will Cerbone, and Eric Newman. I also wish to thank the following, who have contributed to this book in different ways: Rachel Ben-Avi Fast, Doug Burgum, Zuzanna Kobrzynski, Mario Del Pero, Dan Leab, Emily and William Leider, Lawrence Maher, John Rossi, Ellen Schrecker, Bob Swacker, and Marilyn Young. My deepest debt, however, is to Julie Kimber, who read the entire manuscript, made valuable scholarly criticisms, and provided unstinting love and support.

RED APPLE

Introduction

On November 13, 1950, a fifty-six-year-old woman waved goodbye to a handful of supporters, surrendered to the custody of a U.S. marshal, and was committed to the District of Columbia jail in Washington. She was then incarcerated at the Federal Reformatory for Women in Alderston, West Virginia, for a period of three months. Helen Reid Bryan was a Quaker. In her lowly paid role as administrative secretary in an organization deemed "subversive," she had refused, as a matter of principle, to hand over the organization's records to the House Committee on Un-American Activities. This was her crime. Eight years later, while working for a small Congregational church in Vermont, Helen Bryan was once again investigated by Federal Bureau of Investigation officers. They concluded that, for twenty years, the Bureau had gotten it wrong: she had never been a member of the Communist Party.

This is a book about McCarthyism: a phenomenon that, for at least a decade, disfigured the American political landscape. It is a book about the effects of McCarthyism, not its origins. In particular, it focuses on the impact of the prevailing climate of intolerance and repression on the lives of people, such as Helen Bryan. Upon the altar of anticommunism, domestic Cold War crusaders undermined civil liberties, curtailed equality before the law, and tarnished the ideals of American democracy. In order to preserve freedom, they thought, it was necessary to jettison some of its tenets. Crushing domestic dissent from the late 1940s through the 1950s was a vast bureaucratic undertaking. Congressional committees worked in tandem, although not necessarily in collusion, with the FBI, law firms,

1

university administrations, publishing houses, television networks and movie studios, and a legion of government agencies at the federal, state, and local levels. This book focuses on both the persecutors and the persecuted. Of the latter, it examines people from occupationally disparate backgrounds: medicine, law, education, music, and literature. The lives of all were irrevocably altered by their encounters with McCarthyism. Three were jailed and saw their careers derailed. Another took the Fifth Amendment and lost his job. Yet another shifted to the right and was called a "rat." And a Russian who came to New York lost his bearings and, later, feared for his life.

It is easy to overlook the human consequences of the Cold War because the injection of the personal—the "subjective"—into the political is difficult. This study seeks to restore dimensions of personal identity and lived experience to our understanding of the domestic Cold War. The more general analyses of McCarthyism—notably David Caute's *The Great Fear* (1978), Richard Fried's *Nightmare in Red* (1990), Ted Morgan's *Reds* (2003), David Oshinsky's *A Conspiracy So Immense* (1983), and Ellen Schrecker's *Many Are the Crimes* (1998)—are necessarily less concerned with this aim. My focus on individuals silhouettes more directly the corrosive effects of domestic anticommunism and examines, close up, the processes of political repression and the consequences of political activism. I have used the common connection with an overlooked organization, the Joint Anti-Fascist Refugee Committee, and a pivotal event, the Waldorf conference, as the platform for examining the Cold War experiences of six people.

The setting of the book, New York City, is more than a mere geographical backdrop. It is now a truism to state, as E. B. White did in 1949 after the wartime devastation of European cities, that New York was "the capital of the world."[1] Within the United States, New York's political, social, economic, and demographic character and development were distinctive; it deviated from national norms. However, we are not concerned here with the global importance or cultural power or cosmopolitanism of New York. What *is* relevant is its politics. The city became a crucible in which the politics of the Cold War was fought with bitterness and intensity. Huge political gatherings, for example, of both pro- and anticommunists regularly amassed in Madison Square Garden and Union Square, or outside the courthouse in Foley Square. What follows is a brief consideration of political activists: anti-Stalinists, communists, and liberals.

New York was home to that unique but disparate group of political activists, commonly known as "the New York intellectuals," who clustered at different times around periodicals such as *Partisan Review, Politics,* and *Commentary*. In the postwar period, especially after the resignation of Dwight Macdonald in 1943, the previously socialist-inclined *Partisan Review*—and it would not be unfair to categorize many of its contributors and editorial staff as literary Trotskyists—shifted to the right and embraced an anti-Stalinist liberalism that was highly compatible with Cold War anticommunism. Indicative was what one adherent, Sidney Hook, termed a "task of purification": a call to arms for a progressive alliance against the influence of communism.[2] This call was realized with the formation in New York of the American Committee for Cultural Freedom in 1951. That committee had its genesis two years earlier, when 20,000 New Yorkers crowded into Madison Square Garden in 1949 to hear procommunist speakers sponsored by the Cultural and Scientific Conference for World Peace (popularly known as the Waldorf conference). Five of these New York intellectuals—Mary McCarthy, Dwight Macdonald, Nicolas Nabokov, Arthur Schlesinger Jr., and, most notably, Sidney Hook—played a key role in challenging the legitimacy and efficacy of that conference.

By 1955, the number of card-carrying communists in New York had shrunk to 10,626.[3] Yet this far exceeded that of any other city. Such was New York's strong tradition of dissent that it was the sole American city to elect communists to office. One was the African American Benjamin Davis Jr., who represented Harlem on the City Council from 1943 to 1949. New York was, in fact, the epicenter of the Communist Party of the United States of America (CPUSA), and the reactions of New York communists profoundly affected the fortunes of the party. In the wake of Nikita Khrushchev's revelations about Stalin's crimes, the number of party defectors (of whom Howard Fast was one) in New York was disproportionately far greater than elsewhere. In mid-1957, only 3,500 remained. One reason was the high percentage of Jews in the CPUSA— about 50 percent—who were especially affronted by the party leadership's failure to condemn the stark evidence of Soviet anti-Semitism. The communist magazine *Jewish Life* and the Yiddish communist daily *Morgen Freiheit*, located in the same Lower Manhattan building as the *Daily Worker* (whose staff, including the editor, John Gates, born Solomon Regenstreif, was predominantly Jewish) were all based in New York.

Anticommunist crusaders believed that the American Communist Party was "like an iceberg. . . . [O]nly a small part can be seen, [and] the bulk is beneath the surface,"[4] but by the early 1950s, it resembled a sect, not an iceberg. It was diminished, isolated, and on the defensive, its all-important connections with the labor movement severed, its front activity muzzled, its animating presence in alternative political and cultural organizations purged, and even its spy rings long shut down. The party's leadership, based mainly in New York, was a battered remnant of its former state. Prosecutions under the Smith Act in 1949, the decision to go underground in 1951, and the party's own doctrinaire sectarianism saw to that. Largely hidden from view was that pervading sense of fear and anxiety—associated with the advent of McCarthyism—which was experienced privately and silently by a great many rank-and-file party members. Which organizations would next be targeted? Who would next be subpoenaed to appear before an investigatory committee? And which trusted comrade would next transmogrify into a prosecution witness? Although it is arguable that the New York community of communists was sufficiently large for its members to draw inner strength from one another and thereby fortify themselves against the hostile world in which they were political pariahs, the extent of FBI penetration of their ranks created mistrust and suspicion. Friendships were poisoned, marriages broken, and, with widespread blacklisting, employment patterns altered. The ways in which careers in particular were destroyed or stymied is one of the concerns of this book.

If New York was home to the largest concentration of communists in the United States, it was also a bastion, and had long been so, of left-wing liberalism. Indicative was the fact that of the 1.1 million votes Henry A. Wallace secured in his 1948 presidential bid, nearly half a million came from New York state. His Progressive Party ran on the ballot line of the small, left-wing New York–based American Labor Party (ALP), led by Congressman Vito Marcantonio. Many of the New Yorkers who re-elected Marcantonio in 1948 or voted for W. E. B. Du Bois in 1950 when he ran for the U.S. Senate on the ALP ticket would, presumably, have read one, or several, of the politically progressive papers that were distinctive to New York, such as *Daily Compass*, *Nation*, or *PM*. In the 1950s, there would be *I. F. Stone's Weekly* and Irving Howe's *Dissent*. Although the left was besieged during the age of McCarthyism, it was never silenced.

The events and experiences described in this book did not, of course, take place in a historical vacuum. In the postwar years, the political climate in the United States was fundamentally transformed. This resulted from several international developments that saw the wartime alliance with the Soviet Union, symbolized by the Yalta conference, replaced by a continuation of prewar hostility. They included Churchill's "Iron Curtain" speech in Fulton, Missouri, in March 1946, which warned of the extension of Soviet control in eastern Europe; the civil war in Greece, which precipitated President Harry S Truman's doctrine of "containment" of communism in March 1947; the promulgation by the Communist Information Bureau (Cominform) of the "two-camp" thesis in October 1947, which underscored the irreconcilability between East and West; the Soviet-engineered *coup d'état* in Prague in February 1948, which demonstrated that a conspiratorial minority could overturn a stable democracy; the Italian elections of April 1948, which witnessed significant involvement by the Central Intelligence Agency, ensuring the defeat of the frontrunner, the Italian Communist Party; and the imposition of a Soviet blockade of the western sector of Berlin in June 1948, which lasted for another eleven months and brought the Cold War to a flashpoint. By now the bolts of the Iron Curtain had been securely fastened. Despite the tenuous success of "containment" in Europe, American fears about communist global domination continued to escalate.

Those fears intensified in 1949. The success of Mao Zedong's Red Army over the Chinese Nationalist government in the late summer of 1949 diverted attention from Europe to Asia. A monolithic concept of communism was central to Cold War ideology, so Mao's victory became a victory for the Kremlin, whose long-term strategy of world conquest, seemingly, had taken a new and threatening direction. The disquiet of 1947 became the panic of 1949. The explosion of a Soviet atom bomb—President Truman announced this news just two days after the People's Republic of China was officially proclaimed—sent shock waves through America. It reordered America's worldview. And it banished any lingering sense of omnipotence. In the event of World War III, which now seemed imminent and inevitable, the United States would be pitted against a possible military equal. With this realization polarization became complete, and anticommunism, abroad and at home, became obsessive.

The transformative impact of the international Cold War on the domestic landscape, even before Joseph McCarthy's dramatic entrance in February 1950, was profound. Truman's Democratic administration began to take steps to ensure that Republican charges of being "soft on communism" would not stick. The President followed Senator Arthur Vandenberg's advice in 1947 to "scare the hell out of the American people" and initiated a wide range of measures to demonstrate his administration's commitment to meeting the communist menace. A vast loyalty–security program was inaugurated; the Attorney General's List of Subversive Organizations was established; Henry Wallace's Progressive Party was excoriated; and twelve Communist Party leaders were arrested, tried, and imprisoned under the first of the Smith Act trials. The permanent House of Representatives Committee on Un-American Activities (HUAC, for the colloquial "House Un-American Activities Committee"), meanwhile, was in hot pursuit of, among others, the Joint Anti-Fascist Refugee Committee, the Hollywood Ten, and Alger Hiss. (Many of the hearings, and the protests against them, were at Foley Square, in Lower Manhattan.) An array of private groups, organizations, and institutions—for anticommunists were a diverse lot, both ideologically and demographically—joined the swelling tide of government-sponsored activity and, together, engulfed the political culture with a virulent strain of bigotry and intolerance toward leftists and nonconformists. Activists were silenced, intellectual debate was circumscribed, and the legitimacy of radical ideas was discredited or suppressed.

The threat of espionage fueled the mobilization of the anticommunist cause. The defection of Igor Gouzenko, a Soviet cipher clerk, in Ottawa in 1945 sparked a chain reaction culminating in the jailing of British and Canadian scientists who had passed atomic secrets to the Soviet Union. The FBI, assisted by the "Venona" code-breaking operation, arrested Julius Rosenberg in July 1950, just six months after the conviction of Alger Hiss, a former State Department official, and twelve months after the arrest of Judith Coplon on espionage charges. The FBI's Soviet Espionage division in New York was convinced that the Soviet Consulate on East 61st Street conducted espionage operations overseen by the consul general, Pavel Mikhailov, and closely monitored the movements and activities of Soviet diplomats. The search for spies paralleled the hunt in the State Department for those who had allegedly "lost" China. By now, the junior senator from Wisconsin had made his Wheeling speech, the political cartoonist Herblock (Herbert Block) had coined the term "McCarthyism," the Korean War had turned the Cold War hot, and paranoia gripped much of America.

This, then, was the international and domestic context for the experiences of our six case histories. The HUAC hearings on the Joint Anti-Fascist Refugee Committee (JAFRC), resulting in the incarceration of its chairman, Dr. Edward Barsky, and its executive board (Chapter 1); the academic freedom cases of two New York University professors, Lyman Bradley and Edwin Burgum, culminating in their dismissal from NYU (Chapter 2); the blacklisting of the communist writer Howard Fast and his defection from American communism (Chapter 3); the visit of an anguished Dimitri Shostakovich to New York in the spring of 1949

(Chapter 4); and the attempts by O. John Rogge, the JAFRC's lawyer, to find a "third way" in the quest for peace, which led detractors to question which side he was on (Chapter 5)—all these events occurred against a backdrop of mounting anticommunism.

Partly because all of our subjects, with the exception of Shostakovich, were New York–based, there are, not unexpectedly, numerous intersections and overlaps. Like most activists on the left, all were deeply affected by the Spanish Civil War of 1936–39. That influence propelled them directly into membership in, or support for, the JAFRC, whose *raison d'être* was assistance to pro-Republican refugees from Franco's Spain. For anticommunist crusaders, especially Catholic Americans, this was anathema. For Edward Barsky, Lyman Bradley, Helen Bryan, and Howard Fast, their association with the JAFRC was their downfall. All were cited for contempt of Congress in 1947 and jailed in 1950. A year earlier, all attended and some, including Burgum, sponsored, the Waldorf conference. Ostensibly, the conference sought to establish a dialogue between intellectuals from the East and West and thereby reduce Cold War tension. O. John Rogge was a keynote speaker, but Shostakovich was the star attraction. Stalin's pressure on Shostakovich to attend attests to intimidation's being used by both sides of the Cold War. Triggered by this conference, anti-Stalinist intellectuals, led by Sidney Hook, formed a counterorganization: Americans for Intellectual Freedom, which prefigured the Congress for Cultural Freedom. It was from New York University, and with Hook's encouragement, that Professors Bradley and Burgum were fired for their political beliefs. This confirmed that NYU was, to use Schrecker's apt phrase, "no ivory tower" during the early Cold War.

The indefatigable Howard Fast punctuates many of the chapters. Indeed, several of our subjects reappear throughout the book. So do various former communists—Louis Budenz, Herbert Philbrick, and Max Yergan—who were used by different committees and/or the FBI to provide incriminating evidence against many of those examined. The shadowy figure of Gerhardt Eisler, a courier for the JAFRC and a delegate to the Waldorf conference, also recurs. Besides their passionate support for the Spanish Republic in the 1930s, many of our five New Yorkers had a common belief in the 1940s that domestic fascism was on the rise and that another war was imminent. Rogge, who was not a communist, and Fast, who was, repeatedly warned that American politics was displaying totalitarian, fascist-like tendencies. Dimitri Shostakovich experienced this first-hand, in 1948, but Rogge and Fast were conflating fascism with

McCarthyism. The FBI assumed a leading, if not pivotal, role in such red-hunting, and it is no accident that its files on all our case studies, excepting Shostakovich, provide rich source material for the book.

So while each chapter is self-contained, if read as a whole this book will illuminate how the phenomenon of McCarthyism wrecked the lives of a group of American citizens. Through entering the personal world of an individual, the book reveals how living on the left during a time of apparent national crisis can test resilience, destroy careers, and endanger liberties. But as Shostakovich knew too well, the United States in this period was hardly Stalin's Russia, responsible for the largest killing fields of the twentieth century. McCarthyism was not comparable to Stalinism. America was not a totalitarian society. To defy a congressional committee courted unemployment or imprisonment, not death. Yet what happened to thousands of Americans during this time of fear, whose accustomed rights were trampled upon, whose dissent was judged disloyal, and who were often subjected to arbitrary and vindictive behavior, was reprehensible. The limits of tolerance and the boundaries of political debate were very narrowly drawn in those years, and this contains a salutary lesson for America today.

Dr. Edward Barsky, surgeon, New York City, August 28, 1969. (Photograph by Rich-ard Avedon. © The Richard Avedon Foundation.)

1
The Doctor

Edward Barsky

On May 4, 1949, Dr. Edward K. Barsky received some reassuring news. His reappointment as surgeon at Beth Israel Hospital in New York City, where he had worked since 1923, had been confirmed for another two years. Twelve months later, he received some disturbing news that changed his life forever: he learned that the U.S. Supreme Court had upheld a decision that he should serve a six-month sentence in a federal penitentiary. Accordingly, he became Prisoner No. 18907. Upon his release, he learned that his license to practice medicine would be revoked. These misfortunes had nothing to do with medical malpractice or professional incompetence. On the contrary, he was widely respected and trusted by patients, colleagues, and hospital administrators. Instead, Barsky was paying the heavy price for a political decision he made in 1945—that, as chairman of the Joint Anti-Fascist Refugee Committee (JAFRC), he would not cooperate with the House Un-American Activities Committee (HUAC). It was a fateful decision the longer-term consequences of which could not be foreseen. He did not know it then, but for Edward Barsky, the domestic Cold War had started.

This chapter uses the assault on the JAFRC, and Barsky's individual story within that, to illuminate the character of political repression during the early Cold War. The JAFRC was the first to be subpoenaed by HUAC, the first to challenge HUAC's legitimacy, and the first to set the pattern for Cold War inquisitions. In 1950, after three years of unsuccessful legal appeals, the JAFRC's entire executive board was jailed. Coming before the Hollywood Ten trial and the Smith Act prosecutions, this mass political incarceration was the first since the Palmer Raids nearly thirty years before and the biggest during the McCarthy era. Barsky received the most severe sentence. Upon release, Barsky lost his right to practice medicine. By early 1955, the JAFRC had dissolved: like Barsky's career, it had been crippled by McCarthyism. This chapter examines the processes by which a once-flourishing medical career was thwarted and a once-viable organization was destroyed. Although Barsky was but one individual and the JAFRC was but one of many left-wing organizations targeted by HUAC and the FBI, they epitomize the assault on the left by American Cold Warriors. In the context of McCarthyism, both were perceived threats to national security: Barsky was a communist and the JAFRC was a communist "front." However, as a catch-all concept, "communist front" is problematic, not axiomatic. There were degrees of control and autonomy. Some organizations, such as the Jefferson School of Social Science, were instruments of Communist Party policy far more than others. In the case of the JAFRC, its single-minded devotion to the cause of Spanish refugees was consistent with, but not rigidly determined by, the doctrines of party leaders in New York and Moscow. To allege that the JAFRC was a "favorite fund-raising project of the party"—a charge that cynically and "with elaborate virtuosity" played upon public sympathy—significantly underestimates the agency of the JAFRC.[1]

More important, this chapter demonstrates, first, that the punishment of JAFRC members did not fit their "crime" and, second, that such an assault, contrary to received interpretations, commenced very early in the postwar period. For Barsky and the JAFRC, the Cold War commenced in 1945, not 1947 or 1948. It should be remembered, of course, that such a bureaucratic blitz was part of a long historical trajectory. Political intolerance, the crushing of dissent, security service surveillance, deportations, and imprisonment were all familiar to radical activists in the labor movement since the nineteenth century. Even HUAC, established as a standing committee through a congressional vote on January 3, 1945, had an earlier incarnation: the Dies Committee, formed in May 1938.[2] And a legion of historians have catalogued the history of anticommunist repression by the state.[3] However, the actions against Barsky and the JAFRC were a historical marker. They signaled the first flexing of political muscle by HUAC, which saw its confrontation with JAFRC as a litmus test of its legitimacy. As its chairman, John S. Wood (D.-Ga.), pointedly stated: "It is the purpose of our Committee to determine, once and for all, whether an organization such as the Joint Anti-Fascist Refugee Committee has the authority to defy Congress of the United States. . . ."[4] Because

HUAC, not the JAFRC, triumphed, the framework was established for future congressional inquisitions that were to become such an emblematic feature of McCarthyism. But first, who was Barsky and what was the JAFRC?

Eddie Barsky was born in New York in 1897, attended Townsend Harris High School, and was graduated from Columbia University's College of Physicians and Surgeons in 1919. He undertook postgraduate training in Europe and, on return, commenced an internship in 1921 at Beth Israel Hospital in New York, where he became Associate Surgeon in 1931 and where he established a flourishing practice.[5] In 1935, Barsky, along with a great many other New York Jews, joined the American Communist Party. This shaped his outlook on developments in Europe. Fascism was then ascendant, but in Spain there was hope. When the pro-fascist army generals arose against the elected Republican government in July 1936, Barsky realized, like Orwell, that this was a state of affairs worth fighting for. As he told a reporter, "I came to [Spain] for very simple reasons. Nothing complicated. As an American I could not stand by and see a fellow-democracy kicked around by Mussolini and Hitler. . . . I wanted to help Republican Spain. I did. Is it simple or complex?"[6] As casualties mounted, and as a "powerful antifascist coalition" developed in New York,[7] Barsky acted. On "one October night" in 1936, he founded, in a friend's home, the American Medical Bureau to Aid Spanish Democracy.[8] After frantically fundraising and then collecting, storing, and loading provisions to equip an entire hospital in Spain, Barsky—along with sixteen doctors, nurses, and ambulance drivers—sailed on January 16, 1937. This was just three weeks after the first American volunteers of the Abraham Lincoln Brigade had departed. Barsky assumed control of the medical service within the International Brigade; established and headed seven front-line, evacuation, and base hospitals; and refined the operating techniques of medical surgery under fire. He also pioneered a surgical procedure for removing bullets and shrapnel from chest wounds and helped create the mobile surgical hospital that became a model for the U.S. Army in World War II. On at least one leading International Brigadier, Steve Nelson, Barsky made "a terrific impression."[9] In July 1937 he took a brief leave from the front lines—to return to New York to raise funds for more medical aid.[10] He addressed, in mufti, 20,000 at a rally in Madison Square Garden; a photograph of him reveals the intensity of his commitment.[11] When he returned (and he stayed in Spain until October 1938), he was made an honorary major in the Spanish Republican Army. In 1944 he wrote the autobiographical, 302-page *Surgeon Goes to War*, which captures his profound empathy with the Spanish cause. When the celebrated author of *Citizen Tom Paine*, Howard Fast, first met Barsky in late 1945, he described him as "a lean, hawklike man, handsome, commanding, evocative in appearance of Humphrey Bogart, a heroic figure who was already a legend."[12] In 1950, when HUAC found him subversive, Fast found him "a giant of a man, tempered out of steel, yet quiet and humble."[13] Ernest Hemingway transfigured him into a martyr: "Eddie is a saint. That's where we put our saints in this country—in jail."[14]

The Joint Anti-Fascist Refugee Committee

From various organizations (United American Spanish Aid Committee, American Committee to Save Refugees and American Rescue Ship Mission) and individuals (especially veterans of the Abraham Lincoln Brigade) that supported the Spanish Republic during the civil war, the JAFRC was born on March 11, 1942.[15] The driving force was Barsky. With the Loyalists' defeat in 1939, a massive exodus of more than 500,000 Republican Spanish refugees spilled over the Pyrenees into France. Most congregated in overcrowded refugee camps and then, from 1940 after the German occupation, were conscripted as laborers or sent to concentration camps. Thousands died in the Mauthausen camp. Thirty thousand were interned in North Africa. Approximately 18,000 who escaped incarceration fought alongside the French Resistance (as well as de Gaulle's Free French in Algeria) and suffered disproportionately at the hands of the Gestapo.

To remain in Franco's Spain, as many former Republicans soon discovered, was to invite imprisonment or death.[16] Despite this, some remnants stayed on, in hiding. Others escaped to Spanish-speaking countries: Mexico, Cuba, and the Dominican Republic. They lived the rest of their lives in that strange world of exile, some in a "limbo of expectation," others sadly "locked in a sterile polemic about responsibility for their defeat."[17] In the immediate aftermath of the civil war, Barsky—with his direct experience behind him but his visceral attachment to Spain intact—became preoccupied with the plight of these Spanish refugees. This preoccupation led directly to the establishment of the JAFRC, and the refugees were its *raison d'être*. Under Barsky's indefatigable leadership, the JAFRC acquired legitimacy during World War II. Licensed to provide aid by President Franklin D. Roosevelt's War Relief Control Board, it was granted tax-exempt status by the Treasury Department. The committee raised funds, formed sixteen chapters in major American cities, established orphanages, and strenuously opposed Generalisimo Francisco Franco's regime.[18] As

Barsky told dinner guests at the opening of the Spanish Refugee Appeal, which sought to raise $750,000, in March 1945:

> Our program consists of relief, rehabilitation, medical care, transportation and associated welfare services, in many parts of the world. . . . Who will help [the refugees]? We! We are the only people to help them. We help them or they die.[19]

The Spanish Refugee Appeal sent thousands of dollars and tons of food, clothing, and medicines to Spanish refugees in both France and North Africa. The Unitarian Service Committee and the American Friends Service Committee, the latter a Quaker organization, distributed this relief on behalf of the JAFRC. An examination of the records of the Unitarian Service Committee reveals the very close working relationship with the JAFRC and the devotion of both to assisting refugees. The extensive correspondence dating back to 1941, many to and from Helen Bryan, does not contain a whiff of "communist front" about it.[20] Instead, as one report later noted, the work of the JAFRC "was a work of mercy; it sheltered the homeless, fed the hungry, healed the sick."[21] Material and legal support was given to other refugees to emigrate to one of the few countries that welcomed them—Mexico. There, a school for refugee children was built and the Edward K. Barsky Sanatorium was opened when the JAFRC collected $50,000 after a national fundraising campaign in January 1945.[22]

JAFRC: A Ready Target

Eleven months later, HUAC pounced. By now, Franklin Roosevelt was dead, Harry Truman was in the White House, and World War II had ended. On December 10, 1945, HUAC subpoenaed Barsky and the JAFRC's administrative secretary, Helen Reid Bryan, to appear before it at 10:00 A.M. nine days hence in Washington (this appearance was postponed until January 23, 1946). They were to "produce all books, ledgers, records, and papers relating to the receipt and disbursement of money" by the JAFRC, together with "all correspondence and memoranda of communications by any means whatsoever with persons in foreign countries."[23] The executive board held a special meeting on December 14 and unanimously adopted a resolution "to protect the rights of this Committee and its supporters" from HUAC. It would not surrender its records. It also declared that HUAC's demands infringed democratic rights and were "unwarranted and unjustified." It invoked HUAC's own terms of reference by stating that the JAFRC "is truly American in every sense of the word and can, by no stretch of the imagination, be considered un-American, subversive, or an attack upon the principles of our form of government."[24] In early January 1946, Barsky wrote to all contributors explaining the position of the JAFRC executive board. He cited a recent speech by Congressman Ellis Patterson (D.-Calif.), who called for the dissolution of HUAC, describing it as a "sham" that "violated every concept of American democracy." That a showdown with HUAC loomed was implied by Barsky's concluding paragraph: the JAFRC was "determined to continue its humanitarian and relief work" and would "let nothing stand in the way of providing this aid."[25] For its part, HUAC was just as determined that its authority would not be defied by the JAFRC.

Why did HUAC swoop down on the JAFRC? According to Congressman J. Parnell Thomas (R.-N.J.), the trigger was an attack by the "Red Fascist" Harold J. Laski on the Catholic Church in Spain at a JAFRC-sponsored rally of 17,000 in Madison Square Garden on September 24, 1945. Laski, a highly respected professor of political science at the London School of Economics, was also chairman of the British Labour Party. He was a Fabian socialist who opposed the overtures to the Labour Party by the Communist Party.[26] Such political subtleties would have eluded the ideologically myopic Thomas. As a result of Laski's speech, said Thomas, HUAC received "over 8,000 complaints" against Laski, the JAFRC, and the Veterans of the Abraham Lincoln Brigade, and HUAC "decided to investigate the charges."[27] (At least some of those "8,000 complaints" were the work of the popular actor and Catholic Frank Fay, who organized a postcard campaign.[28]) For HUAC's chief legal counsel, Ernie Adamson, the basis for investigating the JAFRC and its subsidiary Spanish Refugee Appeal was that "they both seem to be engaged in political propaganda, not relief."[29] HUAC had jurisdiction over the "extent, character and objects of un-American propaganda activities," and JAFRC propaganda, according to HUAC chairman John S. Wood, was "of a subversive character."[30] Opposing Franco, moreover, which the JAFRC was doing, was considered especially un-American and dangerous to the United States by Roman Catholic red-hunters such as the "Senator from Madrid," Pat McCarran (D.-Nev.), and J. Parnell Thomas, who had close ties to the Franco regime.[31] Both subscribed to a particularly virulent form of Catholic anticommunism that stretched back to Father Charles Coughlin in the 1930s and that now embraced powerful Catholic organizations (the Knights of Columbus and the Catholic War Veterans) and prelates (Cardinal Francis Spellman, Archbishop Richard Cushing, and Monsignor Fulton Sheen).[32] The long-term hatred of communism by American Catholics—fueled by the treatment of Catholic priests both in Spain during the civil war and in "Iron Curtain" countries in the immediate postwar years—found a ready-made target in the JAFRC.

But hostility to the JAFRC went even deeper than this. Congressman Karl Mundt (R.-S.D.) argued that the JAFRC was engaged not merely in disseminating un-American, anti-Franco propaganda but also in "secret and nefarious activities."[33] What were these activities? Newly released FBI files (discussed below) confirm that, by 1944, FBI Director J. Edgar Hoover believed that the JAFRC was actually subversive. He was convinced, by two different "confidential" sources, that veterans of the closely associated Abraham Lincoln Brigade, who had been trained in military warfare, would "lead the vanguard of the revolution in this country."[34] Funds raised by the JAFRC, ostensibly for Spaniards' relief, would assist that goal.[35] Given the symbiotic relationship between the FBI and HUAC,[36] it is arguable that underpinning HUAC's postwar harassment of the JAFRC was Hoover's longstanding anticommunist crusade.[37]

Helen Reid Bryan

The first JAFRC member to travel to Washington and confront HUAC was its administrative secretary, Helen Bryan. She did not travel alone: a delegation of more than 200 supporters accompanied her on the overnight train from New York. When she was inside HUAC's chambers on January 23 and 24, 1946, they were outside lobbying seventy congressmen.[38] As the nominal custodian of the records, she willingly assumed full responsibility for the executive board's refusal to surrender them. This tactic sought to insulate the rest of the board from intimidation and prosecution. According to Fast, it was a defensive maneuver, but legally sound. However, "if we had had any premonition that imprisonment would result from this, not one of us would have allowed Helen Bryan to take the fall."[39] Nevertheless, Bryan pursued a line of action that, according to the introducer of her prison memoirs, "involved risk to herself rather than risk to others."[40] The price she paid was three months in Alderston prison. Again and again the members of HUAC (Chairman Wood and Congressmen Thomas and Mundt, all Dies Committee alumni; John E. Rankin; and five others) interrogated the stubborn Bryan about the whereabouts of the records. Each time she refused to divulge the information. HUAC was not interested in the workings of the JAFRC. Repeatedly she attempted to read an explanatory statement. Each time she was denied, to be met with "I demand that you answer the question 'yes' or 'no.'" Eventually Bryan stated: "How can our organization, created to provide relief for Spanish Republican refugees and their families . . . in good conscience endanger the lives of people by turning names over to your committee?"[41] She then stated that she had not brought the books and records and, as a result, was cited for contempt of Congress on January 24.

It is worth pausing here to reflect on the case of Helen Reid Bryan. One can feel only admiration for her steadfastness and courage throughout this period. She has variously been described as "saintly"; imbued with "integrity," "loyalty," and a "high-minded sensitivity"; and devoted to a "lifetime service to humanity."[42] Yet she has been entirely overlooked by all scholarly studies of this period. Born on June 30, 1894, in Cincinnati, Ohio, she attended Ferry Hall, a wealthy girl's school in Chicago, and was graduated from Wellesley College, Massachusetts, in 1917. Thereafter she became a Quaker. From 1919 to 1925, when her father died, she worked for the Young Women's Christian Association. She was then employed as secretary of the American Friends Service Committee, a Quaker organization, in Philadelphia. In 1929, and for the next ten years, she chaired the Quaker-established Committee on Race Relations. Profoundly affected by the Spanish Civil War, she became executive secretary of the United States Spanish Aid Committee in December 1940 and then executive secretary of the JAFRC from its inception. From all accounts, she was a highly efficient, resourceful, and imaginative administrator. As her FBI file amply demonstrates, she was tireless in her fundraising efforts during the 1940s. In March 1950 she chaired the newly formed Freedom Fund Organization, which sought to raise funds to defray legal expenses associated with court appeals by JAFRC defendants.[43] After her release from prison on February 12, 1951, having served her full three-month sentence, she resigned from the JAFRC because it was apparent that the organization was disintegrating and that she would have no future if she returned to it. She then immersed herself in writing a book, *Inside*, based on her experiences at the Federal Reformatory for Women in Alderston, West Virginia. One review described the book, published in May 1953, as "sincere and highly readable," especially in its discussion of "the unhappiness and loneliness of daily prison life."[44] On June 1, 1953, she secured employment as an officer and counselor at the Massachusetts Reformatory for Women in Framingham. There, she formed a close friendship with the superintendent, Dr. Miriam Van Waters, that blossomed into a long-term lesbian relationship, of which the FBI—ready to conflate "sexual deviance" with political subversion—was fully aware.[45] After only six weeks at Framingham, Bryan was forced to resign following extensive publicity given by two Boston newspapers about her current employment and her past activities. The taint of communism forced the hand of the Reformatory's governor and executive committee. In 1955 she moved to Dorset, Vermont, where she became the treasurer of the local Congregational Church. Her elder brother, Alison Reid Bryan, was a minister in the same church.[46]

Until 1958, the FBI continued to believe that Bryan was a covert member of the Communist Party. Her 310-page file is punctuated with informants' reports confirming that she was "a very active Communist" (1945); was "a member at large of the CP, known only to the higher echelon of the party" (1951); and donated $4,000 each year to the National Reserve Fund of the Communist Party (1957). Throughout 1958, the FBI interviewed numerous residents of the small village of Dorset. None believed Bryan was a communist. Richard Overton, a "pillar" of the community and a trustee for the Congregational Church, knew her well; he was aware that she had "served time." She was, he told two agents on March 7, 1957, a very interesting, intelligent, and well-read woman who was highly active in both the church and civic organizations in Dorset. Furthermore,

> Mr. OVERTON stated that in the many conversations and discussions he has had with Miss BRYAN he has never noticed the slightest suggestion of anything un-American or pro-Communist in her manner, speech or beliefs. He stated that he considers Miss BRYAN to be a loyal American.[47]

Finally, in May 1958, the FBI reviewed her case and concluded that "she has not been a member of the CP" and therefore no longer fit the criteria for inclusion on the Security Index.[48] In short, the FBI had got it wrong. Bryan, who died in 1976, never married. However, in the late 1930s she had an intimate relationship with Dr. Max Yergan, an African American communist, who initiated divorce proceedings against his wife, Susie, and planned to marry Bryan until persuaded otherwise by Earl Browder and other high-ranking communists. A countersuit by Susie Yergan, which named Bryan, was also prepared. At that point, according to a personal letter obtained by Susie, Bryan ended the relationship while professing her deep love for Yergan. The source of this information, and more, which was transmitted by an informant to the FBI, was Reverend Shelby Rooks, pastor of the St. James Presbyterian Church in New York City. He was both Susie Yergan's confidante and the negotiator between her and Max during their marital difficulties. To the FBI, this was confirmation that Bryan was a communist.[49] Max Yergan later became an informant for the FBI.[50] By 1955, it "owned" him.[51]

The mistaken assumption, in the 1940s, that Bryan was a communist meant that no leniency was given during HUAC's investigation of the JAFRC. The reasons—which HUAC members neither heard nor wished to hear—for Helen Bryan's refusal to relinquish JAFRC records were threefold. First, JAFRC records were already available to the U.S. government. As the JAFRC's defense attorney and former U.S. Assistant Attorney General, O. John Rogge (the subject of Chapter 5), repeatedly pointed out, both the President's War Relief Control Board and the Treasury Department had full access to JAFRC reports and records and its investigators had examined them "for a substantial period of time."[52] It would open its books to any authoritative, impartial committee, but not to "this unconstitutional House committee" that was not entitled to them.[53] Second, the JAFRC questioned the constitutionality of HUAC and the scope of its jurisdiction. This was not unusual in 1945–48.[54] Then, a great many American liberals, including congressmen, challenged the legitimacy of HUAC.[55] Even President Truman criticized the purposefulness of HUAC hearings.[56] Former Vice President Henry A. Wallace certainly did.[57] Finally, and most important, the financial records contained two politically volatile lists: one was a list of names of 30,000 American who contributed to relief aid; the other was a list of Republican Spaniards who were receiving relief aid, including those inside Franco's Spain. Barsky, Bryan, and the other JAFRC members were convinced that, if these names were disclosed to HUAC and, presumably, the FBI, the liberties of each group would be imperiled. The board felt a strong sense of obligation to protect both domestic donors from retaliation and Spanish recipients from persecution. To do otherwise, as a board member later recalled, would be a "heinous and totally dishonorable action."[58] A meeting of nineteen members of the executive board on February 1—one of the best-attended—unanimously endorsed Bryan's decision not to cooperate with HUAC.[59] Without knowing it, they, too, were soon to have similar experiences. Ten days later they instructed their national chairman, Barsky, not to produce any records or documents when it was his turn to face HUAC on February 13.[60]

The HUAC Inquisition

The executive (closed) session of HUAC that interrogated Barsky was administratively a shambles. The transcript reveals a distinct lack of unanimity about the procedures to be followed or the degree of latitude afforded the witness.[61] Barsky was twice asked to step outside so that members could decide on procedure. In one instance they even took a private vote. The hearing was punctuated by interruptions to HUAC's own legal counsel (seeking preliminary information on the workings of the JAFRC) from HUAC's John Rankin demanding an immediate "yes" or "no" answer from Barsky regarding the records. Three members (Gerald Landis, J.W. Robinson, and Wood, the chairman) favored permitting Barsky to read his prepared statement; others (Mundt, Rankin, and Thomas) did not. There was also dispute over whether the statement, if not read, could be incorporated into the record. Rankin's demand—"Give it to the Chairman. We will decide later whether it goes into the record or not"—prevailed. Barsky reluctantly handed over his statement, neither read nor tabled. Barsky was no fool whom HUAC could easily intimidate. Dressed in his "impeccably-clad double-breasted suit," and with his "business-like manner," there was a "sureness . . . about his manner, his talk, his gestures."[62] Throughout the hearings, he retained his dignity. Some HUAC members did not. Even at a distance of sixty-six years, their rudeness, intimidation, capriciousness, and sheer bullying during these closed congressional hearings has the capacity to astonish and shock.

The standoff between JAFRC and HUAC began to attract public attention. In addition to the radical press, editorials and articles appeared in the *Los Angeles Examiner*, *The Nation*, the *New York Post*, the *New York Times*, the *New York World-Telegram*, and the *Washington Post*.[63] The newly formed "Citizens to Safeguard the Joint Anti-Fascist Refugee Committee," with such notables as writers Dashiell Hammett and Lillian Hellman, inserted full-page advertisements in three daily newspapers; pressured the Democratic National Committee; contacted trade unions, sponsors, and contributors urging action and donations; and organized two well-attended press conferences and a fundraising dinner at the Waldorf Astoria on March 18. (Two years later, as discussed in Chapter 4, this hotel was the site of a controversial peace conference attended by many JAFRC members.) With the assistance of Helen Bryan, Barsky also undertook a major task: he wrote individually signed letters to every congressman, and he did this twice, on February 18 and March 8.[64] J. Parnell Thomas was not daunted. Indeed, reactions by Barsky and JAFRC leaders emboldened him and confirmed their guilt.

I have been on this committee from its very inception. I was on the Dies committee from the beginning to end . . . whenever we were attacked we [knew] we had struck pay dirt. Now we have struck pay dirt on this Barsky matter. Barsky is doing everything he possibly can. . . . They are getting in touch with members of Congress, telling them that this is an un-American committee. They have used those words.

After labeling the JAFRC as "the leading Communist-front organization today," Thomas told the House that HUAC would be "going right to the bottom" of the JAFRC and would "thoroughly" investigate its leaders. He declared, "You can count on it that when we make our report to this Congress it will astound you all."[65]

Such bravado would prove hollow. There was no more "pay dirt" yielded, no exposé of the JAFRC leaders' alleged clandestine communist activities, no revelation that would "astound" Congress. In fact, J. Parnell Thomas would precede those leaders into jail. Although he chaired HUAC's inquisition of the Hollywood Ten the following year, in August 1948 his past fraudulent salary practices were exposed, and, soon after, he was indicted on charges of conspiracy to defraud the government, tried, convicted, fined $10,000, and sentenced to eighteen months in Danbury federal penitentiary.[66]

"Enemies within our gates"

One piece of information that Barsky provided to HUAC, upon request, was the names and addresses of all executive board members. This enabled the next round in the congressional committee's offensive against the JAFRC. Notwithstanding the "personal opinion" of Benedict Wolf, the JAFRC's legal counsel, that it would be "very difficult" and "absurd" for Congress to cite for contempt seventeen people,[67] this is precisely what happened. On March 16, 1946, every member of the executive board (in addition to Bryan and Barsky) was cited for contempt of Congress. This was hasty, precipitous action. Astonishingly, none of these individuals had been subpoenaed, none had appeared before HUAC, and none had been given any opportunity to answer any questions, even contemptuously. This overreaching was so blatant that, when HUAC Chairman Wood sought congressional confirmation of the contempt citations on March 28, he quickly struck out their names when challenged by the radical American Labor Party congressman Vito Marcantonio (Ind.-N.Y.) and, more efficaciously, by "no better friend" of HUAC than the conservative Eugene

Cox (D.-Ga.).[68] But it was a pyrrhic victory for those supporting the JAFRC. Members of HUAC immediately went on the attack. To Mundt, the JAFRC was "honeycombed" with communists, was "bringing foreigners to America," and was "trying to destroy the things for which our flag stands"; to Thomas, the JAFRC was "a vehicle used by the Communist Party and the world Communist movement to force political, diplomatic, and economic disunity." Rankin hoped that the House would "support the committee and let the world know that we are going to protect this country from destruction at the hands of the enemies within our gates." The House complied. All the strenuous efforts of the JAFRC "pressure campaign" proved to be in vain. By a staggering majority, 339–4, the House voted in favor of citing Barsky for contempt of Congress.[69] That night a naïve or ignorant Benedict Wolf told the executive board: "Possibly it won't go any further than the District Court because of the fact that the books and records were not in the custody of Dr. Barsky."[70]

The following day, it did go further. On March 29, all remaining sixteen executive board members were served with subpoenas. All appeared before HUAC, and all refused one by one to hand over any books and records. All were cited.[71] None was permitted legal representation. Once again, the proceedings became aggressive. Recalcitrance would be met with truculence. When the soft-spoken NYU professor Lyman Bradley was interrogated, a subsequent report noted, HUAC members "were exceedingly abusive in language and demeanor" and the hearing lacked "dignity and order."[72] This is evidenced by the following exchange:

> *The Chairman.* You are a man of intelligence, aren't you? You think so at least. Do you know whether you have got these books or not?
>
> *Mr. Bradley.* May I consult my counsel?
>
> *Mr. Rankin.* Not on this question. . . . Now let us have [your] answer to this question "Yes" or "No" . . .
>
> *Mr. Bradley (reading).* I have been served with a subpoena requiring me . . .
>
> *The Chairman (interposing).* No. I tell you we don't want you to read a statement. Have you got these books with you? . . .
>
> *Mr. Bradley.* Allow me to finish reading the statement.
>
> *Mr. Adamson.* It is the same one the previous witness had.
>
> *Mr. Rankin.* Give it to the chairman. Now, the next question he refuses, just call up the marshal and send him to jail.[73]

One ritual that recurred in numerous subsequent hearing and trials—
"taking the Fifth"—was noticeably absent in these hearings. The fact
that none invoked the constitutional right of protection against self-
incrimination, which may have saved them in 1946[74] (before "guilt by
suspicion" became so ubiquitous), was sharply criticized by Howard Fast,
one of those cited. Fast directed blame squarely at the JAFRC attorney, Benedict Wolf. He judged Wolf as "an unimaginative, plodding man,"
who, "either by intent or by his poverty of invention . . . failed to advise
us on the use of the Fifth." According to Fast, Wolf was responsible for
the overall "woeful mismanagement" of the case, and his actions "never
ceased to mystify me."[75] But Wolf genuinely believed that those cited
would be cleared by the courts, that talk of jail sentences was fanciful,
and that HUAC's investigatory methods (demanding financial records as
opposed to "un-American propaganda") would be declared unconstitutional.[76] It was not until March 1, 1947, that O. John Rogge took over.[77]
By then it was too late. Twelve months earlier the JAFRC board had been
cited for contempt of Congress for refusing to answer its interrogators. A
month later the House of Representatives voted to confirm the citation.

The congressional confirmation of this mass contempt citation was
distinguished by passionate debate for, as Helen Gahagan Douglas (D.-
Calif.) presciently commented, the vote "will directly affect the lives of
17 people, directly and indirectly, to the end of their days."[78] The response
of the red-hunting hardliners was predictable: "Is Congress going to be
subjected to contempt by an element in this country that is plotting day
and night for the overthrow of this Government?"[79] Less predictable was
this plea from Emanuel Celler (D.-N.Y.), who had not previously voted
against the citation of Barsky:

> Mr. Speaker, we are making history, regrettable history, in finding
> innocent people guilty of contempt without trial, without jury and
> without the benefit of counsel. I believe we are turning our backs
> upon our glorious past if we pass this resolution. . . . I predict our
> action will come back to plague us.[80]

However, Congress made its "regrettable history" and voted 292 in
favor, 56 against. There were 82 abstentions.[81]

Interregnum

Notwithstanding these Damoclean swords, the JAFRC attempted to
continue its work. Its monthly executive board meetings for the remain-

der of 1946 recorded activities such as the Women's Division Luncheon, a hootenanny, distribution of "Street Solicitation Cans," theater parties, preparations for a Madison Square Garden rally, and the Christmas auction at the Waldorf Astoria. Twelve months passed before the U.S. District Court of the District of Columbia, on March 31, 1947, heard the indictment initiated by prosecutors within the Justice Department that the JAFRC board was in contempt of Congress. The board had been charged with "having conspired to defraud the United States by preventing the Congressional Committee from obtaining the records."[82] It was, in short, a conspiracy indictment. This changed a misdemeanor into a felony and thereby jeopardized the license to practice of doctors and lawyers (both of whom were well represented on the JAFRC board). When appealing for funds to cover immediate legal expenses, estimated at $17,000,[83] Barsky wrote that "This case against us is a potential threat to the civil liberties of all Americans."[84] On June 16, 1947, the eighteen executive board members of the JAFRC were brought to trial in the Federal District Court of Washington. The trial, which was to last ten days, had been delayed because Rogge charged that Judge Alexander Holtzoff was "guilty of bias and prejudice." Indeed he was. Holtzoff had been assigned by the Department of Justice to advise the FBI when the JAFRC was first being investigated by the FBI in 1944–45. When Holtzoff refused to recuse himself, he made legal history: for the first time, the U.S. Court of Appeals issued a writ of prohibition against a federal judge.[85] There was an unreliable witness as well as a prejudiced judge. At the trial, a key government witness, Robert Alexander from the Visa Division of the State Department, branded the JAFRC "subversive." Twelve months later he was being investigated, at the request of the Secretary of State, on charges of "misconduct and dereliction of duty."[86]

To the JAFRC, however, this mattered little. On June 27, 1947, after adjourning for only one hour, four men and eight women of the federal court jury convicted all eighteen board members of contempt.[87] Immediately after the guilty verdict, five defendants got cold feet. They "purged" their contempt by recanting and resigning from the JAFRC board. Their sentences were suspended.[88] The remainder, except Barsky, were sentenced to jail for three months and fined $500 each; Barsky received a six-month sentence. He also received hundreds of letters of support, from Pablo Picasso in France to this unknown woman in Milwaukee: "My heart is sad by your suffering. I only wish I could give more. All the money I have to give is in this envelope. I gladly give my widow's mite. God bless your work is my prayer."[89] The thirteen convicted JAFRC members served notices of appeal and were released on bond.

Appeals cost money. Simply bringing one case to the Court of Appeals would cost $4,000, so much time at JAFRC meetings was focused on fundraising, not for Spanish refugees but for self-defense: "A fund raising event, possibly in the Golden Gate Ballroom in Harlem, might be planned. Outstanding Negro and white talent could be secured. A counter proposal was made that such an event might be planned by which a larger income could be secured."[90] In its capacity to raise funds to aid refugees, meanwhile, the increasingly besieged JAFRC suffered two body blows. First, the committee was listed as a "subversive" organization in the first of the Attorney General's List of Subversive Organizations, published on December 4, 1947.[91] The American Civil Liberties Union, on behalf of the JAFRC, challenged procedural aspects of the List,[92] but to be on the list was tantamount to a kiss of death as far as broader community support was concerned. As I. F. Stone noted, many contributors and supporters were "frightened" to link themselves to a "disloyal" organization.[93] Until then, support had remained steadfast; a total of only two from the large list of JAFRC sponsors had resigned. Second, on January 23, 1948, the Internal Revenue Service informed the JAFRC that its tax-exempt status (granted on February 8, 1943) was revoked. This meant that donations could no longer be tax deductible and income tax returns since the inception of the JAFRC in 1942 must be submitted. It was little wonder that Barsky, in appealing to supporters for yet another financial contribution to support a legal challenge, felt that "we are now faced with one of the gravest crises in the history of our organization."[94] Curiously, perhaps, recognition of this crisis could not be discerned in any of the addresses or reports heard by delegates to the two-day National Conference of the JAFRC in August. Indeed, an inverse relationship between vulnerability of position and defiance of tone pervaded discussions and resolutions.[95] But the committee's nemesis awaited.

Back in Court

For the next three years following the convictions, a series of complicated but ultimately unsuccessful appeals and petitions for re-hearings was conducted.[96] The many arguments presented to the appellate courts and to the Supreme Court, mainly by Rogge, and the judgements of the various courts, will not be summarized here.[97] Suffice it to say that both the Court of Appeals for the Second Circuit (5–2) and the Court of Appeals for the District of Columbia Circuit (2–1) held that HUAC was not exceeding constitutional powers, or acting in violation of the First Amendment, in questioning witnesses about Communist Party membership or associations. In other words, HUAC had the right to interrogate individuals about their alleged Communist Party affiliations. In his blistering dissenting opinion, Circuit Judge Henry Edgerton wrote that the HUAC inquiry stigmatized unpopular views, abridged freedom of speech, and inflicted punishment without trial.[98] Ten years later Edgerton was vindicated, but too late for the JAFRC.[99] Rogge stated, "We are concerned here with the basic democratic right to be free from intimidation with reference to one's personal beliefs."[100] At a JAFRC-sponsored dinner at the Astor Hotel, Rogge let fly. HUAC, he proclaimed, was "an unconstitutional body acting in an unconstitutional manner and more concerned with advancing the political fortunes of its members than in protecting American ideals."[101] At another meeting, recorded by the FBI, he went even further. The assault on the JAFRC, he claimed, was "plainly part of the first step towards Fascism."[102] On May 29, 1950, the U.S. Supreme Court refused, for the second time, to review two appeals filed by Rogge.[103] That decision opened the gates to the federal penitentiary.

Imprisonment

On the day the eleven Board members commenced their incarceration, June 7, 1950 (Helen Bryan and Ernestina Fleischman were imprisoned separately, on November 13, 1950, after a final, unsuccessful legal appeal[104]), a solitary line of about fifty veterans of the Abraham Lincoln Brigade marched outside the White House. Their placards read "No Jail for Franco's Foes" and "Franco was Hitler's Pal."[105] A more "respectable" protest to the President was made by Francis Fisher Kane, an "old member of the Philadelphia Bar" and U.S. Attorney General under Woodrow Wilson. He "earnestly" requested that Truman commute the sentences imposed, because imprisonment was "a denial of justice and a blot upon American liberty."[106] Washington prison authorities, meanwhile, were itemizing the clothes of their new inmates—in Barsky's case, a green hat, blue shirt, gray and yellow necktie, and brown pants and coat.[107] He became Prisoner No. 18907. The eleven prisoners came from a range of backgrounds— academic, legal, literary, medical, labor union, and business. In addition to Barsky, the most notable members were the head of the German Department at NYU and Modern Language Association treasurer, Professor Lyman Bradley, and the well-known essayist and historical novelist Howard Fast.[108] Initially, Barsky and the other male JAFRC detainees were confined to the District of Columbia prison in Washington. The female board members (Marjorie Chodorov, Ruth Leider, and Charlotte Stern) were sent to the Federal Penitentiary for Women at Alderston, West Virginia.[109] According to one commentator, "In the normal course of events [these individuals] wouldn't see the inside of a jail, or even a courtroom, during their whole lifetime. . . . But these are not ordinary times and these are not ordinary events."[110] They were treated, however, very ordinarily and no different from the "common" criminal: handcuffed, stripped, processed naked, fingerprinted twice, showered, given faded blue uniforms, and locked in a shared cell five by seven feet in a towering prison block. After nine days, the men were scattered. Dr. Jacob Auslander, a physician, joined J. Parnell Thomas—one of the HUAC members who had cited the JAFRC for contempt—in Danbury federal penitentiary in Connecticut; Bradley and Fast were relocated 300 miles away in the mountains of West Virginia; Barsky was sent to the equally isolated penitentiary at Petersburg, Virginia; James Lustig, a trade unionist, went to Ashland, Kentucky; three others were remanded to the Federal Detention House in New York City. The reasons for this dispersal were never articulated, but there is a hint in one source. According to Professor Arad Riggs of NYU: "I don't want to talk too much about it, but I might say that I had a conversation with the United States District Attorney and I am told that when they had this group of eleven serving in the Washington jail, they were afraid they might take over the jail and decided to scatter them."[111]

Barsky was sent to the Federal Reformatory in Petersburg, Virginia, 400 miles from New York. There, he lost twenty-five pounds, suffered from ulcers, was permitted only two visiting hours per month with his wife only, and was not permitted to do any medical work, only menial work. Coupled with the psychological strain of the past four years of criminal and civil litigations and appeals, his months in this remote jail must have tested his resilience. He would also have been concerned by the financial effects on his dependent wife, Vita, and two-year-old daughter, Angela, of his prolonged cessation of income.[112] A heartfelt, handwritten two-page letter was sent to him from a dentist and acquaintance ("I don't know if you remember me"), Samuel Anderman. The letter is worth noting because it illustrates how the persecution of the JAFRC touched a great many Americans beyond the normal reach of JAFRC or communist "front" activity. After telling Barsky that his jailing had had a "profound effect" on him, Anderman continued: "There are many people like myself around, who are not sleeping easily while you and other patriotic Americans are being jailed. . . . Be of good cheer. This period is a severe trial but every great man has had to suffer for his convictions. Your suffering is not in vain. . . ." This letter was returned as the sender was not listed as one of the correspondents from whom Barsky was permitted to receive mail.[113]

Barsky was freed from Petersburg on November 7. Either "good behavior" or the numerous letters from the medical fraternity to the Federal Parole Board[114] earned him one month's reprieve. He was just in time to both greet and say farewell to his loyal, steadfast secretary, Helen Bryan, as she began her three-month sentence on November 13. The night before, 200 friends, including Barsky, attended her farewell party at Fairfax Hall in New York. According to one who was present, "it was a welcome, heart-warming occasion to see this man moving freely again, among his friends."[115] It was the final function he attended as JAFRC chairman. Because of "the demands of my present situation," he resigned as officer, director, and member of the JAFRC in January 1951.[116] It could not have been easy for Barsky to relinquish the organization he had founded nearly a decade earlier. It was pivotal to his existence. According to a JAFRC staffer, "We never saw anybody with such single-mindedness. His entire life is wrapped up in the work of helping the refuges, in helping Spain."[117] He himself told a reporter: "Best committee in America. No committee in America has this tradition." The reporter noted that it was near-impossible to get Barsky off the subject of the work of the JAFRC, about which he slipped into "lyricism."[118] So what were these "present demands"?

Persecution, Again

If he thought deprivation of freedom would end upon his release from jail, he was wrong. Another round of persecution commenced; another fight to resist it became necessary. It concerned not his political or humanitarian activities for the JAFRC, although these continued to stalk him, but his right to practice medicine. And it did not end until 1955, by which time the JAFRC announced its own dissolution. During his time in Petersburg penitentiary, Barsky's medical license was revoked. Upon his release, he was obliged to reapply for it. To that end, the executive director of Beth Israel Hospital, with the approval of the Medical Board and the Hospital's Board of Trustees, wrote to the Board of Regents of the New York State Department of Education, the body responsible for issuing—and revoking—medical licenses. The letter outlined the history and length of Barsky's appointments at the hospital and the type of service he rendered. It continued:

> Dr. Barsky is a skillful surgeon, whose medical ethics and conduct have always been beyond reproach. He is an ethical physician, imbued with the traditional Hippocratic sense of responsibility to his patients and services in their behalf. The patients at the Hospital are well served by him.[119]

The expectation, presumably, was that restoration of his license would be a formality. But by the winter of late 1950 and early 1951, the American political landscape was gouged by anticommunism and paranoia was intense.

In January 1951, the immensely powerful Board of Regents informed Barsky that it was reviewing his case and a subcommittee would decide whether a further penalty (from mere censure to revocation of license) was to be imposed. Immediately, Barsky went on the offensive and wrote to numerous doctors, academics, and Quakers requesting, in effect, character references to be posted to the Medical Grievance Committee prior to its closed hearing on February 15. They obliged.[120] Before the hearing, Barsky's attorney, Abraham Fishbein, mounted (what seems to the historian) a compelling and superbly crafted case revolving around five separate arguments and amounting to thirteen pages.[121] At the hearing Fishbein spoke with much passion: "This man has paid the full penalty. . . . To treat him now as a felon who commits abortions or who deals in narcotics and place him on that level, gentlemen, is too low. . . . I beg of you, gentlemen, don't let's stoop that low to hit this man . . . [who has] paid in full. . . . To do more to this man is to wreak vengeance and not to do justice."[122] On the other hand, the Assistant Attorney General of the state of New York, Sidney Tartikoff, for the Board of Regents, focused on the activities of the Joint Anti-Fascist Refugee Committee, the contempt of Congress citation, the constitutionality of HUAC, and, especially, the Attorney General's List of Subversive Organizations. Considerable evidentiary weight was placed by Tartikoff on the JAFRC's being listed as subversive and un-American; unfortunately for Barsky, this hearing was precisely two months before the Supreme Court invalidated such listings by the Attorney General.[123] None of these issues, for which Barsky had endured five months in prison and five years of litigation, was relevant to medical competence. None of these issues involved "moral turpitude," the customary concern of the committee. None of the dozens of testi-

monials counted. Barsky was found guilty of nothing, other than his failure to produce records subpoenaed by a congressional committee, which
the Grievance Committee itself acknowledged was "the only method
by which legal objections to [HUAC] could be judicially determined."
Even Tartikoff informed the Grievance Committee "candidly and hon-
estly" that he could find "no real evidence" that JAFRC activities were
"Communistic."[124] And, as we know, Barsky was now no longer a member of the JAFRC. All this was to no avail. The Board of Regents' Medical
Grievance Committee revoked Edward Barsky's medical registration, first
issued in 1919, for a period of six months. No reasons were given.

In a rerun of the legal challenges to his conviction that lasted from
1947 to 1950, Barsky launched appeals against this decision. The case was
next heard by the Regents' Committee on Discipline, which overturned
the suspension of Barsky's license—there being no moral turpitude, no
impeachment by evidence, and therefore "no valid basis for discipline."[125]
However, this decision was repudiated by the full Board, which upheld
the original ruling. Barsky then sought review in the Court of Appeals of
the State of New York, which affirmed the order of the Board of Regents
despite noting that the board "ignored weighty considerations and acted
on matters not proper for consideration."[126] One improper matter was
that Attorney General's List of Subversive Organizations. Barsky's last legal recourse was the U.S. Supreme Court. His lawyer prepared a detailed
Petitioner's Brief (which included the plea, "this petitioner has suffered
more than enough"). On April 26, 1954—just three weeks before its his-
toric school desegregation case[127]—the Supreme Court decided (6–3) on
technical grounds not to interfere with the determinations of the Board
of Regents. The dissenting opinions of Justices Hugo Black, William O.
Douglas, and Felix Frankfurter make fascinating reading and, presumably,
must have fortified Barsky. Douglas did not mince words: "nothing in a
man's political beliefs disables him from setting bones or removing appendixes. . . . When a doctor cannot save lives in America because he is
opposed to Franco in Spain, it is time to call a halt and look critically at
the neurosis that has possessed us."[128]

In a final, desperate act, Barsky wrote to the Board of Regents and appealed for clemency. Barsky was a self-effacing man, not given to effusive
displays or the grand gesture. To an interviewer he did not display "the
slightest hint of sentimentality."[129] To his daughter, he was a "very private,
a shy man who did not toot his own horn."[130] So writing the following
soul-bearing letter could not have been easy. The letter also points, in a

microcosmic way, to the psychological damage and financial devastation inflicted on individuals who held political views contrary to the Cold War consensus.

> I have been in practice for 35 years and never once during this time have I been in any difficulty. Not a single patient could or has ever accused me of . . . any lack of sympathy or understanding . . . [and] no medical colleague who has had any contact with me, either directly or indirectly, could point to any improper actions on my part. . . . I am not a young man and my family, a wife and young child, are completely dependent upon my earnings. I am not wealthy, and being deprived of six months income would almost completely wipe out what little savings I have. To pick up the threads of a practice after a lapse of six months would be fraught with the greatest of difficulties and obstacles. . . . I am sure that you gentlemen can understand what havoc a six months suspension could do to a professional career.[131]

The Board was not swayed. In fact its legal counsel wrote to "caution" Barsky on his office procedure: under the suspension order not only was he required to "desist from practice," but his office secretary was forbidden from leaving any impression that he was "still in practice."[132] Four days later, on June 25, 1954, the suspension of Barsky's medical license took effect.

Further Persecution

Eventually, Barsky did "pick up the threads" of his practice. But there was yet another act of "undiluted vindictiveness" that was committed, yet another battle he had to fight.[133] When his medical license was revoked, so too, unbeknownst to Barsky, was his registration with the Workmen's Compensation Board, which he had gained in July 1935. He learned this only when insurance companies refused to honor his invoices from workers' compensation cases, which constituted much of his surgical work.[134] He judged the damage to his reputation and earning capacity as "extremely great."[135] He applied for renewal of his registration, which, with a surgeon of his longevity, qualifications, and unimpeachable record, would normally have been a routine formality.[136] Not so with Barsky, for Barsky was a communist. He was "amazed" by the request that he appear before the Medical Practice Committee but did so, on May 24, 1955, in the hope of "expediting this matter in an amicable way."[137] Further amazement awaited him. He was obliged to take the oath and was questioned by an attorney (who was not a member of the committee), whose questions related to his associations with communists, not his professional capacities. Barsky had not been informed beforehand of these unprecedented procedures, nor had he recourse to legal counsel. So he stopped answering questions. On July 22 he was informed that, because he "refused to answer certain questions which the Committee considered material and relevant," his application for registration was rejected.[138] In what by now was a familiar route, Barsky formally appealed to the Medical Appeals Unit, informally appealed to the chairman of the Workmen's Compensation Board ("to grant an exception so that patients operated upon by me would receive sickness disability benefits"), and enlisted the support of the Provisional Committee of 1000 Physicians Against Imposition of "Loyalty" Oaths.[139] There is no extant record of the outcome of these appeals.

It was in this same year, 1955, that the JAFRC officially disbanded. Its death throes were punctuated by further assaults. In 1952, the Treasury Department demanded payment of the crippling sum of $315,000 in back taxes after its tax-exempt status was revoked. In 1954, the Subversive Activities Control Board (SACB) ordered the JAFRC to register itself as a Communist Party "front" organization. It refused and faced further punitive sanctions. In early 1955, it faced investigation by the New York Joint Legislative Committee on Charitable and Philanthropic Agencies and Organizations, which was attempting, unsuccessfully, to locate and serve a subpoena on the new JAFRC chairman. Another JAFRC appeal to its beleaguered supporters could not save it. In a brief public statement the executive board disclosed that it had voted on February 14 in favor of its own dissolution. It cited "harassments, persecutions and prosecutions" by HUAC, SACB, and the Treasury Department. These activities made it "impossible" to continue the "good and necessary relief work that we have carried on since our inception."[140]

The Role of the FBI

This statement did not mention the activities of the FBI, whose records detailing its ten-year vendetta against the JAFRC have remained classified, until recently. Its vast confidential files on the JAFRC were requested by the author and obtained in nine batches, with the final release on December 22, 2010.[141] Those who have researched the records of security organizations in other countries will find much that is familiar: infinite

details of meetings, speakers, amounts raised, membership lists, publications, correspondence, telephone conversations, mail interceptions, travel
itineraries, photographs of officials, lists of financial contributors, identi-
ties of donors, patrons and benefactors, and extensive deletions. These
previously untapped files constitute a case study of political repression in
the modern age. That repression is an index of the cost of defiance and
the strength of the forces mobilized against the JAFRC, and the JAFRC
was but one of dozens, perhaps hundreds, of left-wing organizations destroyed during the McCarthyist era. To put it simply, the sides were not
evenly matched.

The FBI's relentless pursuit of the JAFRC commenced before World
War II had ended and well before the Cold War had started. Three examples suggest the flavor of the hunt. First, on January 18, 1945, J. Edgar
Hoover contacted the head of the State Department's Division of Foreign
Activity. Hoover made this official aware of a plan by the JAFRC to bring
Pablo Picasso to the United States and, more ominously, that Picasso had
recently joined the French Communist Party. The source—"confidential
and reliable"—was an FBI informant inside the JAFRC; he or she was
joined by dozens of other informants throughout the next ten years, and
the intelligence they provided was voluminous. Second, on February 21,
1945, Hoover disseminated to senior FBI officers information received
from the Military Intelligence Division of the U.S. Army concerning the
activities of Spanish communists inside France. In particular it emphasized
the National Union of Spanish Republicans, formed in Vichy France in
November 1942, and identified members of its Central Committee with
whom the JAFRC was in contact. Third, on March 7, 1945, the director
of the Office of Censorship, Byron Price, forwarded to Hoover a copy
of a cable sent from Dorothy Parker in New York to Lillian Hellman in
London requesting that the latter attend a JAFRC dinner in Hellman's
honor. Referring to this cable (and implying that it had been illegally
procured), the accompanying memo to Hoover stated that "the attached
information was taken from private communications and its extremely
confidential character must be preserved." From this sample we are able
to get some sense of how various arms of the state—the FBI, the State
Department, the U.S. Army, and the Office of Censorship—worked together to counter what were seen as threats to national security.

Embodying such a perceived threat was a national organizer of the
JAFRC, Felix Kusman. Born in Estonia in imperial Russia on March 25,
1909, Kusman immigrated to the United States in 1920 and served with
the Abraham Lincoln Brigade in Spain. There, he met Edward Barsky

and, subsequently, worked with him to establish the JAFRC. Suspicions commenced the following year, when a letter to Kusman, dated February 24, 1943, was intercepted by the FBI; it thanked him for sending monthly checks to Mexico that helped establish a "Latin American Committee of Free Germans."[142] The FBI was convinced that foul play was afoot, that there was "something more to the transaction [of money] than a mere rescue of Anti-Fascist refugees."[143] Consequently, Kusman was very closely monitored. When he visited Seattle in early 1945, the FBI established a "Central Coordinating Committee" to monitor his movements and activities. It made extensive and effective use of "technical equipment" (microphone installation in his Roosevelt Hotel room and recording of all incoming and outgoing telephone calls) in addition to physical and photographic surveillance, which "completely covered" the subject.

> This surveillance was most successful in obtaining information of value regarding KUSMAN's conversations and purposes of his visit to Seattle, and although KUSMAN had the reputation of being a "whirling dervish," a man extremely hard to tail, he was never lost. With this technical coverage it was easy not only to follow KUSMAN, but to anticipate his movements by knowing the identity and time of his appointments.[144]

The use of such microphones and wiretaps was probably illegal.[145] The theft by Los Angeles FBI agents of a duplicate set of Kusman's keys—stolen when his hotel room was entered and his personal belongings searched—was definitely illegal.[146] Surveillance was a labor-intensive activity. A report on Kusman's activities for just one day, February 15, 1945—from 10:40 A.M., when he emerged from his hotel room, until the "time of the subject's retiring," at 11:10 P.M.—runs to seven single-spaced typed pages. Kusman's reputation as a "whirling dervish" had some basis: much to the chagrin of the FBI, which found out only after the event, Kusman illegally exited the United States, illegally entered Portugal, and illegally reentered the United States.[147] The final FBI reference to Kusman, hundreds of pages later, reveals that on June 22, 1953, he was detained on Ellis Island after being arrested by the Immigration and Naturalization Service (INS) under a deportation warrant. The FBI confirmed that the INS had "no objection" to the Bureau's reinterviewing Kusman "to see if he might not now be receptive to persuasion to testify as a Government witness."[148]

The FBI could count on the cooperation of former members of the JAFRC or disaffected communists who were prepared—and sometimes eager—to provide testimony that incriminated their former comrades. The bureau could "openly" produce admissible exhibits and information that had been obtained through clandestine means by informants, burglaries, or "black bag jobs" (illegal entries). Seduced by, *inter alia*, a generous FBI stipend, former communists became professional anticommunists. Lyman Bradley, Helen Bryan, and Howard Fast were all approached in the 1950s but refused to cooperate. Two who did and who gave evidence against the JAFRC were the serial testifier Louis Budenz, the ex-editor of the *Daily Worker*, and the serial liar Harvey Matusow.[149] A less notorious apostate, John Janowitz, identified JAFRC member Ruth Davidow as a member of the Communist Party's Tom Paine Club in Cleveland, Ohio, in 1945.[150] Janowitz had been an official of the Party's Cleveland branch from 1943 until 1950. He was assessed as "a good witness for the Government in 1949" (during the Smith Act prosecutions) and "available and willing to testify" in 1953.[151] This was central to the FBI's *modus operandi*: to find witnesses who could confirm the alleged communist domination of the JAFRC. Once "proven," the organization was obliged, under the draconian McCarran (Internal Security) Act of 1950, to register with the Subversive Activities Control Board (SACB) as a communist "front" and surrender its membership and financial records. The bureau's *modus operandi* is also revealed through its assessments of witnesses who testified against the JAFRC. Stephen A. Wereb, for instance, was not a member of the JAFRC "until contacted by a representative of this [Los Angeles] office." During the period he worked for the FBI, from 1944 until 1948, "he was a regularly paid informant."[152] As an "individual of known reliability," he then testified against the JAFRC. So in its war on "front" organizations, the FBI used Wereb, and innumerable others, in two consecutive roles: first, as an undercover informant and second, as a public witness. Indeed, some of the most recent FBI files released on the JAFRC concern the location, availability, and assessment of these informants/witnesses to testify before the SACB, which, with FBI help, was about to commence its 1954 investigation of JAFRC.[153] The irony is that, by this time, the JAFRC was barely functioning.

After JAFRC

Unlike the organization he founded and to which he was so devoted, Barsky survived. And he continued to support progressive causes. He was involved in a strike at Beth Israel Hospital in 1962, organized by Local 1199, over recognition of union membership of hospital employees.

Two years later, he helped establish the Medical Committee for Human Rights. It provided doctors and medical staff for civil rights activists who went to Mississippi in the violent "Freedom summer" of 1964. He remained active in this committee as well as in the anti–Vietnam War movement. He died at the age of seventy-eight on February 11, 1975. In an echo of the Spanish Civil War, seven ambulances sent from the United States to Nicaragua in support of the Sandinistas in 1985 were named in honor of Edward K. Barsky.[154]

This chapter has shown how one left-wing organization was destroyed in the early Cold War. There was no single persecutor but rather a range of government agencies—the bureaucracy of McCarthyism—whose combined force was formidable. The agencies identified in this chapter were the U.S. Justice Department, the Board of Regents of the New York State Department of Education, the House Un-American Activities Committee, the Federal Bureau of Investigation, the Internal Revenue Service, the Treasury Department, the Subversive Activities Control Board, and the U.S. State Department. They were not necessarily working in unison nor were their different roles and activities coordinated. The absence of overarching coordination should not, however, imply an absence of a bureaucratic consensus and operational framework. While there was no outward conspiracy, the various arms of the state complemented one another through their pursuit of a shared goal: the elimination of any activity deemed "un-American." Against this, the JAFRC; its leader, Edward Barsky; and its legion of supporters were no match.

Howard Fast, 1952. (© Van Pelt–Dietrich Library, University of Pennsylvania.)

2
The Writer

Howard Fast

During the early years of the Cold War, Howard Fast, born in New York City in 1914, was one of America's most celebrated novelists. Until his resignation in 1957, Howard Fast was the single most important literary figure in the Communist Party of the United States of America (CPUSA).[1] The first of his sixty-five novels was published in 1933, when he was eighteen. When *Citizen Tom Paine* appeared in 1943, he was regarded as "one of the few major American novelists."[2] According to an American academic who visited the Soviet Union in 1956, "the name of Howard Fast was on the lips of nearly everyone [I] talked with" and noted that Fast's works were "required reading in universities and schools throughout the country."[3] As a result, he "became *the* representative contemporary American writer in the Soviet Union."[4] Fast was also lionized in the satellite countries of eastern Europe, where translated copies sold in their millions. An East German recalled Fast's books' being "everywhere" in the windows of bookshops all throughout his youth.[5] Until 1956, *Spartacus* alone had sold 800,000 copies in the German Democratic Republic (East Germany).[6] Thus, from "Bratislava to Pyongyang his name [was] a banner and a byword."[7] Although his literary star had faded by 1957, Fast's historical novels remained on the bookshelves in hundreds of thousands of American homes. But as we have seen, Fast, as a member of the Joint Anti-Fascist Refugee Committee (JAFRC) board, along with Edward Barsky, Lyman Bradley, and Helen Bryan, was jailed in 1950. This chapter investigates his encounters with both anticommunism and communism, culminating in his decision to quit the CPUSA in 1957.

"The books are burning"

Fast's confrontation with McCarthyism commenced in February 1947. This was eight months before a group of film industry professionals, who were to become known as the Hollywood Ten, were subpoenaed to appear before the House Committee on Un-American Activities (HUAC). On February 4 the nine-member Board of Superintendents of New York City, the highest administrative unit of the public school system, recommended unanimously to the Board of Education that *Citizen Tom Paine*, Howard Fast's popular novel of the American Revolution, be removed from all secondary schools. The novel had already sold more than a million copies, in 1944–46 was distributed to both American servicemen abroad in the *Armed Services Editions* and to citizens of liberated countries by the Office of War Information (OWI), and was on the "approved list" for all New York public school libraries. Although the associate superintendent responsible for the high school division, Dr. Frederic Ernst, admitted he had neither read the book, nor read even consecutive pages but only pages selected for him with marked passages, he believed that *Citizen Tom Paine* was "vulgar" and "unfit" to be read by children.[8] Ernst told a reporter he was "proud" of the way he was protecting the city's youth from "objectionable" literature.[9] The reaction was quick and robust. A radical member of the New York City Council termed the superintendents' decision a case of "witch-burning," "un-American censorship," and a "cheap insult to one of America's greatest novelists."[10] Two playwrights, Arthur Miller and Marc Connelly, publicly condemned the decision, Miller maintaining that the novel was "a proud addition to any patriotic library" and Connelly that it "communicates Americanism at its very best." Charles Duell, on behalf of the book's publisher, Duell, Sloan & Pearce, was mystified by the charge of "purple passages" and advised protesting citizens to write letters to the publisher for use in future legal action.[11] Three separate petitions signed by seven authors, eleven book publishers, and sixteen workers from the Howard Clothing Company were sent to the president of the Board of Education, A. G. Clauson.[12] The Association of Teachers of Social Studies warned that judging a book on the basis of isolated passages could mean the rejection of "a large proportion of classics."[13] This was a foretaste of the storm that broke three weeks later.

At its scheduled monthly meeting on February 26, the Board of Education came to item number 57485: consideration of the superintendents' recommendation. It was not a typical meeting, for there were also

200 spectators crowding into the Brooklyn boardroom. Eleven of them took the floor to persuade the board to reverse the earlier decision. At one point, a board member, James Marshall, stated: "I think we are here to hear people, not to be cross-examined by them."[14] All their arguments—which revolved around censorship, free speech, incipient fascism, and other books on the approved list that, allegedly, were far more objectionable than Fast's—proved fruitless. The president of the board was dismissive: "There has been a great deal of 'Wolf, wolf' cried here. Or perhaps I should say a lot of political hypochondria, with a cry of 'Paine, Paine.'" By a 6–1 vote the board accepted the superintendents' recommendation. The Manhattan representative, George Timone, gave the fullest account of concerns about the book, calling it "improper, indecent, lewd and lascivious."[15] On the other hand, the sole dissenter, the board's Brooklyn representative, Maximilian Moss, stated that because "I have considered the book as a whole, in its entirety," the objectionable passages are "quickly forgotten" by the overall effect of the book and by "the emphasis by Tom Paine on the dignity of man."[16] He quoted from several passages to demonstrate that defense of dignity.

The longest and most serious "offending" passage in *Citizen Tom Paine* was half a page in length. It concerned the sale of a young woman at a Philadelphia slave market. It illustrated Paine's profound revulsion with such human trafficking. Fast describes how the execrable auctioneer, Miles Hennisy ("one of the greatest slave callers of his day"), generated interest in the sale by emphasizing the slave's virginity and her physical features: "Her blood is royal, and as for her mind, already she speaks enough of the King's tongue to make herself understood. Her breasts are like two Concord grapes, her behind like the succulent hams of a suckling pig. I start the bidding at fifty pounds. . . ." Hennisy ripped off the blanket to reveal her nakedness when the bidding reached eighty pounds. The girl was "frightened and shivering."[17] The overall historical context of this scene, or its role in the development of Paine's character, or the way in which Fast contrived the reader to identify with Paine's revulsion, was of no interest to the Board of Education, only its "vulgar" content that supposedly made it unfit for secondary school students.

Although it is possible that the nine members of the Board of Superintendents and five of the six members of the Board of Education were sufficiently outraged by their selective reading of "purple" passages of Fast's historical novel to ban it, it is equally plausible that morality cloaked ideology. The previous year, as we have seen, Fast had been served with a subpoena, appeared before HUAC, refused to cooperate, and was cited for contempt. Fast thereby took the first steps that eventually led him to Mill Point federal penitentiary, where he spent three months in 1950. In February 1947, the indictment against the JAFRC was reported in the *New York Times*. It is possible, then, that the legal proceedings against Fast and what then seemed his imminent imprisonment may have lent support to the decision to remove his book.[18] The poet and anthologist Louis Untermeyer certainly thought so: "I cannot get myself to believe that the reason given is anything but an excuse."[19] The *Daily Worker* was more explicit: "The Board of Superintendents had a *political motive*, and a pretty shabby one at that . . . to frighten teachers and writers with progressive views."[20] This may have been an overstatement, but the issue soon *became* political. The president of the anticommunist American Writers Association, Rupert Hughes, urged the board to "not yield to a propaganda drive,"[21] while in a remarkable letter to Untermeyer, its executive secretary, Edna Lonigan, wrote:

> The sale of Fast's book has been built up by a powerful political "apparat" using all the techniques which could be used to slant the sale of books in his favor. . . . In addition, the book is acknowledged to be a carrier of political propaganda favoring institutions that are hostile to American political freedom and designed to create hostility among American citizens.[22]

Presumably, private publishers, such as Macmillan as well as Harcourt and Brace, did not belong to this political "apparat": both quickly moved to delete Fast's anthologies, short stories, and excerpts from his novels from school readers. He simply disappeared from these reissued textbooks. At least in the mainstream, Howard Fast was becoming a nonperson.[23] School principals, meanwhile, confronted the problem of how to dispose of *Citizen Tom Paine*. Board regulations stipulated that outworn textbooks be burned, but for a banned novel, there was no precedent.[24]

"The books are burning" was the rallying cry given to a protest meeting to support Howard Fast at New York's Manhattan Center on October 16, 1947.[25] Organized by *New Masses & Mainstream*, it was chaired by Fast's close friend Untermeyer and included speeches by lawyer O. John Rogge (then defending the JAFRC), musician Artie Shaw, playwright Arthur Miller, publisher Angus Cameron (about whom more below), and writer Shirley Graham. The meeting was reported only by the *Daily Worker*. This was to become symptomatic of the public isolation and detachment from the "masses and mainstream" that Fast experienced over the next decade.

Blacklisting

If 1947 opened with Fast's not being read, it closed with Fast's not being heard. After he and the executive board of the JAFRC were sentenced to jail on June 27 and a series of legal appeals were initiated, Fast was invited by several student organizations to speak at campuses. One by one, the administrations of such universities and colleges refused permission. The first was Columbia University. Its provost, Albert C. Jacobs, invoked "university practice" in barring Fast because he was "under sentence." "Any man," he clarified, "who is not under sentence or indictment can speak at Columbia." The college paper, the *Columbia Daily Spectator*, editorialized that this position was "dubious."[26] The fact that Columbia also barred Fast in November 1950, after his sentence had been served, confirms the spurious rationale.[27] Moreover, another JAFRC board member, New York University's Lyman Bradley, also under the same sentence, had been permitted to speak at various colleges (although not at NYU). One of these, Brooklyn College, used the same justification as Columbia, and City College of New York and Hunter College followed suit. Fast had been invited by the Karl Marx Society at City College to speak on "Marxism and Literature." At each of these colleges, protest rallies attended by hundreds of students were held, but all in vain. Even an attempt to circumvent the ban—by successfully booking the auditorium at Midwood High School, adjacent to Brooklyn College—was quashed by the Board of Education.[28]

Of course, Fast was not completely silenced. But the range of organizations he addressed that were not connected to the CPUSA was steadily narrowing. One was the American Library Association. He was the keynote speaker at its 67th national convention, held in Atlantic City in June 1948. Approximately 400 librarians heard Fast reveal that, in contrast to his previous novels that were published in editions of many thousands of copies, "the publishers of *Clarkton*, [my] latest novel, have responded to pressure and printed so few copies of the book that orders cannot be filled, an illustration of the devious methods of the censor."[29] The publisher, Duell, Sloan & Pearce, which had stood by Fast in his battle with the Board of Education, printed only 5,000 copies of *Clarkton*. (In 1946 it had printed 100,000 copies of Fast's *The American*.) Plausibly, this decision was made because, as Barnard Rubin's "Broadway Beat" column put it, Duell, Sloan & Pearce expected "a concentrated effort to boycott it."[30] *Clarkton*, which concerned a Massachusetts strike, was explicitly political. A combination of the size of the print run and the fear of publicity meant that booksellers were not supplied by wholesalers, publicity and promotion were negligible, and interested buyers could not find the book. This development, whereby publishers, past and prospective, were infected by the Cold War climate, meant that Fast struggled to be read. It was not only schoolchildren but the wider reading public whose access to Fast's novels dried up. But such blacklisting involved more than small print runs. In 1951, commercial publishing houses were unwilling even to publish *Spartacus*, and this development had significant repercussions on Fast's life.

Spartacus

Howard Fast first contemplated *Spartacus* while incarcerated, from June 7 to August 29, 1950. Its genesis was a book he found in the Mill Point prison library about the German revolution of 1918–19 in which Rosa Luxemburg, who formed the Spartacists, played a leading role. This revolutionary group, the forerunner of the German Communist Party, was named after Spartacus, who led the Roman slave revolt in 73–71 B.C., and "I read every scrap and thread of information about Spartacus that I could find in that small prison library."[31] In prison, too, "I developed [the book] in my mind and gave it structure."[32] Fast completed the manuscript of *Spartacus* in the first half of 1951. It was perhaps his best-constructed work, and Fast was highly satisfied with it.[33] So was Angus Cameron, vice president of Little, Brown since 1943 and Fast's publisher since 1948.[34] In his in-house reader's report, dated June 27, 1951, he wrote that "It is endlessly engaging, most ingeniously put together, and, all in all, an entertaining and meaningful novel. . . . It is a novel we can publish with pride. . . . This is a fine novel." Cameron sent Fast this report accompanied by a personal congratulatory letter, adding that the trade editorial report "tells briefly what I think of the book. It does not attempt to say all the things I feel about it and it does not do justice, really, to my admiration for the skillful technique of the telling. It shows the sure hand of a real artist . . . [which] never falters."[35] Ominously, copies of both the Little, Brown report and Cameron's personal letter (each on official Little, Brown letterhead) were forwarded to the FBI.[36]

Angus Cameron joined Little, Brown in 1938 and became its editor-in-chief in 1943. He had a reputation for promoting unknown writers such as J. D. Salinger (he published *The Catcher in the Rye* in 1951), iconoclastic poets such as Ogden Nash, and communist writers such as Stefan Heym, Lillian Hellman, and Albert Maltz (one of the Hollywood Ten). In 1951 *Time* magazine described Cameron as the "foremost" book editor in the United States. But that same issue also announced his forced resignation from Little, Brown.[37] The trigger, as we shall see, was the internal wrangle over the publication of *Spartacus*, but the issue went deeper and takes us into the murky minutiae of the anticommunist crusade in the early 1950s.

Cameron first came to the notice of red-baiters when he was attacked in 1947 by Arthur Schlesinger Jr. for Little, Brown's refusal (along with numerous other publishers') to publish George Orwell's *Animal Farm*. Schlesinger continued to campaign against Cameron, writing to the president of Little, Brown (until 1949 Alfred McIntyre, then Arthur Thornhill) and going public with Cameron's sponsorship of organizations close to the CPUSA.[38] Cameron was not formally a party member but was on friendly terms with many communist writers, such as Fast, Albert Kahn, and Maltz. He described himself in one interview as a "philosophical Marxist."[39] Schlesinger's attacks were picked up and developed by the American Legion, George Sokolsky in the *New York World-Telegram*, and, most extensively and damagingly, by *Counterattack*. Published weekly by American Business Consultants, Inc., *Counterattack* was emblematic of virulent domestic anticommunism and liberally quoted in Scripps-Howard newspapers, such as the *New York World-Telegram*.[40] Its six-page August 31, 1951, issue was devoted solely to Little, Brown and Angus Cameron. It not only provided an annotated list of communist "agents and their fellow-travelers and front supporters" whose books have been or would be published by Little, Brown (Fast, of course, was on this three-page list) but also itemized Cameron's "impressive front record": petitions he signed, meetings he supported, organizations he joined.[41] It suggested that Little, Brown was, in effect, a front organization and Cameron, in particular, was targeted. *Counterattack* rhetorically asked: "How long will [Little, Brown] be able to continue publishing the works of so many Communists and front supporters without incurring bad publicity and suffering financially?"[42] According to Cameron, "[M]y colleagues got panicky."[43] These colleagues would also have known that nine days earlier, on August 22, 1951, Louis Budenz, a former editor of the *Daily Worker*, now a professional witness, had testified before a public session of the Senate Internal Security Subcommittee that he knew Angus Cameron to be a member of the Communist Party.[44]

Two days after this issue of *Counterattack* appeared, Cameron called a full board meeting of Little, Brown to discuss *Spartacus* and confirm its earlier policy. In April the board of directors had resolved that the company would not be intimidated, would resist the Cold War climate, and would continue to publish books irrespective of their politics. Now, in August, *Spartacus* was one of those books. But Cameron missed the scheduled Friday meeting: he had met an author in Maine, and because of bad weather the local airport was closed. The board lacked Cameron's resolve, or integrity, and withered. It decided, in his absence, that he must in future submit to the board for approval all his outside political activities.[45] *Spartacus* was not mentioned. The executive vice president, Sidney Salmen, drafted a letter that was delivered the next day, Saturday. On the following Monday, Cameron told the Little, Brown board that "no free publishing house ought to require of its editor" such conditions, which he could not accept, and resigned. By 2:00 P.M. he left his office, quietly but angrily, for the last time.[46] The anticommunist crusaders had claimed another scalp. For the rest of the decade, he was blacklisted by the publishing industry.[47]

Spartacus also exited from Little, Brown quietly: Salmen had not favored publication because of the politics of its author, and, with Cameron's departure, *Spartacus* lost its key supporter and was dropped.[48] This, then, was the context for Little, Brown's not publishing *Spartacus* in 1951. Fast then sent the manuscript of *Spartacus* to several other publishers whose editors he knew personally.[49] Each, in turn, sent it back, either with no comment or euphemistic explanations for rejection ("with cost factors being what they are today . . ."[50]). Publishers' acquiescence to McCarthyism certainly contributed to Fast's increasing separation from mainstream literati. Understandably, he was demoralized:

> It has been a very dreary and unhappy experience. . . . I have behind me seven best sellers and some 10 million books sold throughout these United States, and I did not feel that I could tolerate an endless succession of such experiences.[51]

One of those experiences was his communication with a small publisher who "must remain nameless" because of his and Fast's close personal relationship. It also captures a less dramatic, usually unknown, but profoundly debilitating dimension of the blacklist.

> This publisher, while never actually being in the left camp, has in the past published many novels of independence and radical content. He begged me not to submit my manuscript to him, and not put him in the terrible position of having to reject it out of fear. I abided by his wishes.[52]

Blue Heron

By the end of 1951, Fast was contemplating publishing *Spartacus* himself. At a small, private reception in the home of Haya Hamburg on December 11—also attended by an FBI informant—Fast stated that he and another individual (whose name was noted in the FBI report but redacted in the FOIA copy) were considering establishing a publishing house but lacked the initial $50,000 capital. Instead, all those present at the reception "paid an advance of $5 for a copy of *Spartacus* which it was hoped would be privately published."[53] This, in fact, was how *Spartacus* was bankrolled. He described his *modus operandi* in a promotional piece for a left-wing paper:

> I had no money with which to publish the book, but I had friends and I knew that over ten million people in America had read my books. I wrote to these friends. I asked them to buy in advance, sight unseen, a novel called *Spartacus*, which I would publish if and when enough of them sent me five dollars for a subscription to it. It was a strange offer on my part, and I got a strange response.[54]

That response was that the first, limited self-published edition sold out. There were clearly limits to the hegemony of McCarthyism. A thick, subterranean layer of left-wing opposition persisted. This made it possible, according to Fast, "for me to break through the curtain of silence that has been draped around my work."[55] One who responded at the outset was the noted Percy Bysshe Shelley scholar Kenneth Cameron; his accompanying note conveyed the despair in some literary circles: "I am happy to send $5.00 to rescue Spartacus from oblivium [*sic*]. It is certainly a hell of a commentary on the present situation in American culture when a world recognized author cannot find a publisher."[56] In contrast, the librarian at the University of Kentucky Library, to whom Fast sent a letter of solicitation, immediately contacted "My dear Mr. [J. Edgar] Hoover" with the more sinister comment that "Fast is probably trying to raise money for some other purpose."[57] A cheaper paperback edition went to press in February 1952 and was also distributed, as a selection, through the pro-communist Liberty Book Club. The distribution methods were rudimentary. An advertising flyer soliciting orders stated: "Write to me at Box 171, Planetarium Station, New York 24, New York. Put $2.50 in cash, money order or check in an envelope, and I will send you the book before February 1. If the fifty cents in cash presents a problem, you can use stamps for that amount."[58] For a book that later sold millions and became a $9 million Hollywood film, this does not seem an auspicious start. However, within three months an astonishing 48,000 copies were sold across the United States, mainly through Fast's own direct-mail method. Copies were also sold in Great Britain after it was published by Bodley Head and distributed by Central Books—a development that disturbed the FBI's legal attaché at the U.S. Embassy in London.[59]

It was this success, extremely rare for a self-published work, that encouraged Fast to form Blue Heron Press.[60] He and his wife, Bette, poured all their available assets and savings into it. For four years, until mid-1956, Blue Heron was the sole American publisher of all of Fast's new works: *Tony and the Wonderful Door* (1952, a children's book), *The Passion of Sacco and Vanzetti* (1953), *Silas Timberman* (1954), and *The Story of Lola Gregg* (1956). Although these books were applauded in the communist press for their "socialist realist" strengths, their sales were, by *Spartacus* standards, paltry. Blue Heron also republished both Fast's earlier works (*The Last Frontier, Citizen Tom Paine, Freedom Road*)[61] and W. E. B. Du Bois' classic, out-of-print *Souls of Black Folk.*[62] It also published (with a foreword by Fast) *The Best Untold: A Book of Paintings* (1953) by the blacklisted artist Edward Biberman (brother of Herbert, who was one of the Hollywood Ten).

Steadily, Blue Heron Press slid into insolvency. Fast was constantly concerned about the state of his finances. In a letter to his old friend Angus Cameron, now overseeing the ailing Liberty Book Club, of whom Fast requested immediate payment of an outstanding invoice for $27.59, he wrote:

> I also want to tell you, Angus, that I have had to sell my entire stock of books, some 6 or 7,000 in number to the Remainder Book Company at a mere pittance to meet my obligations. This is the situation I was forced into by the failure to [*sic*] Liberty Book Club to meet their obligations. It also means the end of Blue Heron Press, for what that is worth, and puts me in a position where I shall have to borrow personally to get out of this.[63]

Although Fast never paid himself a wage from his firm—his family lived on the earnings he received from foreign book sales and royalties and his wife's income from fashion designing—there were other writers and publishers far worse off. One was the blacklisted Albert Kahn (who later joined Angus Cameron in the short-lived Cameron & Kahn Publishers in August 1953); he was invited to a dinner function in 1952 with Howard

Fast. "I wish I could attend," he wrote, "but I happen to be in rather difficult financial straights [sic] at the moment, living on borrowed dough."[64] Indeed, the financial hardship of those blacklisted is an easily overlooked reality.

The days of Blue Heron were numbered. In September 1955, Fast wrote to Albert Maltz in Cuernavaca, Mexico, that his struggle with Blue Heron "is just about over. I have laid out so much money for the project in the course of it, that I cannot possibly go on as a publishing house."[65] Elsewhere, he commented that the venture "almost bankrupted me. Cost me about $20,000. Plus leaving me very poor."[66] Yet self-publishing provided a measure of protection against the blacklist, and, in this context, he claimed a pyrrhic victory over the FBI. Because J. Edgar Hoover could send "none of his agents to knock on my door and instruct me not to publish books by Howard Fast . . . I had beaten the little bastard, and whatever it cost, it was my small victory."[67] Blue Heron limped on until June 4, 1956, when Fast immediately dropped it on the same day he read the text of Nikita Khrushchev's "secret" speech denouncing Stalin.[68]

Isolation

Financial difficulties, the almost total absence of retail outlets, and deteriorating health[69] were compounded by denial of recognition: Fast's books were no longer reviewed. For him and, indeed, most authors, critical reviews were as important, intellectually, as oxygen was, physically, to treat his devastating cluster headaches. Fast's historical novel on a phase of the American Revolution, *The Proud and the Free*, published by Little, Brown in 1950, received only one (hostile) review, in the *New York Post*.[70] In the summer of 1951–52 the self-published *Spartacus* was similarly ignored; even the FBI, whose Agent Suttler had written a detailed six-page review of *Clarkton* in 1947, did not repeat the courtesy.[71] The silence that greeted *Spartacus* prompted Maltz, another blacklisted author, to comment:

> . . . any book by a man of your body of work has always gotten reviews everywhere, in every journal and paper. The extent of the boycott upon you is therefore savage and sweeping. I don't think it will soon mend.[72]

Later, Maltz wrote that, as a writer, Fast was being "boxed in by reactionary publishers and critics, and shut up in a very small world of readers in the U.S."[73] The problem of being neither reviewed nor read within the United States deepened with Fast's next three novels; *The Passion of*

Sacco and Vanzetti, Silas Timberman, and *The Story of Lola Gregg* were almost universally ignored. The communist press, of course, especially the *Daily Worker* and *Masses & Mainstream,* carried reviews,[74] but Fast was scarcely heartened by this. He caustically referred to the "superficial reviews of my work that come out of the left" and believed that "book reviewing on the left is usually infantile," followed an "idiotic pattern," and was determined by "the current political nonsense of the moment."[75]

At least Fast was still being read overseas. In 1953, the editor of *Masses & Mainstream,* Sam Sillen, observed Fast's books' being prominently displayed in the bookshops of three European capitals: London, Paris, and Prague.[76] His books were also on the shelves of innumerable United States Information Service (USIS) and American embassy and consulate libraries around the world, and readings from his historical novels were regularly broadcast via the Voice of America (VOA). All this stopped in 1953. And here we come to Fast's final encounter with McCarthyism or, more specifically, with the Permanent Subcommittee on Investigations of the Committee on Government Operations, simply known then (because of the identity of its chairman) as the "McCarthy Committee." In February–March 1953, this subcommittee trained its sights on State Department agencies, the VOA, and its parent body, the International Information Administration (IIA).

Book-burning, Again

Senator McCarthy had already been supplied with "inside" information about alleged communist subversion by "Loyalty Underground," a small cell of anticommunist employees within VOA.[77] Some had testified during closed executive sessions throughout the second week of February. Under the headline "Pro-Americans Spy on Schemers," a journalist—to whom McCarthy undoubtedly fed information—breathlessly reported that those who testified revealed "amazing evidence of a conspiracy to subvert American policy in propaganda broadcasts abroad" and provided "documentary proof [of] deliberate sabotage of American objectives in foreign propaganda."[78] McCarthy also knew that the IIA (established January 1948) was staffed with several employees of the Office of War Information (closed August 1945), an agency with a reputation for employing writers with communist sympathies, including Howard Fast.[79] Here was an opportunity for McCarthy to validate his initial charges made three years before in Wheeling, West Virginia, that the State Department was infested with communists and debunk the Tydings Committee report that those charges were fraudulent. On February 3, 1953, just two weeks before the public hearings commenced, VOA policy writer W. Bradley Connors issued a directive approving the use of material by Howard Fast in VOA broadcasts and the circulation of his novels at USIS libraries. The underlying logic was that his pro-American novels would have "a special credibility" to audiences behind the Iron Curtain, given the Soviets' endorsement of his writings.[80] Ominously, McCarthy acquired Connors' memorandum from an unnamed source, probably a "Loyalty Underground" member. This directive had first been approved by an advisory committee of academics, publishers, and a Truman administration appointee.[81]

All this was grist for McCarthy's mill. In his interrogation of the IIA director, Dr. Wilson Compton, he alleged that the Voice of America had become the "Voice of Moscow" and that overseas libraries had become instruments of communist propaganda.[82] The grilling shook Compton, a former president of Washington State College (1944–51) and an appointee of former Secretary of State Dean Acheson. Two days later, the Secretary of State, John Foster Dulles, accepted his resignation. On that day, February 18, Fast appeared before the subcommittee.[83] It was the only time that the noted communist author and the chief communist hunter were in direct contact, and conflict. It was a dramatic moment. A battery of television and newsreel cameras was present, as was a packed audience that overflowed from the federal courthouse in New York's Foley Square. McCarthy and his chief counsel, Roy Cohn, asked Fast in rapid-fire succession about his communist affiliations and his knowledge of communists past and present at the OWI, the VOA, and the State Department. To all these questions, Fast repeatedly invoked the First and Fifth amendments. When Fast sought to explain more fully the privileges he was claiming in refusing to answer the questions, McCarthy cut him off with "The committee will not receive a lecture from this witness." Even when Senator Stuart Symington (D.-Mo.) taunted him with, "If you are a member [of the Communist Party], why aren't you proud of it instead of being ashamed of it?," Fast again took the Fifth.

The exchanges between Fast and McCarthy were heated and belligerent.[84] The gavel was frequently pounded. When Fast insisted on explaining why he would not give yes/no answers, McCarthy retorted that he would not allow the subcommittee to "become a transmission belt for the Communist party." Fast was questioned in detail about his time with the OWI: his earnings, whether he had signed a non-communist affidavit, the reasons why his employment with the OWI ceased. It seems that these questions were intended to entrap Fast into making perjurious statements. There was nothing duplicitous, however, about the series of questions from Senator Charles E. Potter (R.-Mich.), whose "ire" (according to a reporter present) Fast aroused. He asked Fast whether, if drafted, he would serve in the U.S. Army to fight communism in Korea. Fast "shouted," reportedly, that he had spent his whole life giving service to his country. When Fast fell short of answering whether he would fight communists and was ordered to answer by McCarthy, the conversation continued:

> *Mr. Fast.* Why don't you ask me what you mean, would I . . .
> *Senator Potter.* Why are you so nervous when we say fighting Communists?
> *Mr. Fast.* I am not nervous; angry but very calm. Don't tell me I am nervous.
> *Senator Potter.* If drafted would you fight Communists in Korea?[85]

After a tense hour, the inquisition was over. Fast was still under subpoena, but his testimony could not be cited as constituting contempt and the FBI, closely involved with this investigation, had nothing to act on.[86] A second jail term was avoided. But the "book burners" were not yet finished with Fast. As a result of the committee's investigation, and following the appointment of Robert Johnson as IIA director on March 3, the terse February 18 directive from the State Department—"no repeat no materials by any communists, fellow travelers, etcetera will be issued under any circumstances by any IIA media"[87]—was followed by another, on March 17. Now, all works by communist authors were to be weeded out and destroyed. The library shelves of all American embassies and USIS offices were combed and offending books removed. It was no small undertaking. In West Germany, for instance, more than forty Amerika Haus libraries were under USIS jurisdiction. Fortunately, McCarthy's two traveling investigators, Roy Cohn and Gerald Schine, were on hand to check shelves in the summer of 1953.[88] Officially, sixteen authors were blacklisted, and the historical novels of Howard Fast were joined by the detective novels of Dashiell Hammett. Also proscribed were Bernhard J. Stern's medical books and Morris Schappes' documentary history of American Jews.[89] Unofficially, according to a survey undertaken by *New York Times* correspondents in twenty world capitals, scores of other authors' works were removed arbitrarily by USIS library heads on their own initiative. These included *Witness*, by Whittaker Chambers. Presumably, in their haste, these USIS officials had not realized Chambers' critical role in the conviction of Alger Hiss on the charge of perjury. And presumably, too, they were not yet aware of President Eisenhower's "book-burners" speech at Dartmouth College on June 14.[90]

By mid-1953, therefore, neither a U.S. serviceman stationed in West Berlin nor a high school student in the Bronx could read *Citizen Tom Paine*. But American prisoners of war in Korea could. According to Colonel Robert Abbott, "a victim of communist torture in Korea," captured American soldiers were fed a literary diet of Howard Fast novels. Abbott stated that Fast "is a very vicious writer and should be stopped from publishing."[91] Abbott need not have worried. As we have seen, by the time the FBI received his report, the circumstances of the domestic Cold War had contrived to inhibit publishers, silence reviewers, and stifle access to Fast's books. For several years now, "I was no longer the young genius of American literature. The day of the glowing reviews was over."[92] He had, to use his own description, "taken the wrath of this last decade. . . ."[93] But what of Fast himself? What were the effects of this "wrath" on the quality of his writing, on the nature of his relationship with the CPUSA, and on his personal life?

"Neck-deep in politics"

From a certain perspective, there were some positive effects. Before 1949–50, Fast was a regular commentator and writer for the mainstream media. Being cut out of the commercial press, magazines, and radio meant he had more time on his hands. In the 1940s, he wrote short stories and articles for a wide range of magazines (*Collier's, Coronet, Esquire, Jewish Life, Saturday Review, Woman's Day*) and gave a regular radio commentary.[94] These opportunities dried up.[95] He also had more "free" time because he could not travel. In September 1950 the State Department put Fast on a different kind of blacklist: it repeatedly denied his application for a passport.[96] Before the passport ban was imposed, he traveled overseas in April–May 1949, when he attended the first Soviet-sponsored World Peace Congress in Paris and visited a JAFRC-sponsored hospital in Toulouse.[97] But now, he could not travel to the second World Peace Congress in Sheffield (relocated to Warsaw) in November 1950, to which he was invited by the organizers; to the "world premiere" of his play *Thirty Pieces of Silver* in Prague, in March 1951;[98] to the Youth Carnival for Peace and Friendship in Sydney, in March 1952, at which he was to be the guest speaker; or to Moscow to collect the $25,000 International Stalin Peace

Prize, which he was awarded in December 1953.[99] So how did Fast compensate? He immersed himself in mainstream politics. Quixotically, he ran for Congress under the American Labor Party (ALP) banner.[100] The seat, for the 23rd Congressional District in the South Bronx, was held by Democrat Isidore Dollinger, and Fast (and his wife) believed he had a good chance.[101] With a small band of dedicated supporters under the nomenclature "Independent Citizens Committee to Elect Howard Fast," he campaigned tirelessly and—seemingly—effectively. Indicative of his efforts is the thick folder of twelve transcripts of radio talks and interviews over station WMCA. For three nights every week from October 13 until November 3, Fast was on the air.[102] The issues discussed ranged from the war in Korea and the possible independence of Puerto Rico to the wage freeze and conditions in local schools and hospitals. And this was the tip of the campaigning iceberg.[103] The campaign was exhausting and exhilarating.[104] But it was doomed: he won fewer than 2,000 votes; Dollinger won more than 40,000.

Being marginalized as a writer may have afforded Fast the "space" to mount a campaign to win a congressional seat, but it meant that, to use his own description, he was "neck-deep in politics."[105] This immersion extended, of course, to the CPUSA, which was his fulcrum. It is beyond the scope of this chapter to list for even a three-year period (1953–55) the astonishing number of meetings he addressed, rallies he attended, lecture series he gave, campaigns he waged (for Steve Nelson, Julius and Ethel Rosenberg, and the Martinsville Seven), or the organizations he defended (Civil Rights Congress; Jefferson School of Social Science; National Lawyers' Guild) and represented (National Council of the Arts, Sciences and Professions; Joint Anti-Fascist Refugee Committee; Partisans for Peace).[106] This daunting degree of political activity was in addition to the plethora of columns, articles, and pamphlets he wrote for the communist press; by 1956, for example, he was writing a new column every four days for the *Daily Worker* under the title "The Current Scene." His close friend Albert Maltz was in awe: "You constantly astonish me with your enormous productivity, and . . . I envy and salute your prodigious output in all directions. . . . I don't have your gift of combining solid writing work with so many other activities."[107]

However, a casualty *was* Fast's "solid writing work." As the domestic Cold War became more intense, as his political commitments became greater, and as the effects of the blacklist became more circumscribing, the literary quality of Fast's writing diminished. It became more polemical and further isolated him from wider audiences. Perhaps the most extreme example was not a novel but Fast's only attempt at (vulgar) Marxist literary criticism, *Literature and Reality*. It was an indictment of almost all major American novelists, poets, and critics and condemned modern American literature as sterile, reactionary, and degenerate in contrast to that of the creative and vital Soviet writers. He referred variously to "belly-crawlers" and "hatchet-men"; literature as "garbage" and "filth"; and an award given to Ezra Pound as "overloaded with pus." John Steinbeck "reeks" with "cheap, phony sentimentalism," while George Orwell was a "crass" and "inept" propagandist, responsible for "childish and wicked little opium dreams" that reflected the interests of Wall Street.[108] *Literature and Reality* was canonized in the Soviet Union. It was translated, quoted, and paraphrased. Hailed as "a major event in the history of American literature," the book led Soviet reviewers to claim that Fast had now "defined a path for socialist realism in America."[109] At home, it was ignored or excoriated.[110] To a lesser degree the same applied to his Blue Heron books: *The Passion of Sacco and Vanzetti*, with its overly didactic thematic similarities to the Rosenberg case; *Silas Timberman*, a somewhat one-dimensional tale about a liberal university professor driven from his job and sent to jail (modeled, in part, on his prison cellmate, Lyman Bradley); *The Last Supper and Other Stories*, a book of sixteen short stories; and Fast's last novel as a member of the CPUSA, *The Story of Lola Gregg*, a polemical tale about the wife of a prominent communist being hunted by the FBI (based on CPUSA leader Robert Thompson's actual experience). These novels were the most doctrinaire and propagandist novels Fast ever wrote.[111] Fast attributed this to self-publishing: "When I had to publish my own books, I lost my distance, I lost my cool. . . . I was not objective."[112] The fact that he didn't have an editor, as a result of the blacklist, certainly contributed; also, arguably, Fast was on a vain quest to reconcile art with ideology through the application of "socialist realism." In these dark years, and consistent with *Literature and Reality*, he held that literature must take sides, must align itself with antifascist forces and must repudiate "bourgeois realism," which idealized form over content.[113]

Notwithstanding his commitment to socialist realism, his indefatigable political activism for the communist cause, and his canonical status in the Soviet Union (*Silas Timberman* was compared to Maxim Gorky's *Mother*), relations between Howard Fast and the CPUSA became increasingly strained. Although nothing was publicly apparent until Fast's seemingly sudden and dramatic break from the party in early 1957, there is strong circumstantial evidence of this tension and the art–ideology divide, dating back to 1948. The party leadership, according to Fast, wished to expel him because of the alleged Jewish nationalism in his *Glorious Brothers*. Only the intervention of others saved him.[114] His expulsion was "an unfulfilled dream of certain Party leadership."[115] He clashed with the party—in particular with one leader, V. J. Jerome, editor of *Political Affairs* and chairman of the party's Cultural Commission—over his 1950 play *The Hammer*. CPUSA leaders insisted, in keeping with its anti–Jim Crow casting policy, that the son of a small, slender, pale, orange-haired Jewish father be played by a 6′2″ deep-voiced African American actor, James Earl Jones. Fast was outraged, but lost. The mostly Yiddish-speaking audience laughed.[116] Bette had no illusions. When he told her of the busy schedule the CPUSA planned for him upon his release from jail, she replied: "What the hell is this overwhelming urge [by the party] to start tearing you to pieces again?"[117] By late 1952, Fast recalled, he felt trapped: "I hated the Communist Party . . . remaining in it only because I was a goddamn hero and there was nowhere else to go. . . ."[118] This remark was undoubtedly shaped by hindsight and retrospective judgment, but it reveals some of his inner tensions in being a communist and a writer.

These strains imposed additional burdens upon Fast's health. We cannot be certain whether his imprisonment triggered, exacerbated, caused, or was irrelevant to his emotional or physical condition. Although his bond with Bette was seemingly strengthened during his confinement at Mill Point—"Why is it, Bette, that we seem to find each other only when the going is tough?"[119]—we do know that his cluster headaches commenced then. Five years later, Albert Maltz heard they were so bad that "you had to carry oxygen [for the headaches] in your car."[120] In 1954, Maltz's wife, Margaret, told an FBI informant that Fast "needs rest" and was "recuperating" in Cuernavaca, Mexico. The Maltzs, still in exile, lived in Cuernavaca, a small resort town about sixty-five miles south of Mexico City. In July, Dr. Ernesto Amann, a political exile from the Spanish Civil War, was seeing Fast "nearly every day" allegedly for a "nervous disorder."[121] Amann stated (to an informant) that Fast and his family had "no intention of returning to the U.S." and might (like numerous blacklisted American communists from California and Spanish exiles from the civil war) establish "permanent residence" in Mexico.[122]

The Fasts and their two children, Rachel and Jonathan, did, of course, return to the United States, but not to New York. They settled quietly in a New Jersey suburb. Fast withdrew from the frenetic political activity of earlier years but joined the *Daily Worker* as a permanent staff member and wrote a regular column that was, as Maltz commented, "easily readable, thoughtful and thought-provoking."[123] But his "solid writing work," his creative extended fiction, dried up. He blamed it on the political environment, which meant "I was crippled in my function as a writer."[124] Then, on June 4, 1956, in the offices of the *Daily Worker*, Fast read the full text of Khrushchev's cataclysmic "secret speech."[125]

Defecting

On February 1, 1957, the front page of the *New York Times* carried a story that reverberated across the nation and, thereafter, the world. It began: "Howard Fast said yesterday that he had dissociated himself from the American Communist party and no longer considered himself a communist."[126] The *Times* article was carried by scores of local and state newspapers across the country. Fast was one of the most recognizable public faces of the party, an embodiment of its remaining credibility and prestige. For those Cold Warriors cheering on the collapse of the CPUSA, Fast's desertion of the party appeared to hasten it. We will now focus on why Howard Fast defected, why his defection was so important, the responses of others within and beyond the CPUSA, and the personal impact 1956 had upon him. Fast has already told his story, twice, but it is partisan, incomplete, and, at times, self-mythologizing.[127] It is worth revisiting Fast's predicament not merely to gain a more textured and nuanced picture of the thunderbolt that struck the CPUSA in 1956 and from which it never recovered but to close the chapter on Howard Fast's Cold War, on his encounter with communism.

By 1957, when the rigidly Stalinist William Z. Foster defeated the reformers (or "liquidationists," as he termed them), the party resembled an impotent sect: the *Daily Worker* had closed, its cultural and educative activities had ceased, and its membership, stripped of defecting intellectuals, had shriveled to about 3,000 hardcore cadres.[128] Ten years earlier, it numbered 74,000 members.[129] In understanding both this hemorrhaging and Howard Fast's disillusionment, the explosive "secret speech" is of critical importance.

Close to midnight on February 24, 1956, the First Secretary of the Communist Party of the Soviet Union (CPSU), Nikita Khrushchev, began a four-hour report to a closed session of delegates to the Twentieth Party Congress of the CPSU. His focus was on Stalin, and the speech was excruciating. Khrushchev exposed the mechanism of terror and the system of arbitrary rule that had dominated the country for thirty years. He deployed dozens of documents and a wealth of detail to reveal the brutal character of the terror. One such document, which he read aloud, was the letter by Politburo member R. I. Eikhe, who joined the Bolsheviks in 1905 and whose spine was broken by his interrogator. Khrushchev showed that the history of the CPSU under Stalin consisted of criminal acts such as responsibility for the suicide of Grigory Ordzhonikidze and the assassination of Sergei Kirov; lawless mass deportations of non-Russian peoples; political errors such as the breach with Yugoslavia; incompetent leadership, exemplified by the vulnerability of the Soviet Union to German attack in 1941; the methodical falsification of history written by Stalin himself or at his direction; and the replacement of the Leninist principle of collective leadership with the "cult of the personality." In short, Khrushchev punctured the mystical aura that surrounded Stalin: he had revealed that, instead of the wise and beneficent object of their adulation, Stalin was a bloodthirsty criminal responsible for systematic physical and psychological terror. Within the Soviet Union, only a brief summary of the speech was published, but even the abridged version was a shock, "like the explosion of a neutron bomb."[130] Within eastern European "satellite" countries, the time seemed ripe to challenge the legitimacy of Soviet rule and Stalinist structures. In both Poland and Hungary defiance was expressed openly although resolved differently: the former through compromise, the latter through brutal repression. Within communist parties throughout the world, the impact was profound and its effects convulsive. America was no exception, and it hit Fast hard.

"Ashes of grief"

Vague rumors about a "special report" that referred to "errors" committed under Stalin, and a "cult of personality," had been circulating within the CPUSA but were believed to be baseless. Then, on the evening of April 30, at the Jefferson School of Social Science in Manhattan where the National Committee was meeting, rumor became reality. The Party's political secretary, Leon Wofsy, began to read from a document obtained, ostensibly, from a British comrade. Notes were forbidden and confidentiality was sought. For the next three hours, dumbstruck delegates sat in a deathly, stunned silence as a résumé of Khrushchev's report on the Stalin era was read aloud. The chairman of the meeting, the veteran organizer and proletarian hero Steve Nelson, ruefully remarked, "now I felt betrayed. I said simply, 'This was not why I joined the Party.'"[131] Within half an hour Dorothy Healey was "convulsed with tears" and could not stop crying.[132] George Charney was "too shocked, too unstrung" to say anything. The mood was "eerie," he recalled. "Thus it was on that night each of us went home to die."[133] Indeed, on that night, at home in west Harlem, Peggy Dennis did experience a kind of spiritual death: "I lay in the half darkness, and I wept. . . . For the years of silence in which we had buried doubts and questions. For a thirty-year life's commitment that lay shattered. I lay sobbing low, hiccoughing whispers."[134] These private reactions were a foretaste of Fast's response. Fast personified what soon happened to the party: "With the Khrushchev report, all the accumulated frustrations, discontents, doubts, grievances in and around the Communist party erupted with an elemental force."[135]

One who at this landmark April meeting was John Gates, the recently appointed editor of the *Daily Worker*. In 1955 he had emerged from jail after a five-year sentence imposed under the Smith Act and was now jostling to displace Foster as leader. As a "reformist" opposed to the rigidly orthodox Foster faction, Gates opened the pages of the *Daily Worker* to critical comment; it became a key vehicle for genuine debate within the CPUSA. The staff was strongly aligned with the Gates faction.[136] In comparable communist parties in other countries—for example, in Australia, Canada, and Great Britain—there were debates and ideological fractures but not the bloodletting. One of the reasons was that the *Daily Worker* was the *only* communist paper in the world that printed Khrushchev's "secret" speech.[137] In the face of opposition from much of the CPUSA leadership, it appeared on the same day that it was published, famously, by the *New York Times*. It was accompanied by a long, teeth-gnashing editorial.[138] Thereafter, in the words of Gates, "Readers spoke out as never before, pouring out the anguish of many difficult years."[139]

Howard Fast read the full 26,000 words of this speech the day before, on June 4, 1956, in the offices of the *Daily Worker*. Fast was now on the permanent staff of the paper, for which he wrote a regular column, "The Current Scene."[140] His May 15 column edged, for the first time, toward a less myopic appraisal of the Soviet Union. He noted that Khrushchev's official report to the Twentieth Congress was not only "the record of what socialism brought to . . . a proud and happy people" but also "the record of mistakes, large and small."[141] His next six columns, from May 21 to June 7, steered clear of the Soviet Union. He often received praise. Dr. Edward Barsky, still on the left but no longer with the JAFRC, found Fast's columns "very stimulating, very instructive, and very indicative of new paths of thinking . . . many, many people will be guided and heartened by what you say."[142] But Barsky and other astonished readers would have been horrified, not heartened, by the entirely different tenor of Fast's next column, "Man's Hope," on June 12. For he had now read the "secret" report, and when he did, "something broke inside of me and finished."[143] As he later elaborated, "the edifice that I had become a part of thirteen years earlier came crumbling down in ashes—ashes of grief, horror and helplessness."[144] His column was angry and anguished. It was the last that Fast ever wrote for the *Daily Worker*. It is a remarkable statement for its candor, its bravery, its sense of moral outrage and betrayal and sorrow, and for its unparalleled sharp criticism of Soviet leaders. "There is little one can say," he began, "to take the deadly edge off the 'secret' Khrushchev speech." He continued (and it is worth quoting at length because of its unprecedented character):

> It is a strange and awful document, perhaps without parallel in history: and one must face the fact that it itemizes a record of barbarism and blood-lust that will be a lasting and shameful memory to civilized man. . . . I for one looked hopefully, but vainly, at the end of the document for a pledge that the last execution had taken place on Soviet soil. . . . Instead I learned that three more executions had been announced . . . and my stomach turned over with the blood-letting, with the madness of vengeance and counter-vengeance, of suspicion and counter-suspicion.

He wrote that it was "some small comfort" that, until recently, he was ignorant of the facts in Khrushchev's report. He knew that Jewish culture was being systematically destroyed; that writers, artists, and scientists were being intimidated; that the "abomination" of capital punishment was being enforced. But all these things, he rationalized, were "a necessity of socialism." But now, such blind faith was finished.

> Never again can I accept as a just practice under socialism that which I know to be unjust. . . . Never again will I remain silent when I can recognize injustice—regardless of how that injustice may be wrapped in the dirty linen of expediency or necessity. Never again will I fail to question, to demand proof. Never again will I accept the "clever" rationale, which appears to make sense but under scrutiny does not.

For Fast, the effect was cathartic: "With this said, I feel better—better than I have felt in a long time."[145] The only letter printed by the *Daily Worker* that commented on Fast's column revealed a ruthlessness against which the "reformers" had been fighting.

> When we read of men convicted as accomplices in the crimes of Khrushchev's report being executed, I say good. And let's hope they don't abolish the death penalty until they get them all. My stomach does not turn over like Howard Fast's.[146]

If Fast's stomach turned, it was also knotted with ambivalence. Although he still clung to the party—it was, after all, "the anchor in my life"[147]—the umbilical cord was stretched and damaged. Only Michael Walzer saw what was coming: "It is difficult to see how he can return to the paper. His [*Daily Worker*] article described a despair which, if it is honest, must drive him from the CPUSA."[148]

For the next six months, Fast lived out this despair. He withdrew from party activity and retreated into self-imposed isolation. He and his family were now living in the quiet, leafy suburb of Teaneck, New Jersey.[149] There, he licked his wounds. For another six years, apparently, he suffered from depression.[150] As John Gates later commented, "One of those most shaken was Howard Fast . . . It was to be expected that he would react to the Khrushchev revelations in a highly emotional manner, [but] I know of no-one who went through greater moral anguish and torture."[151] Although he stated privately as early as June 23, 1956, that he intended to resign—this was reported to a highly-placed FBI informant, T-1[152]—no membership card was torn up. There was no cathartic moment, no confessional, no high apostatic drama. Just the full force of that moral anguish and torture. Personal memoirs, and especially institutional histories, tend to sidestep this dimension. Despair is difficult to document or retrieve. Thus, we know nothing of Sam Sillen's near–emotional collapse. Sillen was the well-respected editor of the communist literary magazine, *Masses & Mainstream*; one day in late 1956 he walked out of his office and never returned.[153] Nor do we know much more than a newspaper report about the plea of John Steuben, a communist union organizer and party defector in early 1957, to live out his life "in agony and silence."[154] In Fast's case, we have a document that captures this agony. It was written by the wife of a close friend, Carl Marzani, and it refers to a dinner party that Fast attended just before New Year's eve.[155]

> I am very familiar with pain of many varieties and I felt the night you came [to our house] . . . I wasn't able to reach you. And then all the little clever guests started in on you and if [you] did not feel

isolated when you came you must have felt it when you left. . . .
There were more of us with you than against you that evening—
though you were lashing out wildly in your distress. . . . The Times
article [*New York Times*, 1 February] made me feel very sad that I had
not contacted you in this period. We both wanted to—I called your
home several times to no answer and when Carl did reach you . . .
you were very distant, Carl said. How do we reach you—how do
I reach you? . . . Remember, dear Howie, you are not alone. And
nothing you said to Schwartz indicated that you want to be. Call on
us if it will help—call on me if you want to.[156]

By mid-1957, he was more reflective, but still dispirited. In responding to
a letter requesting some assistance, which Fast declined, he wrote: "I am a
very tired man of forty-three and not in the best of health. I am trying to
write, earn a living for my family, and think. There is a great deal to think
about."[157] These thoughts, as we shall see, became *The Naked God*.

The Jewish Question

It is clear, then, that, as with so many unnamed and unknown rank-and-
file party members, the Khrushchev revelations were a decisive factor in
Fast's defection. But Fast was also a Jew, albeit secular, and his affinity with
Judaism, he believed, was not mutually inconsistent with his commitment to communism. Here we come to the second explanation. When
he joined the CPUSA in 1943, he was a Jew; when he left the party in
1956–57, he was still a Jew. The position articulated by a leading Canadian
Jewish communist also applied to Fast: "I never had a conflict about being a Jew and being a Communist. I became a Communist because I am
a Jew."[158] And yet Fast's Jewishness caused problems within the party. The
leadership, according to Fast, "wanted to expel me" in 1948 because of
his "Jewish nationalist point of view,"[159] and there is strong circumstantial evidence that, even before he had read Khrushchev's "secret" speech,
his awareness of Soviet anti-Semitism severely frayed the bonds of his
CPUSA membership.[160] The seeds of this disillusionment over the treatment of Soviet Jews stretched back to the late 1940s. Before departing for
Paris in April 1949 to attend the inaugural World Peace Congress, Fast
met with two leaders of the influential Jewish section of the New York
District of the CPUSA. One, Paul Novick, editor of the Yiddish communist daily *Morgen Freiheit* (whose circulation was greater than that of the
Daily Worker), was also on the party's National Committee, with whose

authority he spoke. They presented Fast with compelling evidence of anti-Semitic practices (arrests; executions; closure of Jewish newspapers, magazines, printing presses, and schools) in the Soviet Union. Although "dumbfounded," Fast agreed to their request to press the charge with Alexander Fadeyev, the chairman of the Union of Soviet Writers and the political head of the Soviet delegation to the Peace Congress, and who accompanied Dimitri Shostakovich to New York for the Waldorf conference in March 1949.[161] When Fast confronted him, Fadeyev repeatedly denied the accusation with the mantra, "There is no anti-Semitism in the Soviet Union." Fast recalled that "after I came away from the meeting, my own doubts grew."[162] So must have Fadeyev's: soon after the Khrushchev report, he shot himself through the head.

Before Fast read that report, he would have read in *Jewish Life*, to which he subscribed, the formal apology from the editorial board for its specific failure to protest the anti-Semitism that underpinned the notorious Slansky show trial in Czechoslovakia in November 1952 and its general failure to condemn Soviet anti-Semitism since the late 1940s.[163] Perhaps Fast was also aware, as were many Jewish communists (who made up 50 percent of the Party's membership in New York[164]) in April 1956, of the article in a Polish communist paper, the Yiddish *Folks-shtimme*, which accused Soviet leaders of anti-Semitic actions, including the disappearance or death of Jewish poets, writers, and artists. The article was reprinted in *Morgen Freiheit*.[165] According to I. F. Stone, the detailed 1956 attack on Soviet anti-Semitism by J. B. Salsberg, the Canadian Jewish communist leader, published in *Jewish Life*, was "the final blow for Fast."[166]

One Jewish poet, whom Fast knew personally and whom Paul Robeson met memorably in Moscow in June 1949,[167] was Itzik Feffer. He had been a decorated officer in the Red Army and a "beloved" Russian poet. Fast heard a rumor "a good while" before the Twentieth Party Congress that Feffer had been executed.[168] Fast asked the *Pravda* correspondent at a diplomatic reception at the Russian consulate in Manhattan about Feffer. The angry reply—which, if correctly recalled (and Fast swears by it), is, for its time, remarkable: "Howard, why do you make so much of the Jews? Jews? Jews? That is all we hear from you! Do you think Stalin murdered no one but Jews?"[169] Another Jewish poet whom Fast knew was Lev Kvitko, executed in August 1952. Fast's "moral anguish and torture" (to use Gates' phrase) over Kvitko's execution is captured in a letter he wrote to the Russian writer Boris Polevoy: "And why—why, Boris, did you tell us here in New York that the Yiddish writer, Kvitko, was alive and well and living in your apartment house, when he was among those executed and long since dead? Why? Why did you have to lie? . . . Why did you lie in so awful and deliberate a manner?"[170]

Hungary

Anti-Semitism and the "crimes of Stalin," as reasons for quitting the party, were compounded by Hungary. Throughout 1956, it was a gradual break, not an abrupt rupture. Until January 1957 it remained a largely private decision. But the decision was confirmed by events in Hungary. In November 1956, Russian tanks rolled into Budapest for a second time and crushed its "Spring in October": the reform movement, the workers' councils, the embryonic multiparty political structures, the quest for greater national independence. Hungary was the country most profoundly affected by the Twentieth Party Congress. Within the Hungarian Workers' Party, a movement seeking greater democratization and independence gathered momentum. In July the first secretary of the central committee, Matyas Rakosi, was dismissed; in early October, László Rajk and other victims of the 1949 Stalinist trials were rehabilitated; and in late October the new leadership of Imre Nagy replaced that of Ernö Gerö. Reform, invasion, rebellion, and pyrrhic victory. Then occupation and doomed resistance. Each punctuated the brief story of the Budapest uprising of autumn 1956. The brutality of the Soviet regime, exposed by Khrushchev in February, had reasserted itself in November.[171]

On October 24, on the very day Russian tanks first entered Budapest, Fast wrote a despondent, almost self-pitying letter to his friend Stefan Heym. "Here I sit, 42 years old, 25 years of literary effort behind me, and apparently at the end of the road. It would seem that I have no place in my own country, no one to publish my books, no one to distribute them, no one to read them. What do I do and how do I start life at 42?"[172] The answer, of course, was to leave the party. Although Soviet military intervention in Hungary confirmed this decision, Heym, and the world, was unaware that Fast had, in his mind, taken this step. In subsequent correspondence, after Fast had expressed opposition to the Soviet response to Nagy's reforms, Heym upbraided Fast for not recognizing that the uprising was the work of counterrevolutionaries, not freedom fighters, who had been responsible for "liquidat[ing]" the workers' state.[173]

Very soon after these events in Hungary, Howard Fast received a mauling in a public debate at the hands of Irving Howe. Like Fast, Howe had grown up in poverty (in the West Bronx) and was Jewish and socialist. In 1956, he was a leading anti-Stalinist intellectual, but still a radical social democrat, having founded *Dissent* three years before. He was also "a brutal debater."[174] There was no newspaper coverage of this debate, so we must rely on the recollections of Jeremy Larner, who moderated the debate, and Howe himself.[175] Fast had been invited to debate Howe at Brandeis University, where Howe then taught, on the topic of "Politics and the Novel," which was also the title of Howe's soon-to-be published book. To Howe's "astonishment," Fast agreed. It was not a wise move. "I'd been lying in wait for something like this, and I really went after him," Howe recalled. "I lashed Fast without kindness or mercy" and "I beat the hell out of him." In addition, bitter, bottled-up feelings were released by many of Howe's friends who were present, such as Rose Coser, who repeatedly heckled Fast. Fast, who had not yet declared his breach with the CPUSA, was obliged to defend the indefensible. During his address, which, apparently, was long and rambling ("belying his name") and lacking cogency and conviction, he upheld the principles of Stalinism. Howe was restless and asked "how long I was going to let this go on." At this point, according to Larner, "I'd fallen into a semi-doze when a bellow woke me with a jolt. 'You have got blood on your hands!' Irving cried, rising to shoot quick, sharp arrows into Fast." He then demolished Fast's arguments about the supposed freedom of Soviet writers by pointing to Fast's (and others') willingness to bend the truth to fit the party line. "The sad thing," Howe recalled, was that Fast "was on the verge of breaking from the CPUSA. . . . I didn't realize [this] until later . . . he was helpless."[176] This was indicated, Howe continued, by "the way he lied, for example, about the Jewish/Yiddish writers. And I knew he was lying and he knew he was lying."[177] As Howe commented, Fast was "stupid" to put himself in that untenable position of having to defend Stalinism "straight down the line." Evidently Fast was bruised and shaken by this experience—it is absent from his memoirs—and propelled him to go public to avoid repetition.

At the end of 1956, *Fortune* magazine phoned Fast for an interview about the CPUSA; it was then that he told *Fortune* that he had left the party. This news was included in its January 1957 article about the Communist Party and the Soviet Union.[178] It was picked up by Harry Schwartz, the Soviet specialist for the *New York Times*, who contacted a "reluctant" Fast on January 31, 1957, and then interviewed him.[179] The outcome was the front-page article the next day.[180]

Outside the Party

Thereafter, Fast did not go quietly into the night. He wrote an important and lengthy reflective piece, "My Decision," for *Masses & Mainstream*; answered critics and letter writers in the *Daily Worker*; completed a manuscript, *Moses, The Prince of Egypt*, that he sent to a commercial publisher, Crown; submitted the entire fascinating exchange of letters between himself and a Soviet author, Boris Polevoy, to Harrison Salisbury, former Moscow correspondent at the *New York Times*;[181] and was interviewed by communist journalist A. B. Magill in the *Daily Worker* for a long article focusing on the Jewish issues[182] and, curiously, for an "exclusive" three-part article by art critic and gadfly Florence Berkman, in the relatively obscure *Hartford Times*.[183] And of particular significance—in response to an approach from the publisher Frederick Praeger, armed with a contract and $2,000, to write a companion volume to the more theoretical *The New Class*, just completed by Milovan Djilas, a dissident Yugoslav communist[184]—Fast started working on *The Naked God*. It was finished by August and published in November 1957. By then, his position had evolved into a less equivocal, more uncompromising one. Fifteen months earlier he would never have stated that his party membership amounted to "a long and terrible nightmare."[185] Before we examine *The Naked God*, let us consider the reactions to the public announcement of Fast's disillusionment and defection.

There were four sets of responses. First, the plaudits. Because there was so little public applause, we can assume that Fast was immensely heartened to receive this handwritten note from one he admired, the famous writer Upton Sinclair: "My dear Fast, thought I'd write + tell you how happy I am over your recent statements over the Soviet horror. Now I can love you!"[186] More grounded were the encouraging words from the historian Bertram D. Wolfe and author of the 1948 classic *Three Who Made a Revolution*: "I have some notion of what you must be going through, for I experienced something like it myself."[187] But the most poignant epitaph to his time in the party came from a rank-and-file communist who wrote this to the *Daily Worker*:

> Howard Fast has left us—the words are cruel but true. A hole has been left in my heart. My body aches with the sorrow of his loss. It is as if a brother has left me. For was he not my brother in the battle for all that is good and right? But though he may march in different ranks[,] all that he has taught us will march with us. . . . [A]nd

though his own flame has grown dim—it will burn within us. Hail and farewell Howard Fast. . . . We weep that you may have left us. We hope you may return soon.[188]

Fast, too, may have wept upon reading this letter. The impact of Fast upon a generation of communist activists was underscored by this, more critical but equally remorseful, remark: "It sure was a personal tragedy for me when Howard Fast turned on the movement. I sure had believed in him."[189]

Second, the CPUSA apparatchiks, who were far less generous. Some context: by mid-1957, William Z. Foster was firmly in the saddle. He had beaten his centrist and "right" factional CPUSA opponents by default, since those who would have supported Gates at the February 1957 convention (and initially Gates had "the numbers") had by now left the party. Foster failed to see that his victory was merely pyrrhic.[190] Cleansed of reformers, the party shrank further and was reduced to political impotence. When Foster, whose politics were as hard as granite, was challenged by Dorothy Healey in the spring of 1957 about his indifference to the hemorrhaging of membership and the loss of valued comrades, he replied, "Let them go, who cares?"[191] As one commentator noted, Foster had "foresworn the very possibility of moral shock."[192]

On the same day as the *New York Times* announcement of Fast's defection, a friend of Fast's wrote to him: "I've no doubt the furies will descend upon you as a result of your statement in the Times this morning."[193] He was prescient. As Gates wrote, "Party leaders leaped on him like a pack of wolves and began that peculiar brand of character assassination which the Communist movement has always reserved for defectors from its ranks."[194] Foster castigated Fast for his "emotionalism" instead of Marxist analysis; for his "hopelessly incorrect" understanding of developments in the Soviet Union, and for sowing "confusion and despair" among the workers. The events of 1956 had scraped off Fast's "thin veneer of Marxism" to reveal the "bourgeois nationalism lying not far beneath it."[195] Privately, he said that Fast was "worse than Max Eastman"—the ultimate epithet.[196] Joseph Freeman believed that Fast was an opportunist who stayed in the party only sufficiently long to win the prestigious Stalin Peace Prize.[197] To V. J. Jerome, Fast was a "renegade" and an "embittered turncoat,"[198] while Fast's *Masses & Mainstream* article of March 1957 elicited this jaw-dropping, invective-laden response from Jim Jackson, invoking political rodentry and mirroring Joe McCarthy at his worst:

Howard Fast, continuing his psychotic conduct of wallowing in his own retchings in public print, is heard from again, this time way up a dirty creek without a paddle, in "Mainstream." This piece is a fair exercise for entering into the lush "guts and gore" market . . . with a pen copiously filled and dripping with his own enormous gall. . . . [T]he chicken scratches of this chicken-hearted one . . . [are] the rabid desecrations of such a delinquent mind of such a smut-scribbler-on-subway-ads as this Howard Fast. . . . Those whose heads are pointed and whose tails are long enough will follow him.[199]

The *Masses & Mainstream* article was published as "Ma Décision" in the April issue of the French Communist Party's *La Nation Socialiste*. Its editor, Pierre Hervé, wished to use it "as a weapon against those who would continue the Stalinist practices of arriving at truth by fiat."[200] We do not know if French communists were shocked by Fast's tormented words, even in translation:

I was filled with loathing and disgust [after reading the "secret" speech]. I felt a sense of unmitigated mental nausea at the realization that I had supported and defended this murderous bloodbath, and I felt . . . a sense of being a victim of the most incredible swindle in modern times.[201]

Third, the FBI. We can see a quite different response to Fast's "My Decision" from the FBI's clandestine Counter Intelligence Program (COINTELPRO), which had commenced operations only seven months before, in August 1956. Its main aim, in the wake of the Khrushchev revelations, was to use defections to cause disruption and increase factionalism within the CPUSA. It focused on Fast. His resignation, a COINTELPRO memo to J. Edgar Hoover stated, "has provided an excellent psychological weapon to utilize in connection with wavering CPUSA members[,] especially those who come from families of Jewish faith or who have spouses of Jewish faith." It printed and distributed, to dozens of FBI offices across the United States, from Boston to Seattle, multiple copies of "My Decision." Each office was instructed to select active CPUSA members who might be persuaded by Fast's arguments for leaving the party or who were disturbed by his allegations of Soviet anti-Semitism. We can obtain a rare and fascinating insight into the *modus operandi* of this early COINTELPRO operation through the following instructions:

Each office should anonymously mail a copy of this article to each of the selected CPUSA members in plain envelopes and in such a manner that they cannot be traced back to the FBI. The mailings should be varied, using different types of envelopes, and should not be sent to individuals who are closely associated, thus limiting discussions relative to the source for same. Each office should advise of any tangible results obtained from this mailing. . . .[202]

The efficacy of such an operation is notoriously difficult to gauge. But in light of the exodus of active rank-and-file communists in 1956–57, it seems plausible that at least some were influenced, via COINTELPRO, by Howard Fast's decision to quit the CPUSA.

Finally, the Soviet Union. Until 1957, Fast had been a pin-up boy in the socialist sixth of the world. He was "*the* representative contemporary American writer in the Soviet Union,"[203] where his name was a "household word."[204] He was only one of two American recipients of the $25,000 Stalin International Peace Prize, the East's version of the Nobel Prize.[205] No other living American writer was similarly celebrated. The royalties he earned from Soviet sales totaled a staggering two million rubles (or US$500,000 in the 1950s).[206] His writing perfectly suited the needs of Soviet literary policy. As Deming Brown put it: "Not until their discovery of Fast had the Russians found an American who conformed so closely to their political and aesthetic demands that they could embrace him wholeheartedly."[207] So the Soviet literary world had invested heavily in Fast—emotionally, politically, and financially.

For six months after "My Decision," Fast heard nothing from the Soviet Union. He was being liquidated, albeit silently and in absentia. All mail ceased (the Russian post office seized the many letters addressed to him); all reviews stopped; all references to him disappeared. He was becoming a nonperson. As Fast himself put it: "I simply ceased to exist. . . . I not only was not but had never been."[208] Then, on August 24, 1957, Moscow's chief literary magazine, *Literaturnaya Gazeta* (*Literary Gazette*), which had been the principal Russian publisher of Fast's journalistic articles, burst into denunciation. Entitled "Desertion Under Fire," the article accused Fast of serving "the most bellicose reactionary agents of Zionism." He had made a "malicious attack" on the Soviet Union and in "a tone favored by anti-Communist fanatics from overseas propaganda centers, he borrows their false arguments and slanderous methods."[209]

In what was, perhaps, a reciprocal relationship between the level of abuse and the sense of betrayal, *Literaturnaya Gazeta* published a second article, on January 30, 1958. Written by Nickolai Gribachev, it was far longer, occupying most of the issue (the fully translated version runs to twenty-two pages). For its almost visceral, splenetic hatred of Fast, it outdid the August tirade. He was called a swindler, a renegade, a coward, a right-wing opportunist, a frightened bourgeois, a worshipper of Wall Street, and "not a Marxist, not an internationalist, but a militant Zionist." Because he conflated religion with Marxism, Fast was "never capable of good, logical thought" and in essence was "never a member of the party." In addition, Gribachev went on, he was sly, ignorant, indecent, craven, self-aggrandizing, and ready to be squeezed "as an orange" by "yellow journalism," especially the "yellow Harry Schwartz into whose waistcoat Howard Fast wept during the first interview." Gribachev, who had visited the United States in 1957,[210] preferred "to argue with an honest enemy than to rub noses with a chameleon" whose "spiritual fornication gives birth to only one monstrous child—doubledealing." The tone ranged from icy contempt to scathing sarcasm to the invective of the betrayed; the scope from Hungary and the Suez crisis, to Fast's "hysterical" new book, "The Denuded Idol" [sic]—"197 pages of intellectual trash and eclectic hodge-podge!"[211] It would appear that such vitriol was deemed necessary by Soviet propagandists to destroy, in one knockout hit, the literary reputation that they themselves had so assiduously cultivated, if not created.[212] Excommunication of the canonized is not pretty.

Regaining an Audience

The Naked God was eclectic. In structure, it was a jumping narrative lacking logical development. In tone, it took a breathless moral high ground implying that Fast was the first, and not merely the most recent, to have discovered the psychopathology of Stalinism. In content, it sidestepped any measured reflection or self-analysis or self-exploration: it was no *Darkness at Noon* (1940).[213] Nor did it have the intellectual weight of *The God That Failed* (1949).[214] Instead, there was "rage and grief and anger," for "when I wrote *The Naked God*, there was no perspective . . . I was very angry."[215] So the book vacillates between calm analysis of social fact (his boyhood poverty and conversion to socialism) and explosive outbursts of deep hurt (his reaction to Khrushchev's speech and experiences with the CPUSA leadership). This was an anguished apostasy. The author Hershel Meyer commented on Fast's "orgy of exhibitionism," in which, martyr-like, he "flogs himself in public."[216] And as another reviewer noted, "Each break of tight human relationships leaves a scar; often a painful scar. All scars are ugly. Fast has scars and his scars show in this book."[217]

Far more focused and coherent than the book was a 25,000-word, 26-page article on which it was based, entitled "The Writer and the Commissar." The central intent was a literary–political analysis, not an emotional–political catharsis. Although it constituted nearly two thirds of the book, it was stripped of the vignettes, anecdotes, observations, and private correspondence (with a Soviet writer, Boris Polevoy) that made *The Naked God* so disjointed and montage-like. The outlet was a new periodical, *Prospectus*. This handsome, ambitious publication, which sought to find a niche as a social democratic monthly magazine, appeared only once and is now completely forgotten.[218] In the same month that *Prospectus* appeared, a substantial article by Fast appeared in the far more widely read *Saturday Review*. A half-page photograph of Nikita Khrushchev introduced the piece, generating further comment in the commercial press. Again, it was drawn from *The Naked God* (whose imminent publication was advertised), and, again, it was more focused and, therefore, more cogent.[219] It cannot be said that Fast was publicity-shy. For those who missed these publications, Fast could also be seen on NBC television: first, on Dave Garroway's popular *Today Show* on August 29, then on Martin Agronsky's authoritative *Look Here* program two weeks later. He told Garroway that the Communist Party should go "out of business" but insisted he did not subscribe to "the cult of anti-communism."[220] He told Agronsky that for "a sincere and devoted communist, expulsion was almost as bad as death—and sometimes worse." He referred to the now-irretrievable $500,000 in lost royalties from the Soviet Union, which showed he "did not leave [the CPUSA] for financial gain."[221] One viewer, an academic, wrote to Fast: "On Sunday, October 13, I saw you in the interview conducted by Mr. Agronsky. I felt that you . . . must have had a very high sense to an ideal to have suffered as you have."[222]

In none of these publications or interviews did Fast adopt the confessional "I have sinned" tone of so many repentant former communists.[223] His *Naked God* may have been a *cri de coeur*, an angry and agonized personal testament, but it belonged to an entirely different genre from that anticommunist memoir literature which many Americans had recently been reading: Louis Budenz's *Men Without Faces: The Communist Conspiracy in the USA* (1950), Elizabeth Bentley's *Out of Bondage* (1951), Whittaker Chambers' *Witness* (1952), or Bella Dodd's *School of Darkness* (1954). As a result, he was not taken to the bosom of the red-hunters. To their disappointment, his apostasy was only partial. His commitment to communism was over, he wrote, but "I am neither anti-Soviet nor anti-Communist."[224] So despite repeated assertions by erstwhile comrades that he had "gone over" to the enemy, the FBI knew better. Under the Top Level Informant (TOPLEV) program, the FBI typically interviewed defectors from the CPUSA. Many disaffected party members had cooperated by becoming informants or prosecution witnesses. Permission was twice requested, internally, to interview Fast, and twice refused: intelligence was needed to confirm that Fast had "crossed over sufficiently," so that an approach would be "more likely to be productive."[225] The FBI report noted that evidence of insufficient repudiation of communism was his appearance before the House Committee on Un-American Activities: he repeatedly invoked the Fifth Amendment and refused to name names. In his own words, and much to Louis Budenz's disappointment, "I made no bones about showing them, not only that I was an unfriendly witness, but that I utterly despised all they represented."[226]

Fast's broadcast over Radio Liberation in November 1957 was, similarly, less a conscious selling out to the class enemy—as a veteran labor reporter for the *Daily Worker,* Art Shields, alleged[227]—than a vain and naïve attempt to reach otherwise inaccessible Soviet writers. He implored them to make known their "anger and indignation" over the imprisonment of communist Hungarian writers connected with the 1956 uprising for "anti-State activities."[228] His impassioned letter to the *New York Times* on October 23 against "watching and waiting in silence" was his attempt to arouse domestic opinion. Consistent with this, we find Fast in 1958 speaking out, vociferously and repeatedly, against the successful Soviet pressure on Boris Pasternak to reject the 1958 Nobel Prize for *Doctor Zhivago.* He referred to "the filthy slanders directed against [Pasternak], the evil threats, the dirty names that he was called—the whole exhibition of degenerate boorishness on the part of the paid and directed Soviet critics." Downgrading, or forgetting, the impact on him of Khrushchev's revelations, he continued, "I don't think anything that has happened in the Soviet Union in my lifetime was quite as disgraceful, as sickening, as this spectacle around Boris Pasternak."[229] Fast's statement was carried by innumerable papers across the country. In a mirror image of the situation three years earlier, Fast was ignored by the communist world but applauded within the United States.

Fast's congratulatory telegram to Pasternak for winning the Nobel can be read as a literary doppelgänger: as a summation of Fast's *own* life since the Khrushchev revelations. "I congratulate you with all my heart," he cabled, "for you have endured and must win a lonely and terrible and noble struggle—the struggle of a writer to write as his conscience dictates."[230] Loosened from that "hook upon the soul"[231] and, consequently, from the ideological moorings of the CPUSA and its straitjacket of socialist realism that so disfigured the quality of his writing, Fast now felt free.

Moreover, he had come in from the cold. His *Moses, The Prince of Egypt*, was published commercially by Crown, sold 18,000 copies in hardcover, and received favorable reviews in the mainstream press. He had returned to his early successful genre of the historical novel, but with a religious, not political, theme. "This was my first touch of legitimacy after all those years of blacklisting."[232] He hired an agent (a well-connected Bostonian, Paul Reynolds), received dozens of letters of invitation to speak to "respectable" professional groups and organizations (such as Sarah Lawrence College), wrote a Broadway play—a comedy about George Washington ("The Crossing")—and was deleted from the FBI's Security Card Index as a "Key Figure."[233] In the year that Joseph McCarthy died,[234] the film director Stanley Kramer bought the rights to Fast's 1948 historical novel, *My Glorious Brothers*.[235] Throughout 1958, Fast began working with Kirk Douglas and Universal Studio on the film script of *Spartacus*.[236] Although he was ultimately dissatisfied with Stanley Kubrick's movie version, he would have been heartened by the imprimatur of a freshly inaugurated President. On February 4, 1961, John F. Kennedy crossed an American Legion picket line to see *Spartacus* in a Washington theater.[237] This would have been unthinkable in 1947, when the Board of Education's banning of *Citizen Tom Paine* marked the beginning of Fast's ten-year struggle for survival against blacklisting, isolation, and bitter disillusionment.

Lyman Bradley, c. 1946. (Courtesy Emily Leider.)

Edwin Burgum, c. 1950. (Courtesy
Doug Burgum.)

3
The Professors

Bradley and Burgum

O n Monday, April 16, 1951, Professor Lyman Bradley received a telegram from James L. Madden, the Acting Chancellor of New York
University. It informed Bradley that the University Council had resolved
"to remove you from the faculty of New York University."[1] We do not
know which emotion Bradley most felt when he read the telegram that
day: astonishment, anger, despondency, or bitterness. But we do know
that the genesis of his dismissal lay in events external to the university
and that had commenced six years earlier. Eighteen months later, on
October 13, 1952, another telegram was delivered from NYU. It was
addressed to Edwin Berry Burgum, a literary critic, erstwhile editor of
Science & Society, and associate professor of English at NYU. The instructions given to Western Union were to "Drop If Not Home," but Burgum
was at home, in his Upper West Side Manhattan apartment, on that day.
The telegram was from the chancellor, Henry T. Heald, and it read:

> I regard membership in the Communist Party as disqualifying a
> teacher for employment at New York University. . . . Because of
> your refusal to answer questions before the United States Senate
> Internal Security Subcommittee regarding your connection or for-
> mer connection with the Communist Party, I hereby suspend you
> from your duties at New York University.[2]

These dismissals, which were not unusual in the age of McCarthyism,[3]
did more than permanently disfigure the lives of two academics. They also
provide sharp silhouettes of the fragility of academic freedom and illumi-

nate the bureaucracy of political repression: the institutional processes by which a particular university, renowned for its defense and promotion of liberal values, sacrificed those values on the altar of anticommunism. So this is a story of persecution, of the ways in which a university dealt with two of its own: long-serving, respected professors whose alleged "unfitness to teach" arose from political positions or actions that had nothing to do with the university. It is a story disturbing in its implications for university governance and for the dark shadows it threw over these men's lives.

★ ★ ★

Lyman Richard Bradley, known to friends as "Dick," was first appointed to NYU as lecturer in German in 1924 and was promoted to both associate professor and chairman of the Department of German in 1942.[4] Since 1931 he was an office-bearer of both the Modern Humanities Research Association and the venerable Modern Language Association (MLA), established in 1883.[5] He was treasurer of not only the MLA. Significantly, he was also treasurer of the Joint Anti-Fascist Refugee Committee (JAFRC) and, *ipso facto*, a member of the committee's executive board. That membership was Bradley's undoing, although this was unforeseeable in 1945.[6] The fate of the JAFRC was closely entwined with the fate of Lyman Bradley. As we saw in Chapter 1, on December 19, 1945, the JAFRC was ordered to produce all its "books, ledger sheets, bank statements, documents and records" that would reveal both the names and addresses of all contributors to its funds, as well as the names and addresses of all recipients of such funds for 1944 and 1945.[7] The entire seventeen-member board of the JAFRC appeared before HUAC and each, including Bradley, refused to surrender the required records.

Bradley's involvement in the JAFRC was a natural extension of his earlier commitments. As with Edward Barsky and Helen Bryan, the Spanish Civil War loomed large. In 1937 he chaired the NYU Faculty Committee to Aid Spanish Democracy; in 1938 he sponsored the National Emergency Conference for Aid to Spain; in 1940 he was treasurer of the American Rescue Ship Mission; and in 1941 he was a member of the American Committee to Save Refugees. Throughout these years he made speeches, wrote articles, signed petitions, and gave money on behalf of the Spanish Republic, Spanish refugees, or the anti-Franco cause. In March 1946 Bradley was cited for contempt of Congress for refusing to answer his interrogators. A month later the House of Representatives confirmed the citation. With that vote, his imprisonment and subsequent academic dismissal moved inexorably closer.

When, in the autumn of 1947, Lyman Bradley referred to "the hesitancy and apathy of many of the faculty" at NYU, he was right.[8] Few faculty members were aroused by the case against the JAFRC.[9] His own professional organization, the MLA, of which he was an office-bearer, took a "wait and see" attitude.[10] So, too, did the American Association of University Professors (AAUP), of which he was a member.[11] Even the chairman of the NYU chapter of the AAUP acknowledged that "I should have made a bigger fuss."[12] The NYU administration, however, was less reticent. Two days after the executive board members of the JAFRC were convicted on June 28, 1947 (but before they were sentenced), the dean of Washington Square College of Arts and Science, Thomas C. Pollock, removed Bradley from his position as chair of the German Department. Pollock himself became acting chair with the assistance of an advisory committee. This decision was conveyed to members of the German Department, who did not react, and to the University Council, which did. On October 27, on the motion of the chancellor, Harry Woodburn Chase, it approved and confirmed Dean Pollock's action.[13] There was, however, a rally organized by the quickly formed Students Committee for the Defense of Prof. Bradley. At the rally, attended by an estimated 200, Bradley attacked HUAC and denied that the JAFRC was a communist front, while the editors of Washington Square College's *Bulletin* stated they would fight for Bradley's reinstatement.[14] Further protest rallies were held in Washington Square Park on August 6 and October 14, addressed by O. John Rogge, and on December 22, addressed by Howard Fast. When Fast spoke, more than 1,000 students and faculty attempted to crowd into the 450-seat auditorium in the School of Education; the overflow required him to repeat his talk.[15] At each of these subsequent rallies, Bradley was banned from speaking by Dean Pollock. Leaflets began appearing that depicted Bradley with a gag over his mouth.[16]

"Stalin's chief agent"

A document in Pollock's files, prepared in late 1947, badly tainted Bradley. By signing several checks for $150 each payable to Gerhardt Eisler, Bradley, as treasurer of the JAFRC, was seemingly implicated in something shady if not conspiratorial.[17] This well-known German communist and recipient of JAFRC aid was an FBI *bête noir*. Eisler used various pseudonyms—Hans Berger, "Edwards," Julius Eisman, and Samuel Liptzen—

which contributed to the FBI's conviction that he was previously a senior Soviet Comintern agent and now a figure of "paramount importance" and "unlimited authority" within the American Communist Party.[18] He had entered the United States in 1941 en route to Mexico but instead was interned. After the war, he tried again to leave and was arrested and jailed. J. Edgar Hoover's long report on Eisler was read into HUAC testimony when Eisler appeared before it in early 1947. It described Eisler as a "Kremlin terrorist" and the "Soviet mastermind in the United States" and included specific reference to the checks signed by Bradley, regularly collected by Eisler at the JAFRC offices and endorsed by "Julius Eisman."[19] The report reinforced the FBI's and, thus, HUAC's view of the JAFRC as subversive. The full text of Hoover's damning report was also in Pollock's files; it was to become Exhibit 11 in the 1951 case brought by NYU against Bradley.[20] But there was a more innocuous explanation: Eisler, who had been imprisoned in 1940 in a French concentration camp with other Spanish refugees, was the conduit between the JAFRC and German-born veterans of the Spanish Civil War who had become refugees during World War II. Indeed, an FBI file on Eisler stated that "he was a sort of a dictionary as he knew the people and the conditions" in Europe.[21] Twelve of the Spanish refugees named Eisler as a trustee of a fund that provided them with aid, derived from the $150 monthly checks. That fund was established in the name of a German killed in Spain—Julius Eisman.[22] Correctly anticipating further incarceration (following a perjury charge from 1942 and a contempt citation from 1946), Eisler illegally fled the United States on a Polish ship, *Batory*, after buying a twenty-five-cent visitor's pass and hiding on board until it sailed.[23]

Suspension

While Eisler hid, Bradley waited. On March 18, 1948, the U.S. Court of Appeals upheld by a 2–1 vote the conviction of Bradley and the other JAFRC members for contempt of Congress. The NYU chancellor contacted the university's legal counsel. He queried whether any moves against Bradley should be made in advance of the outcome of a Supreme Court appeal. He was troubled by the absence of rules of due process: "I know of no academic precedents in dealing with this situation . . . which might give us guidance."[24] As we shall see, external legal advice increasingly determined university governance. Chase's uncertainty diminished on June 14 when the Supreme Court refused to review the conviction.[25] One week later he wrote to Bradley, notifying him that he had been suspended from the university.[26] Bradley learned of his suspension from the newspapers before he received the chancellor's letter; he was at this time not in New York but in Reno, Nevada. He was finalizing a divorce from his wife, Francine, whom he had charged with "mental cruelty."[27] It is possible that the success of his divorce suit may have tempered his response. Uncharacteristically, he replied to "My dear Chancellor Chase" that "I am grateful to you for the opportunity promised me to state my case before some agency of the University. I welcome this proposal as an orderly, dignified procedure which may end rumors and deflate the headlines of this past year."[28] As the chancellor commented to his dean, Bradley's reaction to the notice of his suspension was "unexpectedly mild."[29] Bradley's conciliatory words were to be oft-quoted by the NYU administration when it publicly defended its actions.[30] One such occasion was the University Council meeting of October 25, 1948, which voted to approve and confirm the suspension. Attached to the Council minutes was Exhibit F, which outlined "l'affaire Bradley" (as the vice chancellor and University Council secretary, Harold O. Voorhis, condescendingly termed the case). In language that resonated through FBI reports of student protest against the Vietnam War twenty years later, it stated:

> With the reopening of school this fall, outside agitators have been doing what they can to foment student unrest against this action. A protest meeting, instigated by Bradley, strongly surcharged with Communist elements, was held on University premises with Bradley's lawyer [Rogge] as one of the speakers.[31]

It also noted, in even more wooden language, that refusal by the administration to permit Bradley to speak at this meeting "rekindled radical remonstrance."

"Preserving democracy"

The protest meeting, on Friday, October 8, to which the Council minutes referred, had a dramatic aftermath. Rogge was again granted permission to speak; again, Bradley—because of his "suspension until further notice"—was not. After the meeting, two NYU students, representing "Students for [Henry] Wallace" from the Schools of Commerce and Education, attempted unsuccessfully to meet with Dean Pollock, who had left the building. An appointment was made for 4:00 P.M. on Monday, October 11. On the morning of that Monday, hundreds of five different handbills were distributed to students and inadvertently to either informants or NYU security. The date, location ("Washington Square"), and the identity of the sponsor ("Young Progressives of America" or "Students for Wallace") were typed on the handbill and retained in NYU's administrative files. Each handbill urged students to fight the threat to academic freedom, "preserve democracy" on the NYU campus, and join a delegation to Dean Pollock's office at 4:00 P.M.[32]

Approximately 150 to 200 students heeded the call and assembled in the foyer outside the dean's office. A delegation of 26 students (whose names were recorded), plus Bradley himself, was admitted to his office. The meeting was recorded and a verbatim 11-page transcript was made. It is difficult to discern the work of "outside agitators." All of the students who crowded into Pollock's office were enrolled at NYU. None was impolite or disorderly, as the original recording makes clear.[33] Although the transcript of the recording was stamped "Confidential—Not For Publication," Pollock appears to have been sufficiently pleased with the outcome to send a copy to the chancellor. He marked with a red pen on five pages the passages where Bradley spoke. He need not have bothered; Chase replied approvingly: "When I say I have read it, I mean it; I read every word, and your handling of the situation was a masterpiece."[34] Astonishingly, three years later, this meeting was to haunt Bradley. It became one of three grounds presented by Pollock when moving for Bradley's permanent dismissal.

The student body at NYU was in the vanguard of the protest movement far more than his colleagues, from whom Bradley received (according to his recollection) "No reaction; no support."[35] Yet opposition to Bradley's suspension developed throughout 1948. A wide range of individuals (from lawyers to housewives) and organizations (from the Civil Rights Congress to the Carmel Country Club) wrote to the university's senior administrators; overwhelmingly, they were protest letters.[36] Typical was the sentiment expressed in one handwritten, only semi-legible letter: "I was stunned to hear of the dismissal of Dr. Lyman Bradley . . . you should instead *commend* Dr. Bradley for his brave stand and fine American attitude. He's a *real* American, not un-American Committee brand, but the Jeffersonian kind! Shame on you!"[37] As with most letters, this received no reply. Voorhis claimed they emanated from "the lunatic fringe."[38] Pollock specifically recommended that the chancellor *not* respond to correspondence from the Bureau on Academic Freedom because of its "general impudence"; it stated, *inter alia*, that NYU had "run for cover before this Committee [HUAC]."[39]

NYU Acts: Round One

The extent to which the administration of NYU had "run for cover" is difficult to determine with any precision. Being a private university, NYU was a relatively autonomous institution and was under no obligation to take HUAC's contempt citation as a reason for taking punitive action of its own. It knew that the legitimacy of HUAC was then contestable. It knew there was no internal precedent for the Bradley case, and it could have chosen an alternative path. It knew that Bradley's long teaching record was unblemished. Yet the university sheltered behind the argument that HUAC was a duly constituted authority of the Congress, that its insistence that the JAFRC surrender its books was constitutionally proper, and *ipso facto* Bradley was defying the U.S. government. He must carry the cost of this defiance. If NYU defended Bradley, that defense would be interpreted as a repudiation of HUAC, the Court of Appeals, and the Supreme Court. This could affect endowments, on which NYU was reliant. Although the university generally was regarded as a stout defender of academic freedom,[40] and Chase and Pollock in particular as liberals,[41] it was not prepared to swim against the rising tide of political intolerance. This required courage and conviction. The Bradley case displayed neither.

With the petition to the Supreme Court for a rehearing still pending, in January 1949 Bradley sought some redress from NYU. For more than six months now he had been suspended, his salary stopped and his public voice silenced. The assumption on which his suspension was made—that he would be in jail by the end of summer 1948—proved to be false. In fact he did not expect to go to prison.[42] At the least, because the Supreme Court had decided to first review the Eisler and Hollywood Ten cases, he believed there would be no final disposition of his appeal for another year. Events proved him correct. Bradley was still "unclear" why he had been suspended in the first place.[43] Indeed, the Washington Square College *Evening News* report in late 1948 that "The University has as yet not publicly stated the reasons for its suspension of Professor Bradley" was accurate.[44] From Bradley's perspective, "I have received no complaints concerning my work as an instructor or as an administrator at the University." If his suspension was due to his expected imminent imprisonment, then it was unwarranted and unjustified. Given that the Supreme Court had not yet considered the issue and, when it did, might reverse the conviction,[45] and given that Bradley remained "ready, willing and able to teach at the University," Bradley seemed to have a compelling case. He concluded:

> To suspend a man without a [university] hearing for taking a stand
> which may yet be decided by the Supreme Court to be in proper
> defiance of an unconstitutional agency of the government . . . is not
> only unfair but a serious breach of the academic freedom in which
> we both believe.

In short, Bradley sought either a hearing or reinstatement. The chancellor sent copies of Bradley's letter to his vice chancellor. Voorhis was
completely without compassion: he sought Bradley's "elimination from
our midst." Personal animosity merged with political ideology. Voorhis
continued,

> [H]e is manifestly a bad egg and will continue, particularly if white-
> washed, to give us trouble. I don't see that leave of absence for the
> duration at full salary is other than a measure of condonation. . . .
> Besides it will give comfort and encouragement to other fellow
> travelers in our camp who are already a distinct menace.[46]

On February 8 the chancellor replied to Bradley. If he feared the worst,
he got it. Although Chase acknowledged—for the first time to Bradley—
that the "presumption of your imprisonment" underlay his suspension, he
denied both Bradley's requests. Until the Supreme Court decided, one
way or another, he would neither be reinstated nor given a hearing.[47] It
was not until May 29, 1950—that is, nearly two years without salary—
that the Supreme Court finally decided not to review the conviction of
Bradley for contempt of Congress.[48] This "cleared the way" for Bradley to
enter jail.[49] On June 7, 1950, he began serving his three-month sentence.
Helen Bryan, meanwhile, told the JAFRC board that, because NYU was
engaged in intimidation based on Bradley's political beliefs, she intended
to undertake a study, "documented in a scholarly way," of hiring and firing actions throughout the United States in institutions of higher learning. That study never materialized, perhaps because she, too, was soon
in jail.[50]

Initially, Bradley was confined to the District of Columbia prison in
Washington. Three female JAFRC members, including Bradley's wife,
Ruth Leider, and, later, Helen Bryan, were sent to Alderston, West Virginia.[51] After nine days, Bradley and Howard Fast were relocated 300 miles
away to the Mill Point prison camp, also in West Virginia. This isolation
made visiting (such as by Fast's wife, Bette) difficult, but it was a relatively
congenial place for inmates. Bradley was given the job of librarian, shared
a cell with Fast (and two other convicts), and had access to books (includ-

ing an unabridged edition of *Don Quixote*, which he found daunting) and newspapers—in which he read of a huge meeting in Madison Square Garden to protest their imprisonment. According to Howard Fast, "Dick Bradley took the entire experience with scientific interest and unflagging curiosity, never relaxing a sweet professorial manner." Fast described Bradley as "a wonderful, modest gentleman" and, when he had earlier been handcuffed to him, "I could not have asked for a more pleasant, erudite and philosophical partner."[52] Indicative of Bradley's generosity of spirit, he wrote to the Department of Interior, after his release, praising the warden and staff at Mill Point.[53] When Bradley and Fast were released, they ruefully left behind Albert Maltz, one of the Hollywood Ten and one of Fast's close friends. The FBI, ever vigilant, knew the precise details of their respective journeys back to New York City.[54]

NYU Acts: Round Two

Having served his sentence, Bradley assumed that he would be reinstated to his teaching position by NYU. Soon after his release from jail, Bradley wrote to Chancellor Chase requesting the internal hearing promised him on June 21, 1948, in the letter of suspension.[55] From Bradley's perspective, such a hearing would enable him to state his case; but from the university administration's perspective, it would be the mechanism, to use Harold Voorhis' telling phrase, for his "elimination from our midst." NYU was not caught flat-footed by Bradley's request. In fact, on the day after Bradley went to jail, Voorhis had decided that, because Bradley's "future usefulness to us is so obviously impaired," there was no need to wait for a hearing and his dismissal should be made retroactive to May 29, the day of the Supreme Court decision.[56] Pollock was less rash. The day before, he penned a dense five-page letter to Chase concerning policies and procedures that should be "carefully considered" well before Bradley's release. For example, given that no charges had been brought against Bradley, would this occur when Bradley was given the opportunity to state his case? If so, "these charges should be very carefully prepared from the point of view both of the legal aspects of the case and of public relations." And if so, who would prepare and present these charges?[57] The last question may have been rhetorical. It was Pollock who picked up the gauntlet. Judging by the specificity of detail, the number of consultations with legal counsel, the amount of correspondence he conducted, and the length of the report, the case must have preoccupied him for much of the summer break and beyond.[58]

On October 23, 1950, Pollock dispatched his thirty-three-page report to Chase. It is unlikely that either he or Chase was inoculated against the swelling chorus of anticommunism.[59] Nineteen-forty-nine was that "year of shocks," when the United States "lost" China and her atomic monopoly, and when the Alger Hiss and Smith Act trials were in full swing. Nineteen-fifty saw Hiss sentenced and Julius and Ethel Rosenberg arrested. And undoubtedly, Pollock would have read two recent and influential articles by Sidney Hook, professor of philosophy at NYU.[60] Pollock concluded that Bradley's actions, primarily his deliberate and willful refusal to recognize the authority of the U.S. Congress, were "adequate cause for terminating his services."[61] A week later, Pollock had crystalized his long report into three specific charges. Bradley was unfit to teach at NYU because "he had been convicted of a crime, to wit, contempt of Congress"; because he had made "deliberate falsehoods" to the faculty and students; and because on October 11, 1948, he "participated in and was responsible for an impetuous, improper, and potentially disorderly demonstration." Developments now moved quickly. In preparation for the hearing, Pollock began a systematic collection of substantiating evidence for each of these charges; on November 9 the chancellor appointed an advisory committee, consisting of the elected faculty representatives on the University Senate of each of the twelve colleges and schools, to review the charges and report its findings; on November 13 Bradley was informed of the composition of the committee, the three charges against him, and the procedure of the hearing; on November 27 the University Council approved this course of action; and on December 5 the University Senate hearing was scheduled. The date was Wednesday, January 3. It seemed that Bradley's fate would soon be determined.

The hearing continued for three days, until January 5, 1951. No attempt will be made here to summarize the 310-page transcript or the 50 exhibits compiled by Pollock. Instead the following relies on an 8-page confidential summary sent to the newly appointed acting chancellor, James Loomis Madden,[62] by Pollock's formidable legal counsel, Arad Riggs.[63] In short, Pollock obtained a majority on only one of the three charges. On the most serious charge, conviction of contempt of Congress, the Senate committee found that Bradley "may be dismissed." Seven were in favor, two remained neutral, and one was opposed. On behalf of Bradley it was argued that Bradley had a right to test his constitutional rights in a legal contest with an arbitrary congressional committee. Pollock's position, which he had never before stated and which was delivered in highly charged language, was that Bradley's "concealment" of records, "which would have disclosed the source of support for Gerhardt Eisler[,] a top espionage agent for foreign communists[,] was a vicious crime involving moral turpitude." On the second charge, concerning misrepresentations and falsehoods, the committee—despite the detailed case that Pollock made—voted 9–1 against dismissal. In deciding the third charge, the committee was played a tape recording of the protest demonstration. The vote was deadlocked: 5 found the charge proved, while 5 did not.[64] Madden then informed both Riggs and Fowler Harper (Bradley's legal counsel and Yale University law professor) that they, and Bradley, could attend the next Council meeting, scheduled for March 26, 1951.

NYU and the FBI

The acting chancellor, James Madden, was not a disinterested arbiter. An astonishing document in Bradley's FBI file reveals Madden's connection with the FBI. At 4:18 P.M. on March 5, 1951, he telephoned the office of J. Edgar Hoover. According to the note made of the call, he stated that "Mr. Hoover would know him," that he would be in Washington on Wednesday, March 7, and would "appreciate an appointment with the Director to pay his respects and to discuss the Lynn [sic] R. Bradley case at the University."[65] He left his contact details in Washington for the FBI to confirm the appointment. What follows is highly revealing. On March 7 Madden arrived at the office of an unnamed assistant of the director to be told that Hoover was "testifying on the Hill" and was unavailable. Madden then stated to the FBI official that Bradley, "now that he is out of jail, is going to continue to make trouble for New York University" but that

> As long as he is [BLANK] of New York University, Bradley will be canned; however he has to go through the motions of having him furnished a hearing by the Board of Trustees [Council] and under the code of the Association of American College Presidents [sic], [BLANK] is going to let Bradley have all the rope that he needs. . . .

Madden was "quite sure that Bradley is going to sue the University for firing him and will demand back pay, etc." He advised that Professor Harper was taking Bradley's case and requested any information on Harper. Hoover's assistant told Madden that a check would be made, and if it was possible to provide him with information on Harper "for his guidance" then "the Director would, of course, consider it." A six-page "summary" report, dated March 8, 1951, on Fowler V. Harper, was attached to the memorandum. It is therefore reasonable to assume that

Hoover's consideration was favorable and that Madden received a copy. From the perspective of the ardent anticommunist, it was a damning report, replete with guilt-by-association activities and sponsorships and petition signings. This needs to be borne in mind when we consider the complete failure of Harper's cogent and eloquent plea to the University Council seven days later. Madden then asked an FBI agent present "if I could tell him whether Bradley was a Communist." Agent McGuire replied obliquely. He stated that it was "most difficult to understand" how anyone who wore "the robes of a truth-seeking professor" by day could participate in activities by night sponsored by organizations that the Attorney General had declared subversive. Madden obligingly replied that "he understood." The assistant to the director noted that Madden then "again remarked that Bradley was through at New York University as far as he was concerned."[66]

However, there was another purpose in Madden's seeing Hoover. It transcended Bradley. And here we come to a remarkable statement. It is remarkable not merely because Madden assumed it would remain private and therefore could speak freely. It is also remarkable for the dark shadow it casts over the management of NYU, for its cavalier discarding of the tenets of academic freedom, and for the readiness of its most senior administrator to practice deceit and persecution. Rarely do successful deceivers and persecutors leave footprints. Here, one has. The memorandum is worth citing at some length.

> He wanted to have the Director know that as long as he was [BLANK] at New York University he wanted to clean up the campus as much as possible and he has the opportunity now in view of the fact that the University's budget will be down next year due to less [sic] enrollments because of the draft situation and that some of the courses will have to be dropped and this gave him the opportunity of cutting off the staff any professors who might be of a suspicious or subversive category. He stated that if there was anything the Bureau could do whatsoever in the way of furnishing him [leads] personally not at the University but at his office at the Metropolitan Life Insurance Company . . . they would be the basis for him to take any action that might be needed to clean up the school. . . . [H]e did want the Director to know that he would appreciate any guidance that we could give to him on a personal and strictly confidential basis.

The memorandum concluded with the recommendation that the FBI's New York office and Security Division determine which members of the faculty at NYU were either members of the Communist Party or "Security Index subjects" and that Agent Scheidt "personally contact" the acting vice chancellor and pass on to him "such data which could then be the basis of an independent investigation" of communist activity at NYU.[67]

Judgment Day

At 4:45 P.M. on March 26, 1951, Bradley, Harper, Pollock, and Riggs entered the Council chambers of New York University. This would be Bradley's last chance, and his legal counsel, Professor Harper, knew it. He spoke passionately and persuasively—less as Bradley's representative, he said, and more in "the cause of academic freedom."[68] He argued that the judgment of whether or not Bradley was fit to teach had nothing to do with his political opinions. Yet, he alleged, throughout the three days of the Senate committee's hearing, "over my repeated remonstrations and objections, evidence after evidence, document after document, was presented, incorporated into the record, which were relevant to nothing but the political ideas of Professor Bradley." In particular, Harper focused on Pollock's and Rigg's persistent references to, and tabling exhibits about, Gerhardt Eisler. Harper challenged the relevance of Eisler's Departure Permit or J. Edgar Hoover's assessment of Eisler to Bradley's contempt conviction. If Dean Pollock wished to charge that Bradley was unfit to teach because he had associated with communists, "I will defend Bradley but I want another hearing. The one thing we don't do in this country is to charge a man with one crime and convict him [of] another." What Bradley had done was "to exercise the right of every American citizen . . . to challenge the validity of Governmental action which he deemed venal and evil." Harper then invoked at great length the historical precedents of Henry Thoreau, Thomas Jefferson, Oliver Wendell Holmes Jr., and the Founding Fathers in defying unjust laws. Harper pleaded for mercy:

> This is a great institution. It has great responsibilities . . . to stand up for the things on which it is founded. . . . Let me beg of you . . . let me plead, do not dismiss this man because he has exercised the right of every American citizen. . . . To my knowledge the scandal of academic freedom has never touched New York University. I hope it

never will. Save yourselves. Save him. Let him leave this institution with honor to himself and honor to the University.[69]

It was all in vain. He had just "gone through the motions," as Madden foreshadowed. After Bradley, Harper, Pollock, and Riggs were excused, a motion was moved and seconded that "because of conduct involving moral turpitude," Bradley's existing suspension be ratified, confirmed, and made permanent, and that his name be stricken from the roll of the faculty at NYU. However, after an intervention by John W. Gerdes, NYU's Wall Street lawyer, Madden ruled that a university statute necessitated deferral of action on the resolution until the next full Council meeting on April 23.[70] Then, that bureaucratic panacea, the subcommittee, was appointed to recommend "proper procedures to be followed." The subcommittee, which consulted with Gerdes and examined forty-six of Pollock's exhibits, was ready to report to the next Council meeting, on May 28, 1951, but "because of the lateness of the hour," it was deferred to the following meeting, on June 20. Finally, the Council adopted a resolution, 20–1, that officially dismissed Bradley without any severance pay.[71] There was no reference to moral turpitude, which would have increased the vulnerability of the university to litigation. The official minutes were certified and signed by the secretary of the Council, Vice Chancellor Harold Voorhis.[72] In that capacity, on June 26 Voorhis sent by registered mail a copy of the Council resolution to both Bradley and Harper.[73]

This brief discussion of protracted decision making has a point. The acting chancellor could not wait for this formal process to be worked through. As we saw at the beginning of this chapter, he sent Bradley a telegram on April 16, more than two months before the dismissal was finally ratified by the Council. What prompted him, it seems safe to assume, was a meeting of the executive committee of the Council on the afternoon of Friday, April 13. At Madden's initiation, it discussed the Bradley case and recommended "that the Council should not compromise" on the issue of withheld salary but should "stand firm" and dismiss Bradley outright without any recompense.[74] This thwarted any chance of compromise. Apparently Riggs had earlier privately offered Bradley $15,000 to "get out."[75] Madden's premature notification was directly inconsistent with Section 313 of the university statutes, which required various advance notices of motions and final actions, and which he himself abided by when deferring action until April 23. But Bradley would know none of this. He had been—to use Madden's term to the FBI—"canned," and comprehensively so. Madden's belief that Bradley was "through" at NYU was now fact. Riggs told Dean Pollock that "we were able to accomplish the result that we did" because of "your painstaking preparation of the case," but this was only partially true.[76] It underestimates the determination, influence, and sway of the acting chancellor and the vice chancellor, who were dedicated to Bradley's "elimination from our midst."

Aftermath

The denouement of the Bradley case was desultory. In early 1953, Bradley hired Royal W. France to bring a lawsuit against NYU for arrears of $13,883 in salary payments between his suspension (August 1948) and his dismissal (June 1951). It alleged that there was no provision in the charter or statutes of NYU permitting nonpayment of salary prior to a faculty member's dismissal. The university hired the firm of Townley, Updike and Carter, which specialized in litigation.[77] After two adjournments and two appeals, the case was eventually dismissed in May 1954 without trial.[78] In the process, it revealed a little about how the Cold War was fought. *Bradley v. New York University* was assigned to one of the firm's partners, Robert Reagan. In defending NYU, Reagan wished to show the court that "Professor Bradley injected Communist ideology in[to] the classroom." To that end, he requested a list of the courses Bradley taught stretching back to the late 1930s, together with a list of his students and their names and addresses. In a breathtaking repudiation of the jurisprudential presumption of innocence until guilt is established, Reagan stated that "we may not be able to prove" that Bradley injected his students with communist ideology, but "the truth is that he did."[79] Indicative of how McCarthyism was shaping the cultural landscape, Reagan would sign off his legal letters to Thomas Pollock and Harold Voorhis by wishing them "a pleasant summer" free from "our subversive brethren" or "a pleasant trip in Europe free from Communist Party representatives."[80]

In fact, Bradley was never a member of the Communist Party, despite the sustained efforts by FBI agents over many years to prove otherwise. In 1946, when he refused to cooperate with HUAC, the New York office was instructed by the FBI director's office to "obtain admissible evidence which will prove directly or circumstantially his membership in or affiliation with the Communist Party." The FBI obtained and painstakingly recorded evidence of (seemingly) every petition Bradley signed, every magazine to which he subscribed, every public meeting he attended or public lectures he gave, every organization he sponsored or supported, every job applicant for whom he wrote a reference—hence the thickness of his file. However, by 1951 the FBI acknowledged that it had found no proof that Bradley was a communist and his name was deleted from the so-called "Key Figure" list.[81]

However, his FBI file remained active until 1966, when "it is felt subject no longer meets the criteria necessary" for the Security Index file.[82] He retained his FBI number, 4869055, but there was nothing to report. In fact, the last piece of potentially incriminating intelligence was provided in December 1950 by the African American former communist Max Yergan, who "was of the opinion that Bradley was a communist."[83] In 1955, five informants of "known reliability" were contacted for any information on Bradley, but none could oblige; the same occurred in January 1959 and again in August 1960 when all six informants advised "the subject is unknown to them" or were "unable to furnish any information."[84] So he had ceased to be politically active. This "wonderful, modest gentleman," according to Fast, tried to reconstruct his life. He began selling art books to local schools. He then established a business, the curiously named Association Conventions Exhibits, which he ran from his home in Brooklyn and which involved arranging book exhibits for different publishers. He had to start from scratch because, he recalled, "Most colleagues fled and [those] who had been bosom friends vanished."[85] In 1961, when he applied for a passport, his occupation was listed as "freelance writer." In 1974, Bradley and his wife moved from New York to San Francisco; Ruth died two weeks after the move. According to his stepdaughter, this "very nice, softly-spoken man" was never bitter, unlike Ruth, and handled what had happened to him "very philosophically."[86]

Twenty years earlier, his philosophical convictions had been a bulwark against "naming names." Had he desired, he could have joined the long ranks of FBI informants, like Max Yergan. In 1955, there were 1,353 security informants and confidential sources in New York division of the FBI.[87] Under the TOPLEV (Top Level Informants) Program, whereby potentially disillusioned ex-communists and fellow-travelers were enlisted to assist the FBI, J. Edgar Hoover authorized the New York office to interview Bradley. The approach was made on the morning of October 5, 1954, at a "discreet distance" from his home. Two agents followed him, called his name, identified themselves, and indicated their desire to conduct "a confidential and personal conversation" concerning matters of "great interest to this government." They explained that, because of "his associations," he would be in a position to furnish valuable information. "BRADLEY at this point became nervous and stiff in his attitude and stated, 'I know of no way that I could help you.'" It was evident that Bradley was no Max Yergan, but the agents persisted. They wished to discuss with him, curiously, the "whereabouts of certain persons of the CP who are now fugitives from justice." Curious, because Bradley would not have been privy to the Communist Party's underground network. His response was: "'I am sorry gentlemen, I do not want to talk to you' and began to walk away." The agents made further attempts to engage with and accompany him, but "when it became obvious that BRADLEY would not stop further or allow the conversation to continue, the interview was discontinued."[88]

It is impossible to know how many left-wing activists "walked away" from the FBI during the McCarthy period in the way that Bradley did. What we do know from FBI files containing informants' reports is that thousands did not. To resist the anticommunist crusaders in the 1950s took courage and integrity. Noncooperation brought retribution: suspicions were confirmed, surveillance was continued, and files remained open. This happened to Bradley. The agents' evaluation of their "interview" recorded: "BRADLEY adopted the typical CP response to the agents' approach and it is believed from his attitude that he is still loyal to the CP and its purposes."[89] Any agent, or informant, who observed the lone figure of Dick Bradley standing behind a publisher's book stall at an educational convention would have been hard-pressed to detect that alleged loyalty to the Communist Party or to its ideology.

★ ★ ★

Edwin Burgum received his fateful telegram at 1:00 P.M. on Columbus Day 1952—one year after Bradley's sacking—from the NYU chancellor. It informed him that he was being dismissed as a result of his refusal to answer the questions of a congressional committee. His immediate reaction was surprise and shock.[90] He had completed his testimony, during which he "took the Fifth," only two hours earlier. The speed of the chancellor's action, the absence of protection afforded by constitutional rights, and the relationship between political affiliation and fitness to teach form the backdrop to his case. Although Burgum was the only NYU faculty member subpoenaed to appear before the McCarran committee, his story was, and remains, largely unknown beyond the academic community.

Edwin Berry Burgum (known as "Berry" to friends and colleagues) was born in Concord, New Hampshire, on March 4, 1894. He was educated at Dartmouth College (B.A., 1915), Harvard University (M.A., 1917), and the University of Illinois (Ph.D., 1924).[91] He commenced his academic career at NYU in the fall of 1924.[92] For the next twenty-eight years, he wrote prolifically. His published books included *The Literary Career of Edward Bulwer Lord Lytton* (1926), *The New Criticism* (1930), *Ulysses and the Impasse of Individualism* (1941), *The Works of James Joyce* (1947), and *The Novel and the World's Dilemma* (1947).[93] He was also a regular contributor to literary journals such as *Accent, Antioch Review, Kenyon Review,* and *Virginia Quarterly Review.*[94] But, and this was his undoing, he was also the editor of a Marxist journal, *Science & Society,* that he had helped found in 1936. Moreover, his innumerable book reviews, critical essays, and opinion pieces appeared not only in the *New York Times*[95] but also in several communist "front" publications: *Jewish Life, Labor Defender, Mainstream,* and *New Masses.* It is unclear precisely when Burgum joined the Communist Party. His FBI file was created in June 1942, after he testified before a stormy hearing of the Rapp-Coudert committee in April 1941 and obliquely denied past or current membership in the Communist Party. The Rapp-Coudert committee, known as New York's "little Dies Committee" (the congressional Dies Committee on Un-American Activities operated from 1938 to 1944), purged New York college faculties of innumerable suspected communists.[96] Its use of informers, its inquisitorial techniques, and even its personnel were replicated or redeployed by its successor committees, especially the Senate Internal Security Subcommittee (or McCarran committee), that similarly focused on identifying and exposing "subversive influences" in educational institutions.[97]

On each occasion, in 1941 and 1952, Burgum was the only NYU professor to be subpoenaed by both committees. In 1941 he was subpoenaed because he was an official of a union that the Rapp-Coudert committee wished to destroy: the New York College Teachers Union, Local 537 of the American Federation of Teachers. It was formed in January 1938 and Burgum became its first president. With nearly 1,000 members it was the biggest union of college educators in America.[98] Much was made of a photograph taken of Burgum marching with the union on May Day 1938.[99] This same photograph became an exhibit in NYU's case against Burgum in 1953. In 1941, he refused to sign a waiver of immunity—he wished "to avail myself of any legal right I may have"—and survived.[100] In 1952, he invoked the Fifth Amendment and was incriminated. Burgum had long been an activist. In 1935, for instance, he helped organize a rent strike among tenants of Knickerbocker Village on the Lower East Side and edited the Tenants' Association paper, *The Knickerbocker News.*[101] The same year he actively supported a students' peace strike and chaired a meeting of the Metropolitan Student Strike Committee.[102] His local activism was underpinned by ideals of social justice: "We began with all the glow of idealism engendered by the New Deal. . . . We sought to promote the extension of educational opportunities. We wished to free education from dry rot and political control."[103] By1940 he was an active supporter of the United Spanish Aid Committee, the forerunner of the JAFRC.

In addition to his prolific pen and political activism, Burgum was an inspiring teacher. When he was suspended, a vast number of students wrote personal letters, many passionate and heartfelt, to the chancellor about his classes. It is worth rescuing a few from the correspondence files because, in contrast to the silence of Burgum's faculty colleagues (consistent with Bradley's experience), these students were prepared to take a stand.[104] A group of Burgum's past and present students signed a collective letter describing him as "a brilliant, fair-minded critic" who provided a challenging but "most rewarding" classroom experience.[105] Numerous others referred variously to his "inspiring," "memorable," "stimulating," and "popular" classes, which "always filled early" and which left indelible intellectual imprints. Many, like Robert Gold, were "deeply grieved."[106] Reading these many letters makes it clear that, insofar as educators can shape students' attitudes to learning and outlooks on life, a whole cohort, if not generation, of English students at NYU was deprived of Burgum's erudition. In this way the sacking of Berry Burgum touched the lives of scores of young Americans.

Although there were frequent insinuations that Burgum's political philosophy shaped his scholarship and entered his classroom, not a shred of evidence was found or presented to support this claim. Burgum emphatically told the Senate Faculty Committee hearing, "I deny that I have ever used the classroom to indoctrinate communism" and that he "never followed dictation from any source either in my writings or my teaching."[107] It also proved difficult to discern the influence of Marxism punctuating his many publications, acquired and perused by Pollock in search of incriminating traces. Even Pollock's legal counsel acknowledged that Burgum's preoccupation with psychological analysis in his 1947 *The Novel and the World's Dilemma* meant that he appeared not to follow "the Marxist line."[108]

Appearing before the "Senator from Madrid"

Burgum's "fitness to teach" was not a concern of the McCarran committee in 1952.[109] But it was his appearance before that committee which triggered the chain of events that transfigured his life. Its official title was the Senate Internal Security Subcommittee, but it was known after its first chair, the powerful Pat McCarran (D.-Nev.), nicknamed the "Senator from Madrid" for his pro-Franco sympathies.[110] It was a subcommittee of the Senate Judiciary Committee, also chaired by McCarran, established by the 1950 Internal Security Act, framed by McCarran.[111] The subcommittee operated in tandem with the equally formidable Permanent Subcommittee on Investigations of the Senate Committee on Government Operations, chaired by Senator Joseph McCarthy, and HUAC. From September 8 to October 13, 1952, its sights were fixed on "Subversive Influence in the Educational Process."

There are three interlocking reasons why the McCarran committee subpoenaed Burgum. First, Rapp-Courdet. As we have seen, Burgum escaped the clutches of the Rapp-Coudert committee, precipitating the creation of his FBI file. Because this committee was in many respects a precursor to the McCarran committee, it is arguable that institutional memory meant Burgum was not forgotten. Indeed, a former communist and Teachers Union activist, Benjamin Mandel, directly assisted both the Rapp-Coudert committee and the McCarran committee, to which he had been appointed director of research. Similarly, Robert Morris, the McCarran committee's special counsel, had connections to Rapp-Coudert. So too did Bella Dodd, the former leader of the Teachers Union; she masterminded the union's response to Rapp-Coudert, turned anticommunist, and named names before the McCarran committee. Second, the FBI. Louis Budenz, the ex-editor of the *Daily Worker*, professional anticommunist, and serial government witness, named Burgum in 1946 as a "concealed Communist."[112] That identification was recorded in Burgum's FBI file in mid-1950 accompanied by a request to "bring subject's activities up to date."[113] The subsequent report, dated January 16, 1951, was twenty-two pages long. In compiling this report, the FBI agent at the New York office was authorized to contact "any of your confidential informants or established reliable sources who are connected with the university." Accordingly, an informant of "known reliability" at NYU confirmed that Burgum was a "concealed CP member."[114] The FBI's close cooperation with HUAC by the late 1940s[115] extended to the McCarran committee in the early 1950s. The FBI's top-secret "Responsibilities Program," under which derogatory personal and political information on, *inter alia*, state college professors and public school teachers was offered to selected governors, college presidents, and, presumably, Senate investigating committees, had also commenced in 1951.[116] Third, the university itself. In addition to NYU informants' assisting the FBI, there was also the NYU chancellor, Henry T. Heald. An NYU paper carried a report, albeit without corroboration, that Heald had investigated Burgum *before* he was subpoenaed by the McCarran committee.[117]

Even if this were not the case, and even if the McCarran committee already intended to subpoena Burgum through its access to extant Rapp-Courdet files and/or intelligence forwarded by the FBI, it is quite conceivable that an investigatory committee into alleged communist educators may have been given Burgum's name by NYU administrators. Relations between some administrators and some congressional investigators were close. The vice chancellor and Karl E. Mundt were on a first name basis. Mundt, a Republican senator from South Dakota, was a powerful member of McCarthy's Government Operations Committee and Investigations Subcommittee. He thanked "sincerely" the vice chancellor for his "gracious and encouraging" correspondence regarding the Burgum case and added: "I am greatly gratified by the splendid leadership being provided by New York University in a very important field of present-day academic activities."[118] The last phrase was a euphemism for red-hunting in the universities. Of course, none of this was known to Burgum when he testified before the McCarran committee on October 13, 1952, and stated that "New York University has always had a very sensible and liberal policy. I should say it has one of the most liberal charters" and has always practiced "the free flow of ideas."[119] Curiously, he neglected to mention the dismissal of Lyman Bradley a year earlier.

Before this public testimony, however, was the private testimony to the executive (closed) session of the McCarran committee three weeks earlier, on September 25. Transcripts of this testimony are unavailable, but a summary, contained in Burgum's FBI file, is. Burgum foreshadowed his subsequent stance. He was asked "if he had ever been a member of the Communist Party and if he had ever been active in the National Committee to Secure Justice in the [Julius and Ethel] Rosenberg case." Burgum refused to answer these questions and based his refusal on his privilege against self-incrimination. Indicative of the symbiotic connection between the McCarran committee and the FBI, the FBI compared the testimony from this executive session with its own data developed during its "Security Matter—C investigation."[120] It made "appropriate Photostats" of Volume 6 of the transcript and returned it to the McCarran committee.[121] At this point, Burgum was in a more fortunate position than that of Maurice Ogur, a chemistry teacher at Brooklyn College. Unlike Burgum, when asked at the closed hearing of the McCarran committee whether he was or had ever had been a member of the Communist Party, he answered with a denial.[122] The FBI had a file on Ogur (100–11624) and therefore knew that he had been identified by two witnesses as a communist at the Rapp-Coudert hearings. The FBI report recommended that proceedings be initiated "with the view of prosecuting him for perjury."[123] Yet, as Burgum and a great many other witnesses before anticommunist congressional committees were to discover, taking the Fifth did not provide any bulwark against employers' persecution. It was not "freedom's bastion."[124]

Because Burgum was an uncooperative witness at the executive session, he was subpoenaed, again, to appear before a public hearing at 10:00 A.M. on Monday, October 13. This was to be the final day of the subcommittee's hearings, which had commenced on September 8. When he entered the Federal Court House in Foley Square, he was cheered by 200 university students who chanted "Pat McCarran, Hit the Sack. We Want Our Professors Back," and "Get the Committee out of Our City."[125] Rhyming slogans or strident editorials[126] could not save Berry Burgum. He invoked the Fifth Amendment fifteen times. A member of NYU's administrative staff, James Armsey, was present, and he speedily conveyed the gist of the proceedings to the Office of the Chancellor. Burgum vacated the witness chair at about 11:00 A.M. and returned to his apartment at 110 West 94th Street in time to receive that fateful telegram from the chancellor at 1:00 P.M. Of those who appeared before the McCarran committee, Burgum was the sole professor from a private university to be suspended. When asked by an NYU paper if he thought he would be fired, Burgum gave a circumspect reply: "NYU has long been a liberal college. It still is at the present time."[127] He would soon change his mind.

Fighting Back

Consistent with the close, reciprocal relationship that existed between Burgum and his students, he wrote to them the day after the hearing. "I deeply regret," he stated, "that I am unable to continue as your teacher because I have been forbidden to appear before my classes by Chancellor Heald." He then explained his position: his refusal to cooperate was "a matter of principle" because the McCarran committee had no moral or constitutional grounds for attacking the "right to private opinion and social action." Indeed, the committee was so "ruinous" of American democracy that "no honorable citizen can be expected to cooperate with it."[128] The student body again rallied. On October 17 a meeting was held in Washington Square, a letter of protest to the chancellor was drafted and signed by seventy-two students, and a Student Organizing Committee for Academic Freedom was formed.[129] From a makeshift office on nearby West 4th Street, this committee planned further mass meetings and mapped out its campaign. It then distributed thousands of mimeographed leaflets, conducted at least three debates, organized a symposium ("In Defense of the Open Mind"),[130] appeared before the Student Council, visited all active NYU clubs, and mobilized fellow students to protest outside Vanderbilt Hall, where the University Senate hearings were held.[131] Soon, "leaflets are being pushed into any outstretched hand, meetings are being held in every nook and cranny and petitions are in the offing."[132] The NYU administration was sufficiently concerned by this committee that Vice Chancellor Harold O. Voorhis requested that an informant from the Registrar's Office attend one of its meetings. If he was seeking evidence of "an outside agency,"[133] he was surely disappointed. The resultant report noted that "There seems to be no financial support from outside inasmuch as the hat was passed to help defray expenses."[134] Voorhis was also concerned by a leaflet entitled "Defend Prof. Burgum," issued by the Labor Youth League. He again requested assistance from the Registrar's Office to locate the source of this "tripe": "Is there any way we can trace this or check up on [the] Labor Youth League?"[135] After an investigation yielded nothing, Voorhis concluded, "It is manifestly a red outfit through and through and it may or may not be a student enterprise."[136]

Student newspapers overwhelmingly supported Burgum.[137] In summary, their position was this: unless Burgum was guilty of academic misconduct or dereliction of duty or used his classes for propaganda purposes, his holding unpopular political views should be defended, not punished. This was the essence of academic freedom. The chancellor's action was not only excessively hasty but also a capitulation to political pressures. That NYU was the first privately endowed school to take disciplinary action for noncompliance with the McCarran committee was further evidence (alongside the Bradley case) of its denial of liberal values and open exchange of ideas. Even the conservative *NYU Commerce Bulletin*, initially the sole paper endorsing Heald's action, soon became critical that a full explanation was not provided.[138] What, then, underlay Heald's action?

Why Dismissed?

Notwithstanding Bradley's experience, at first glance Heald's action seems surprising. At Harvard University, Chancellor James B. Conant had recently upheld the right of dissent, directly criticized "governmental agencies" that inquired into educational institutions, and argued that the damage done to the university by an investigation aimed at "finding a crypto-communist would be far greater than the conceivable harm such a person might do."[139] At Columbia University, whose status and prestige NYU envied, two professors (Bernhard Stern and Gene Weltfish) had appeared before the same set of hearings of the McCarran committee. Both took the Fifth; neither was suspended.[140] The same applied at New Jersey's Rutgers University, which, initially at least, actually supported one of its professors (Moses Finley) after he took the Fifth.[141] NYU was under no obligation, unlike New York's public colleges, to comply with any federal, state, or municipal law or regulation requiring action against Burgum. His refusal, on professional legal advice, to answer certain questions asked of him by a congressional committee could not reasonably be considered a "breach of duty" to the university (as alleged in Heald's telegram) because an obligation to answer such questions was never a condition of his employment. We must remember that Burgum had not been cited or indicted or sentenced; legally, he was guilty of nothing. His only "crime" was to take the Fifth—something the McCarran committee grudgingly accepted but the NYU chancellor did not. Burgum certainly seemed qualified as "fit to teach." As a renowned Harvard University academic told Heald, "no complaint has been made about Professor Burgum as a teacher. He has not indoctrinated anybody. His scholarship is good. He enjoys good professional standing. He has the confidence and respect of many of your faculty."[142] Heald himself had come to NYU from the University of Chicago with a reputation for ardent defense of political tolerance and academic freedom. This is suggested by his address to the NYU Alumni Federation on March 27, 1952, prior to his formally commencing his duties:

> I deplore the irresponsible charges made against university faculty members because someone thinks they represent an unpopular point of view. A faculty member can express himself as his conscience, his learning, and the total set of his experience dictates. As a citizen he can talk about political matters, just as readily as he can talk about cultural matters.[143]

Heald's appointment, then, seemed consistent with NYU's liberal traditions. Indeed, when Burgum was asked about his reactions to the chancellor's telegram, he replied that he was "amazed" given the "liberal attitudes" previously expressed by the chancellor and long enshrined by the university.[144] So, too, was the AAUP, which saw the suspension as an abridgment of academic freedom.[145] Similarly, one of Heald's former Chicago colleagues, who had praised his previous "courageous civic

leadership," now bemoaned his "retreat" before the McCarran committee.[146] So why did he do it?

No definitive document exists that explains Heald's extremely hasty
action, so we must hypothesize. Leaving aside the possibility that he
had the ear of his immediate predecessor, James Madden, who was now
on the University Council, two overlapping motivations emerge. The
first was financial. When Heald was angrily asked, "Is your University
so poverty-stricken that it must throw a man to the wolves to remain
solvent?"[147] the question, when stripped of its emotion, was legitimate.
In late September 1952—less than a month before the Burgum affair
blew up—NYU launched the most ambitious building and development program in its history. Presumably, this was part of the incoming
chancellor's brief. Expansion costs money—the budgetary estimate was
$102 million—so hand-in-glove with this program was a major public
relations campaign to garner business support. As one paper noted, "This
is a time when [NYU] is sorely in need of funds, and must look for them
from outside elements—elements that will look with sharp eyes before
investing."[148] It seems plausible to assume that Heald was conscious of
donors, benefactors, and investors to whom he could demonstrate his
tough anticommunist credentials by acting quickly and decisively against
a resident communist. As one NYU paper put it, in suspending Burgum,
"Chancellor Heald's action can place NYU's stock up in the gilt-edged
category," while another believed the course Heald took "was the only
feasible one considering the new building expansion program."[149] Less
generously, other papers referred to NYU's "compromis[ing] with principle in order to expand its facilities" and Heald's reassuring the public
of its "impregnability from Communist infiltration" in order to "insure
community support for its program of development."[150]

But more tellingly, Heald, who thought of himself as a "hard-headed
businessman,"[151] delivered a speech to the state Chamber of Commerce
on November 6, 1952, in the financial district. Gown was meeting town.
Entitled "A Chance to Serve," it was the centerpiece of the university's
public relations and fundraising campaign and explicitly sought the support of private business. The lengthy and somewhat predictable speech
had been written some time previously, but subsequently Heald added
a seven-paragraph "insert." It dealt with the threat of communism and
how the Communist Party could not be considered "just another political party" because of its commitment to overthrowing the American
system of government, by force if necessary. However, there was reassur-
ance: "Businessmen sometimes ask me if our educational institutions are

hot-beds of communism. . . . I can assure you that this is simply not the case."[152] In other words, businessmen could endow or support New York University with confidence. He had taken care of Burgum, who was, in this larger scheme, expendable. Heald did not spell out (at least in the prepared version) his recently acquired credentials. They were by now well known. NYU's Office of Information Services disseminated this insert and it received considerable publicity.[153] Heald reproduced this same speech when he addressed the opening session of the annual meeting of the American Institute of Electrical Engineers on January 19, 1953.[154]

The financial imperative implies pragmatism. But the second motivating factor, ideological conviction, involves principle. Heald, it seems safe to conclude, was an archetypal Cold War liberal.[155] His action against Burgum was consistent with, not a betrayal of, his principles. In his mind, there was no contradiction between, for example, the AAUP's most recent statement on academic freedom and tenure[156] and his denial of those customary rights to Burgum, if Burgum was a communist. "He is not the same as any other person expressing an unconventional opinion. He cannot claim academic freedom because he has forsaken his claim to academic freedom. He is restricted to a line of thinking and action dictated by a foreign power."[157] In short, Heald believed in the right to dissent but not the right to conspiracy. His views closely approximated those of Sidney Hook, the chairman of the Philosophy Department at NYU, with whom Heald corresponded during this period.[158] As we shall see in Chapter 4, Hook was the main instigator of Americans for Intellectual Freedom, established at the same time as the Waldorf conference in March 1949, and the American Committee for Cultural Freedom, formed in January 1951. By then, the internationally recognized Hook was a highly influential voice at NYU. According to Alan M. Wald, he was "garrulous and aggressive . . . with a street-brawler's willingness to jump into a fray at the slightest provocation."[159] In late October 1952 he wrote a long philosophical article that dominated all NYU papers when it appeared. It revolved around what he termed the two central questions of the Burgum case: "(1) Is membership of [sic] the Communist Party a legitimate ground for excluding a teacher from the profession? (2) Is refusal to answer questions about membership in the Communist Party a legitimate ground for expulsion?"[160] His affirmative answers to both provided Heald with an authoritative intellectual underpinning.[161] The second of Hook's two issues was linked to the first. As Heald stated, because educational institutions must be "seriously concerned" about the communist affiliations of its teachers, "it becomes the duty of all teachers to cooperate fully with duly constituted authorities investigating communism." But he went one step further: "To do less as a faculty member is to create reasonable doubt as to one's fitness for the role of teacher in a free society."[162] Here we get to the heart of the matter. To his detractors, Burgum *was* unfit to teach because of his political beliefs. Invoking the Fifth provided him (and countless others) with no refuge or protection. Paradoxically, it self-incriminated him. Through a form of guilt by association, it "exposed" him so he could then be penalized. This, of course, was central to the *modus operandi* of the congressional committees in the McCarthy era.[163]

That Heald believed NYU was no place for a communist was demonstrated by his response to a private letter from Herbert Philbrick. Philbrick was a professional anticommunist, a former FBI double agent, a prosecution witness at the Smith Act trials in 1949, and the author of the just-published *I Led Three Lives*.[164] Although an undercover member of the CPUSA from 1940 to 1949, he was never a key communist. The highest position he held was literature director of his local cell in Massachusetts, which had five members. In 1952, he congratulated Heald for his "forthright" stand on communism (he had read a newspaper report of the "Chance to Serve" address) and wished there were other university leaders "of your caliber" who "felt the same way." He then recommended that universities and colleges take much more initiative and "fire the subversive teacher long before a Congressional committee moves in."[165] Replying to Philbrick, the chancellor knew of "the excellent work" he had done, found himself in "complete agreement" with his "helpful suggestions," and acknowledged that university faculties "should have been able to recognize the dangers to their freedoms and taken care of them themselves."[166] This was the first time the two communicated, but it was not the last: three months later Philbrick returned as an "expert" witness, employed by NYU in its case against Burgum.[167]

"Conduct unbecoming"

Burgum, one of those "dangers to [university] freedoms," formally requested a university hearing on his suspension. This request was in accord with the Statement of Policy on Academic Freedom and Tenure, adopted by the University Council on September 1, 1948. He also requested that the appropriate faculty committee, the Board of Review of Washington Square College, conduct the hearing.[168] The board unanimously agreed to accept this responsibility, noting that it was "specifically charged with the duty of protecting the interests of the faculty of Washington Square College in matters of tenure."[169] Ominously, on November 24, the University Council overruled this agreement and resolved that the University Senate (potentially, a far less sympathetic body) assume jurisdiction of the case.[170] Burgum protested, but in vain.[171] The chancellor's statement to the Council included verbatim the text of that inserted section on communism in his address to the Chamber of Commerce. He recommended that the Senate review the suspension, James Madden made the motion, and the Council acquiesced.[172] But the Council had additional business. The chancellor distributed a letter written to him that same day, November 14, from the dean of Washington Square College, Thomas Pollock. That letter was concerned not with reviewing Burgum's suspension but with calling for his dismissal: "Since in my judgment Dr. Burgum is unfit to teach in New York University because of conduct unbecoming a teacher I recommend that his services be terminated by [the] University Council."[173] His "conduct unbecoming" consisted of two misdemeanors. The first we know: it was a reiteration of the charges in Heald's original telegram—refusal to answer questions asked by the McCarran committee—but with a curious twist. In so doing, Burgum "violated an obligation of a member of the teaching profession who has the privileges of academic freedom." If this was somewhat confusing, the second charge was even less self-evident. It is worth citing in full because it was this charge that proved to be Burgum's nemesis.

> 2. He refused to tell the truth frankly in this connection not, in my considered judgement, because of his stated desire to uphold freedom of speech, but rather because of his fear of testifying to acts which would reveal the truth concerning the relation of himself and others to the Communist Party and subject him to criminal prosecution.

These charges were a mixture of obfuscation, subjective judgment, and false inference. Burgum was quite right to insist, "As a matter of elementary due process, the charge should be clear and precise so that I may be in a position to know what it is that I am expected to defend myself against."[174] Heald replied to Burgum that Pollock's letter already contained the charges and that they had been "carefully prepared and are in the judgment of Dean Pollock specific."[175] We are seeing here an instance of appalling university governance. An increasingly, and justifiably, frustrated Burgum complained that Pollock's letter contained "personal conclusions couched in . . . allegations of fact" and that he could not tell whether that letter was merely a restatement of the charge in the original telegram or whether there was "some other reason" and "something different." He further stated that he was entitled to know the "*facts*" of any charge against him and insisted, again, that he be informed in writing of the precise charges and in sufficient time before the hearing to prepare his case.[176] Five weeks later, Burgum received a simple acknowledgment. There was no clarification of charges.[177] It was now January 5, 1953, and the hearings were scheduled for January 19.

By the beginning of 1953, America's political landscape resembled a permafrost. Joe McCarthy was at the peak of his power. The two committees he chaired (Senate Committee on Government Operations and its Subcommittee on Investigations) may have sounded benign, but their activities were both iniquitous in effect as well as ubiquitous in scope. In that year he initiated 445 preliminary investigations, conducted 157 investigations, and held 17 public hearings. His subcommittee's far-reaching tentacles ensnared thousands.[178] Owen Lattimore, a Johns Hopkins professor who had been repeatedly interrogated by the McCarran committee, had just been indicted for perjury; the Rosenbergs were appealing their death sentence; and the loyalty–security program was about to be further tightened under President Eisenhower's Executive Order 10450. Internationally, Josef Stalin's life may have ended, but the Korean War had not. In the summer of 1953, the Soviet Union exploded the world's first H-bomb, and domestic attention turned, again, to the loyalty of physicists such as J. Robert Oppenheimer. In short, red-hunting was still in full swing. Moreover, NYU (or at least its senior administrators), once a bastion—and proud custodian—of liberal values, had now fallen into line and joined the anticommunist chorus. To use the phrase of one of Heald's correspondents, NYU found it easier, "in this period of hysteria," to "run with the hounds."[179]

The hearing of the Senate Faculty Committee, which both reviewed Burgum's suspension and decided on his dismissal, opened at 2:00 P.M. on Friday, February 18, 1953 (postponed from January 19). Representing Burgum's Washington Square College was Professor Hollis Cooley. Two years earlier, he had opposed the dismissal of Professor Bradley, but, as he later remarked, "I shouldn't have been so polite."[180] Also present at the hearing were Pollock, the dean who had brought the charges against Burgum (as he had also done against Bradley) and, once again, Pollock's legal counsel, Arad Riggs. There was no warmth between Pollock and Cooley. Indeed, the former would "freeze" when he saw Cooley.[181] After the first day the chairman suffered a heart attack and was replaced. The press was excluded and an embargo on all comments was imposed. The 11 hearings continued daily, Monday through Friday, until March 6, 1953. Throughout, a "tight curtain of secrecy" was maintained.[182] The committee then met an additional 6 times, between March 13 and April 8, to review proceedings, read the 985-page transcript and deliberate on its report to Council.[183]

The Senate hearing resembled a HUAC hearing. Burgum's legal counsel, Martin Popper, constantly punctuated proceedings with objections that evidence was not pertinent. That evidence—and there was a voluminous amount of it—linked Burgum to a wide variety of "front" organizations. Indeed, Dean Pollock's Exhibits 45 through 62, which described each organization (including why it was believed to a "front" organization, the evidence for that belief, and the character of Burgum's involvement in each), were all presented and discussed in detail.[184] Some of the detail drew on a remarkable 5-page list in Pollock's files of every petition, letter, guest lecture, speech, sponsorship, contribution that was signed, given, or made by Burgum dating back to 1933. The research involved was prodigious, and the bulk of it had been undertaken by Pollock's "consultant," the indefatigable J. B. Matthews. The fact that Pollock used him suggests that NYU had firmly embraced academic McCarthyism. Matthews had been an energetic and prominent Communist Party fellow-traveler from the late 1920s until the mid-1930s, holding office in 15 "front" organizations. In 1938, he turned apostate; "struck the trail of repentance"; published his confessional, *Odyssey of a Fellow Traveller*; and became research director of the Dies Committee.[185] Fifteen years later, in June 1953, he briefly held the position of executive director of Mc-Carthy's Permanent Subcommittee on Investigations, which interrogated Burgum. In that period, he was pivotal to the anticommunist inquisition. His contacts were wide, his knowledge was deep, and his influence was immense. By 1944, Matthews had written a 7-volume report on communist fronts; the final volume contained 22,000 names and became "virtually a bible for intelligence officers in the witch-hunt era."[186] He has rightly been called the "dean of professional anti-Communists" and the "*éminence grise* of the anti-Communist network."[187] The vastness of his collection of Communist Party and "front" organization publications and materials, enlisted by Pollock in his case against Burgum, can be measured by the scale—479 linear feet—of his papers at Duke University.[188]

Popper's objections, that Burgum had not been charged with being a member or supporter of any organization and therefore the exhibits were irrelevant, were regularly overruled. So Riggs continued unimpeded in his effort to prove the obvious—that Burgum was a member of the Communist Party. He introduced as evidence transcripts from the Rapp-Coudert hearings in which Burgum was identified as the editor of *Science & Society* and, *ipso facto*, a communist. As at Rapp-Courdet, much was made of a photograph of Burgum marching in the 1938 May Day parade under the Teachers Union banner.[189] Riggs also referred to fifty-one issues of the *Daily Worker* (with precise dates, pages, and columns) from November 6, 1933, to November 21, 1952, in which Burgum was mentioned. An astonishing collection of photostats of no fewer than forty-three issues of *New Masses* from July 1934 to January 1946, in which Burgum had an article, book review, or other contribution, was presented.[190] An exasperated Popper stated: "I object to the introduction of that sort of material as pure hearsay. May I have a ruling, sir, at least one time, on the record?" Later, he exclaimed: "This is not due process in any kind of proceeding. It is pernicious and evil."[191]

In an effort to establish Burgum's unfitness to teach, Riggs sought to link Burgum's classes with left-wing student activism—to, in other words, allege "an unusually close relationship between a leader in these student organizations and being a student of yours."[192] It was an absurd causal correlation that ignored numerous other variables, but Exhibits 45 and 46, extracted from NYU administrative records from 1935 to 1943, cross-listed the names of all the student leaders with the dates, number, and titles of courses they took with Burgum (but with no other lecturers).[193] Yet Pollock had no exhibits showing nor did Riggs present any argument that Burgum at any time attempted to inject communist ideology into his teaching. As with Bradley, the evidence simply did not exist. Not only did the hearings resemble those of HUAC, they also relied on HUAC. Riggs admitted to Popper nearly every one of Pollock's sixty-two exhibits was provided by HUAC, that "it took about a month to get them," and that they had been copied and returned to HUAC.[194] One of Pollock's exhibits (no. 2) was a sixty-one-page HUAC publication that identified Burgum and nine other individuals as being "affiliated with from 31 to 40 Communist-front organizations."[195] One such group organized the Waldorf conference: the National Council of Artists, Scientists and Professionals. Once again, we find evidence of cooperation between McCarthyite legislative committees and the university. The use of HUAC documents—that, in turn, most likely emanated from the FBI[196]—prompted Popper to ask:

Mr. Chairman, here we have a situation where, without being confronted by his accuser, without the right to cross-examination, without the right to determine the things that are being said here, we are not even given the politeness of knowing where a quotation such as is passed off here came from. Is that too much to ask when a man's character is being judged by the Faculty Committee?[197]

A significant amount of time was preoccupied with discussions of academic freedom, the Fifth Amendment, communist ideology, and defining the wording, meaning, and consistency of the actual charges.[198] As the hearing entered its third calendar week, it became apparent that the two sides not only were profoundly polarized but were operating from different premises, within different paradigms. For Pollock and Riggs, the aim was to demonstrate that Burgum's association with Marxist ideas, communist-friendly organizations, or communist-related activities was both longstanding and inimical to the business of a university. For Burgum and Popper, one's fitness to teach had nothing to do with one's political beliefs as a citizen and everything to do with one's professional conduct and competence as a teacher.[199] They also emphasized the legitimacy of taking the Fifth, the illegitimacy of the McCarran committee's methods, and the sacrosanct nature of tenure and academic freedom. In retrospect, it appears that Burgum and Popper concentrated on the first charge, which they believed to be the more important, and Pollock and Riggs on the second charge, which they believed easier to prove once communist connections had been established.

One way in which those connections were illuminated was through "expert" witnesses. Here we find that customary McCarthyist technique of "smearing with the communist brush."[200] Riggs first called Herbert Philbrick, now already known to the chancellor. By now, Pollock had read Philbrick's very popular *I Led Three Lives* and had underlined and annotated it.[201] As Hollis Cooley later recalled, "Pollock believed the anti-communist stuff."[202] Just as Philbrick's "dramatic appearance" at the Smith Act trial of twelve Communist Party leaders in April 1949 "was far more impressive than the substance of his evidence,"[203] so his testimony at this hearing fizzled after he admitted he did not personally know Burgum.[204] The same applied to Manning Johnson, another professional anticommunist witness. Johnson had been a member of the Communist Party in Harlem from 1930 to 1940, when he resigned to work for the FBI and then, from 1941 to 1944, infiltrated several "front" organizations. Thereafter, he worked as a "consultant" for the Justice Department and received a substantial income ($25 per day plus $9 per day expenses) by testifying before HUAC, the McCarran committee, the Subversive Activities Control Board, and the U.S. District Court.[205] The May Day parade photograph of Burgum was again introduced, and again Burgum was identified. Johnson implied Burgum was in a communist cell. But he had never met Burgum and the value of his testimony was further diminished, when, under questioning by Popper, he confirmed earlier statements that he had lied under oath in a court of law in 1951 and would continue to lie under oath willingly and repeatedly (if necessary, "a thousand times") if the FBI requested it.[206] Irrespective of their efficacy, the use of such witnesses by Pollock and Riggs (possibly sanctioned or suggested by Heald) confirms how NYU became entangled with the anticommunist crusaders and exemplifies the bureaucratic rationality of McCarthyism. Such entanglement was formalized when, in October 1952, the director of the FBI's New York office, Leland V. Boardman, was invited to speak on the role of the Bureau at an NYU campus club meeting.[207]

The formal hearing ended on Friday, March 6, 1953, but the Senate Committee met in closed session an additional six times between March 13 and April 8. It had in front of it a further document from Arad Riggs. It was a major document, fifty-five pages in length, that skillfully wove together inchoate threads into a seemingly compelling case. While Popper had previously emphasized the irrelevance of Burgum's political beliefs, Riggs argued that it was those beliefs which Burgum sought to conceal and that such concealment made him unfit to teach. He concluded that Burgum "had no professional right to conceal the truth on an important issue from the American people or to wrap the flag of freedom of speech and academic freedom around him in the effort to shield himself from the consequences of his own overt acts." Thus, taking the Fifth meant that he was not "telling the truth frankly."[208] This, indeed, was the substance of Pollock's second charge.

The Senate committee submitted its report to the University Council on April 15, 1953. The report was brief and pointed.[209] By a vote of 3–9, the first charge was not sustained. The committee found that "no member of the teaching profession should be denied the legal protection accorded to all citizens under the Fifth Amendment of the Constitution." This was significant given that Burgum's refusal to answer those fifteen questions had been the basis of Heald's telegram of suspension. In 1951–52, after a series of Supreme Court and District Court decisions enlarging the interpretation of witnesses' recourse to the Fifth,[210] there was widespread public debate in the *New York Times* and elsewhere about the legal precedents, constitutional limits, and tactical legitimacy of taking the Fifth.[211] It is unlikely that the committee would have been ignorant of this. It seemed that invoking the privilege against self-incrimination was too deeply embedded in the American legal system for this committee to deny it.[212]

But it was a double-edged sword. Witnesses, like Burgum, who relied on the Fifth appeared to be hiding behind it in order to conceal the truth; they therefore seemed disreputable or unethical. The second charge, that Burgum refused to "tell the truth frankly" because he was a communist, was sustained 9–3. Over Cooley's objections, a full explanation for this decision was not given.[213] So again, the report was cryptic but vague: a teacher must be expected "to conduct himself so that his activities meet the tests of responsible exercises of his rights."[214] Because Burgum, on legal advice, declined to answer the same questions before the Senate committee that he had refused to answer before the McCarran committee (for fear of a contempt citation), the chairman reported that Burgum "conducted himself with something less than the honest effort of cooperation I would expect from a colleague who had nothing to conceal." In other words, Burgum's refusal to state whether he was a communist proved that he was one. Proof was also available in the "patterned conduct over a quarter of a century."[215] Dean Pollock's sixty-two exhibits had paid off. Inferences had become facts. Evidence of teaching and scholarly qualifications, or testimonials from students, was deemed inadmissible. Fitness to teach was gauged, in the end, by political allegiance. One of the three dissidents privately commented that, in the army (in which he had served in World War II), "We wouldn't have tried a dog on charges like these."[216]

Events now moved rapidly. An executive committee of the University Council considered the Senate report and adopted a motion (moved by ex-Chancellor Madden) that Burgum be dismissed. That motion was considered by a full meeting of the Council on April 27 along with a thirty-minute address by Riggs and a prepared statement from Burgum.[217] Council members may not have been enamored of Burgum's assertion that the university had become "the actual, but not frankly stated, arm of the [congressional] investigating committee."[218] On this occasion, veracity surpassed diplomacy. On April 30, the Council unanimously endorsed a motion, again made by Madden, that the earlier executive committee motion be adopted.[219] Burgum's twenty-eight-year association with NYU was terminated. In quick succession, Voorhis sent Burgum a telegram, Heald made a public statement, and Armsey (Information Services) issued a press release. On May Day 1953, all New York newspapers carried the news.[220]

Aftermath

The ordeal of Edwin Berry Burgum was not over. Two months later, on July 1, he was subpoenaed to appear, along with 21 other authors, before Senator McCarthy's investigations subcommittee. McCarthy's specific target was the removal from the nation's libraries of books that did not "serve the interests of democracy." Throughout the spring of 1953, more than 300 titles had been removed, and some burned, from the U.S. State Department libraries at 189 information agencies overseas. They included novels by Howard Fast. Several administrators' scalps had also been claimed.[221] Now McCarthy turned to the authors themselves. He was undaunted by Eisenhower's speech at Dartmouth College on June 14 warning against "book burners" and criticizing the purging of Dashiell Hammett's detective stories. Why Burgum? Because one of his books, his 1947 *The Novel and the World's Dilemma*, was found in the U.S. Information Services library in Paris. Burgum, now obliged to describe himself as a "freelance" literary critic, was interrogated mainly about this book by McCarthy and his chief counsel, Roy Cohn, to discern its communist leanings.[222] He invoked the Fifth freely; in fact, during his brief testimony he used it 15 times—the same number as before the McCarran committee 9 months earlier. But being unemployed diminished the risks. It is clear from his testimony that Burgum was not intimidated by McCarthy and Cohn. Nor did he retreat from self-defense. Although in June he had "not yet recovered from [his] astonishment" that NYU had based its case upon the files of HUAC and "conduct[ed] it in the same fashion,"[223] by the winter of 1953 he was busy preparing a booklet that showcased his side of the Senate hearings. The resultant 80-page *Academic Freedom & New York University: The Case of Professor Edwin Berry Burgum* consisted of 7 chapters and 6 appendixes, was printed in February 1954, and was widely distributed. According to an NYU paper, its appearance "fanned" the "smoldering embers of the Burgum case." But to a condescending Harold Voorhis, it confirmed that Burgum was "so wedded to his beliefs that he failed to see reason" and should "be pitied."[224]

Three years later Burgum warranted pity. His wife, Mildred, whom he had married in 1927, committed suicide. She had just turned fifty-one.[225] According to a family member, "the pressure and public disgrace" proved too much.[226] Incognito phone calls from the FBI may have contributed to this pressure; one was made to the Burgum apartment shortly before Mildred took her own life; the call was taken by "an unidentified woman" who confirmed that Burgum lived at the residence.[227] Burgum took over her psychotherapy practice. Not surprisingly he needed "much re-education" and had difficulty adapting to an unstable income. He withdrew from political activity because it took "all my time to earn a living."[228] Nevertheless, Burgum's FBI file continued to grow. Except for his leading role in organizing a petition to President John F. Kennedy in 1961 protesting a Supreme Court decision that upheld the Internal Security (McCarran) Act of 1950,[229] there was little to report. Curiously, the FBI missed Burgum's signature on a petition in 1964 concerning civil rights,[230] and another to President Lyndon B. Johnson in 1965 against the Vietnam War.[231] He met the Security Index criteria (and therefore his file remained active) for three reasons: invoking the Fifth before the McCarran Committee in 1952, his "Dear Colleague" letter in which he showed no repentance,[232] and "his long history of CP affiliation and/or sympathy."[233] He was judged "a potentially dangerous individual" who could "commit acts inimical to the US."[234]

Consequently, for the next two decades Burgum was monitored. Every twelve or eighteen months the records of the New York Police Department's Bureau of Special Services and, later, Intelligence Division (Security and Investigation Section) were checked, informants contacted and queried, "pretext interviews" conducted, fresh photographs taken, and subscribed reading matter recorded.[235] The FBI believed it had struck pay dirt when it discovered that Burgum had visited Cedric Belfrage in Cuernavaca, Mexico, for two weeks in July 1966. As poetry editor, Belfrage had worked with Burgum on his short-lived literary journal, *Contemporary Reader*, in 1953, and the two were old friends.[236] However, Berry Burgum's summer visit was invested with a sinister interpretation. Apparently using an alias, "Barry Bergman" (he was heard to use this name in Mexico), he was making contact with the ACGM—the American Communist Group in Mexico.[237] The alias assumed its own reality. A separate subfile on "Barry Bergman" was created, a new "indices search" was conducted, hotel bookings were checked, and security informants in Mexico were advised. Other than generating considerable paperwork, nothing came of it. The final report in his file, a memorandum from the New York office to the director's office in Washington, was dated June 14, 1972; Burgum was now seventy-eight. The summary of Burgum's "most recent subversive activity" consisted of his membership on the editorial board of *Science & Society*.[238] On July 2, 1979, Burgum's death was noted perfunctorily only by the *New York Times*,[239] which had so often reported his activities in the 1930s, published his book reviews in the 1940s, and carried news of his encounters with the inquisitors from the frightening 1950s.

These two stories, of Lyman Bradley's and Edwin Burgum's battles with McCarthyism, are poignant, even quietly tragic. Outside the New York academic community and a dwindling band of left-wing activists, few people were aware of or interested in their fate. But their stories are a powerful testimony to the corrosiveness of Cold War anticommunism, which could not only destroy the most distinguished academic careers but also blemish the most liberal of educational institutions.

Dimitri Shostakovich at the Waldorf Astoria, 1949. (© CORBIS.)

4
The Composer

Dimitri Shostakovich

At New York's opulent Waldorf Astoria hotel in March 1949, the internationally famous Soviet composer Dimitri Shostakovich experienced "the worst moment in my life."[1] His nadir occurred when he was asked publicly if he supported *Pravda*'s recent denunciation of several Russian composers.[2] Forty years later, the American playwright Arthur Miller still remembered that moment: "It is the memory of Shostakovich that still haunts my mind when I think of that day."[3] William Barrett saw him as "unhappy" and "nervous,"[4] while to Nicolas Nabokov "he seemed like a trapped man."[5] According to another participant at that conference, Dwight Macdonald, Shostakovich was "very pale . . . [and] sat hunched over, eyes downcast, often with hand over mouth or shading eyes; unsmiling." He was "truly a tragic figure."[6]

This chapter focuses on Shostakovich's encounter with McCarthyism in New York. It examines why he went to the United States in 1949, why he experienced such extreme discomfort—"I still recall with horror my first trip to the USA"[7]—and what it suggests about the paradoxical position of the creative artist from a communist country during the early Cold War. Using Shostakovich as its primary focus, the chapter reveals the contradictions between his officially sanctioned role and his private doubts and misgivings. Because the first subsumed the second, the costs were considerable: his creative work diminished and his self-respect suffered. This public/personal disjuncture was most acute from February 1948, associated with the ideological assault on his music led by Andrei Zhdanov, until the death of Josef Stalin in March 1953. In March 1949 it

113

reached its apotheosis. In this chapter we also see how the Cultural and Scientific Conference for World Peace (or Waldorf conference, as it is commonly termed) became, at least for New York intellectuals, a critical and defining moment in the cultural Cold War.

Significance of Waldorf

The ostensible, if naïve, intention of the Waldorf conference was the promotion of cultural exchange across international boundaries, peaceful coexistence, and the diminution of the growing tensions between the Soviet Union and the United States. Its more specific aim was to gather artists, intellectuals, and scientists "to meet, to discuss and to seek a basis for common action on the central question of peace as it affects our work and our aspirations in the various fields of culture."[8] It was initiated either by the National Council of the Arts, Sciences and Professions (NCASP), whose leading light was the left-leaning but non-communist Harvard University astronomer Harlow Shapley,[9] or by the Communist Party of the United States of America (CPUSA) with Soviet backing.[10] A State Department official who escorted the Soviet delegation confirmed the former: "I had the impression that the conference was not actually communist-run" and that it was primarily run by "naïve, well-meaning, and vague [Henry] Wallaceites."[11] By taking much—far too much—of the credit, Howard Fast confirmed the latter. He claimed that he was "the major stimulating force for the Waldorf conference." In short, "It was my idea."[12] This was a gross overstatement. But his comment that it was "a conference created by the Communist Party . . . and no-one [sic] at the conference had any illusions as to who the organizers were"[13] is more telling. While there was a twisted rather than straight line from Wrocław to Waldorf, and while claims that "Moscow gold" bankrolled it are fanciful, there is no doubt that the CPUSA was central to the organization of Waldorf.[14] One example: Hannah Dorner, the executive secretary of the NCASP and a driving force behind Waldorf, was undoubtedly a party member.[15] According to one observer, she "insistently" whispered directions to Shapley, which he apparently took, during the conference proceedings.[16] The assessment of Mary McCarthy, the noted author and literary critic, approximates the reality: "There's no doubt of its having been a Stalinist engineered affair. But it was not the type of totalitarian affair pictured by Sidney Hook."[17] It is not the purpose here to settle conclusively this vexed question; however, the weight of evidence suggests that Waldorf was a Communist

Party "front" initiative with the blessing of the Communist Information Bureau (Cominform).

Irrespective of whether its origins were local or international, the Waldorf conference represented a pivotal and defining moment in the Cold War. To Guenter Lewy and John Diggins, it marked the beginning of both a "new peace campaign" and the cultural Cold War.[18] To New York's anti-Stalinist intellectuals, it provided the stimulant for the American Committee for Cultural Freedom[19] and was therefore, according to a CIA officer, a "catalytic event."[20] To Arthur Miller, the conference was something "brand-new in the post-war world," established "a new and higher level of hostility in the Cold War," and thereby became "a hairpin curve in the road of history."[21] To Arthur Schlesinger Jr., March 1949 was a "moment of transition" in the postwar history of American liberalism, when it redefined its attitude toward communism.[22] Robbie Lieberman, in contrast, sees Waldorf playing a major role in the "fragmentation of American liberalism."[23] For Michael Wreszin, it was a turning point: Waldorf was the last hurrah of the left to "engage in the political dialogue"; after Waldorf, the left became a "beleaguered remnant suffering abuse and isolation."[24] Hugh Wilford also uses the term "turning point" when assessing the role of Waldorf in the "Cold War struggle for hearts and minds." At Waldorf, he argued, the Cominform "staged its most startling provocation of the whole Cold War."[25] But after Waldorf, asserts Solomon Volkov, Stalin no longer attempted to "actively" influence American public opinion.[26] Notwithstanding Garry Wills' comment that "the Waldorf Conference is largely forgotten now,"[27] it has received intermittent but usually fleeting attention from scholars.[28] None has focused on Shostakovich. On the other hand, the Waldorf meeting itself not only generated considerable publicity, invariably hostile, from all the mainstream newspapers but also attracted considerable comment from columnists, writers, and government at the time.[29] Henry Luce's *Life* magazine even published a dramatic two-page photo gallery of fifty prominent "dupes and fellow travelers" who "dress up communist fronts" such as the Waldorf conference. This mixed bag of dignitaries included Leonard Bernstein, Lyman Bradley, Charlie Chaplin, Aaron Copland, Albert Einstein, Lillian Hellman, Langston Hughes, Norman Mailer, Thomas Mann, Clifford Odets, Dorothy Parker, and Harlow Shapley.[30] According to Frances Stoner Saunders, Luce personally oversaw this rogues' gallery, which "prefigured" Senator McCarthy's unofficial blacklists.[31] There is also circumstantial evidence that Arthur Schlesinger Jr. wrote the accompanying article.[32]

Stalin Speaks

On the morning of March 16, 1949, a telephone rang in the Moscow home of Dimitri Shostakovich.[33] He was told to wait for an important phone call, from Comrade Stalin. At first, Shostakovich thought it was a joke, but then he thought better and, in his own words, "took fright." According to one who was present, Yuri Levitin, Shostakovich "froze" and simply said, "Stalin is about to come on the line." Shostakovich soon recognized Stalin's strong Georgian accent from a meeting six years earlier at the Bolshoi Theatre. Stalin asked him why he had spurned the request of the Foreign Affairs Minister, Vyacheslav Molotov, to attend a forthcoming peace conference in New York. Shostakovich explained that performances of his symphonies were forbidden in the Soviet Union, but regularly played in the United States. The Americans would ask him ask why this was so, and the answer would be "humiliating." Thus, he was reluctant to go to America.[34] According to Shostakovich, Stalin feigned surprise: "What do you mean, forbidden? Forbidden by whom?" Disingenuously, Stalin denied having given any such order to the censors. By the end of the day, the ban had been lifted, on Stalin's personal instruction.[35] Order No. 3197 declared the February 1948 repertoire ban (Order No. 17) "illegal" and directed the reprimand of Glavrepertkom (the Committee on the Arts under the aegis of the Council of Ministers of the USSR) for publishing an illegal order.[36] Shostakovich relented.

> So finally I agreed and made the trip to America. It cost me a great deal, that trip. I had to answer stupid questions and avoid saying too much. They made a sensation out of that too. . . . I felt like a dead man. I answered all the idiotic questions in a daze, and thought, when I get back it's over for me.[37]

The 1948 Purge

The reason Shostakovich's symphonies were prohibited in the Soviet Union from 1948 is encapsulated by one word: *Zhdanovschchina*. In January 1948, the Central Committee of the Communist Party of the Soviet Union (CPSU) convened a conference of musicians in Moscow. The three-day meeting—in effect, an elaborate show trial—was dominated by the chairman, Andrei Zhdanov. He was Stalin's cultural commissar and a high-ranking Politburo member. In October 1947, it was Zhdanov who had promulgated the "two-camp" thesis (which divided the world into progressive and imperialist camps) at the inaugural meeting of the Cominform; more recently, he had overseen the purging of anti–Lysenko geneticists.[38] His power was formidable and his decrees were far-reaching. Shostakovich, the highest-ranking composer summoned to the congress, was singled out. Indeed, his revered status made him a prime target. As one biographer noted:

> That Shostakovich . . . was perceived to be above criticism, that as a composer and teacher he exerted enormous influence on rising generations of Soviet composers, that as a leader in the Composers' union he wielded inordinate control over the welfare of Soviet music and musicians, made him all the more vulnerable.[39]

Zhdanov pronounced that Soviet music was threatened by an insidious "formalism" whose methods were "fundamentally incorrect." Formalist music, of which Shostakovich was a principal exponent, reminded him of "a dentist's drill or a musical gas-wagon, the sort the Gestapo used."[40] These "formalists" also happened to be composers whose work was appreciated in the West. Zhdanov's cultivated philistinism was menacing. He castigated classical music as worthless and alien to the "life-affirming" doctrine of Socialist Realism and to the artistic tastes of the Soviet people, who (according to him) wanted mass songs with "melody and harmony."[41] Zhdanov's acolytes continued the assault in language dripping with invective. Shostakovich's *Eighth Symphony*, declared Vikto Belyi, was "repulsive, ultra-nationalistic"; Tikhon Krennikov dismissed his later work as "frantically gloomy and neurotic," and Vladimir Zakharov stated it was "not a musical work at all" and that his symphonies generally were the preferred listening "of nobody except foreign bandits and imperialists."[42]

Outwardly, Shostakovich was contrite, self-critical, and in search of atonement. In short, he conformed. "I have always listened to criticism addressed to me, and have always tried to work harder and better. I am listening now, too, and will listen in the future. I accept critical instruction."[43] Inwardly, he was humiliated and traumatized. Shostakovich learned that on the last day of the congress, January 13, 1948, the Jewish actor Solomon Mikhoels, his close friend, had been murdered.[44] On his way home that night, he visited Mikhoels' grieving family. Mikhoels' daughter recalled that Shostakovich remarked of her dead father: "I envy him."[45] One protégé, the cellist Mstislav Rostropovich, observed that Shostakovich was then "like a lunatic. He didn't sleep. He drank a great deal. . . . Terrible."[46] On February 10 Zhdanov issued his "anti-Formalism" decree.[47] Its effects were profound, reaching even into schools where children were instructed to despise "mercenary Formalists," who had been apprehended before they could fully contaminate Soviet music.[48] In April Shostakovich was subjected to a further week of relentless criticism and vilification by Zhdanov and others at the First All-Union Congress of Soviet Composers; again, he dutifully acquiesced. Shostakovich was dismissed from both his professorships at the Moscow and Leningrad conservatories, was sacked from the directorate of the Composers' Union, lost access to elite medical care at the Kremlin hospital, was probably under security police surveillance, and, with his performances proscribed, was reduced to poverty. During this period, the family's longtime servant, Fenya Kozhunova, spent her own savings to feed them.[49] During the next two years of silence, he performed only once—in New York's Madison Square Garden.

This, then, was the all-important background to Shostakovich's first spurning Molotov's request and then accepting Stalin's. He had recanted, but his punishment continued. He had been humbled but remained isolated. Yet he knew that the path to rehabilitation lay in traveling to New York. He embarked reluctantly and grudgingly and, notwithstanding the blacklist at home being partially eased, the costs—as we shall see—proved high.

Arriving in America

Shostakovich was not alone in viewing his impending visit in a negative light. The Attorney General of the United States, Tom C. Clark, told the FBI that he "would like to keep [the Russians] out," especially Shostakovich, because "they could carry back information to Russia as couriers."[50] Many Americans agreed and requested that the FBI shut the doors into America. One, Mrs. George Lenhart from Toledo, Ohio, wrote, "Let us not give men such as Dimitri Shostakovich a chance to spread their alien doctrine"—the "real reason" for the Russian's trip—and "plan a way to pave the way for Communism into this country."[51] Most letter writers beseeched J. Edgar Hoover to deny visas; Hoover politely reminded them that permission for foreign nationals to enter the country was given not by the Justice Department but by the Department of State. The American Legion knew better. Its "national commander," Perry Brown, wrote directly to the Secretary of State, Dean Acheson, protesting that the Russians were coming only to "support an obviously subversive group."[52] Émigré groups, conservative women's organizations, and trade unions also protested.[53] The president of the American Federation of Musicians, Local 802, wrote to the NCASP alleging that

> Shostakovich's arrival will emphasize more than any other event the utter debasement of artistic freedom in the Soviet Union. Just a few months ago Dimitri Shostakovich, now hailed by your organization as one of the immortals, was being pilloried and denounced by leaders of the Soviet Union who, by some strange alchemy, are able to read into a concatenation of musical notes and symbols the most sinister political meanings.[54]

Initially, the State Department was indecisive and inconsistent. It issued some visas, then revoked them; denied entry to all Hungarian delegates to the conference, then accepted some; and delayed its decision on the Russian delegates. Eventually and controversially, visas for representatives from Russia and the Iron Curtain countries of eastern Europe were granted.[55] A report in the British press stated that these delegates received visas because they had the backing of their governments, held diplomatic passports, and could be regarded as "official" representatives.[56] In the American press, the rationale given by the State Department was that, despite its being "fully aware" of communist manipulation of the Waldorf conference, it "approved the issuance of these visas because of its unswerving devotion to freedom of information and free speech on any issue, however controversial it may be."[57] Hypocrisy aside, this signaled the willingness of the Truman administration to use Waldorf as a propaganda instrument in the cultural Cold War.

The Russian delegation witnessed the Cold War directly when it arrived in West Berlin on March 22 en route to the United States. The Allied airlift was in full swing at Templehof airfield and, allegedly, they "gazed bug-eyed."[58] Asked what he thought of the airlift, Alexander Fadeyev, carrying a Sinclair Lewis novel, replied: "That's a political question; I am a poet."[59] Fadeyev was the Secretary General of the Union of Soviet Writers. In August 1948, he led the Russian delegation to the World Congress of Intellectuals for Peace in Wrocław, Poland, which launched the Cominform-backed peace movement and, in several respects, was a precursor to the Waldorf conference. In a long, chilling speech, he likened American writers (with the exception of Upton Sinclair and Sinclair Lewis) to "jackals," who "learned to use the typewriter" and "hyenas," who "mastered the fountain pen." American culture was "disgusting filth" with "the dollar sign written all over it."[60] Until 1956, when he committed suicide, he was a faithful apparatchik. Possibly, he was more than that. Sidney Hook's Americans for Intellectual Freedom alleged that Fadeyev had been sent to New York under instructions from the MVD, the Soviet secret police, to "protect" Shostakovich from "any anti-Soviet contacts."[61] Wherever the truth lay, he quickly became, while in New York, the villain of the piece, "a sort of cultural Vishinsky."[62]

At 5:00 P.M. on March 23, 1949, after a long flight from Berlin, the seven Russians landed at La Guardia airport in New York. Given Shostakovich's notoriety, they were greeted on the tarmac by seventy reporters and newsreel, television, and newspaper photographers. "Fadeyev, a heavily-built blonde with a Slavic face, led the way down the sloping ramp. Shostakovich, a meek, shy-looking man of 43 with spectacles . . . followed."[63] One shouted, "Hey, Shosty, look this way! Wave your hat!"[64] It is little wonder that Shostakovich should criticize Western journalists as "uneducated, obnoxious, and profoundly cynical."[65] A heavy police escort formed a wedge and ushered them through to Customs and Immigration. A press conference set up in an airport lounge, complete with camera floodlights, was ignored by the Russians. Instead, a group of Soviet diplomatic attachés eluded the press by shepherding the visitors through a side door to waiting taxis.[66] The opportunity to create a small bridge between East and West was lost.

Protests and Pickets

Even before the plane landed, a plan for picketing the Waldorf Astoria had already commenced. The escalation of picketing became a litmus test of the intensity of pockets of anticommunism in New York City. And it became a major logistical operation for the New York Police Department. Initially, picketing was organized only by local Catholics. The New York County Commander of the Catholic War Veterans, Richard McTigue, instructed units in all five boroughs, plus Hudson County in New Jersey, to recruit pickets for a mass demonstration at the hotel for the opening of the conference on March 25.[67] In addition, the chairman of the United Catholic Organization for Freeing Cardinal József Mindszenty stated that the twenty-nine groups in his organization would supply an additional 50,000 demonstrators. A third Catholic-sponsored, Brooklyn-based group, the People's Committee for Freedom of Religion, also announced its intention to picket.[68] All three would target delegates from communist countries, especially, as one angry demonstrator later shouted, the "Russian skunks."[69] Catholic Americans had openly allied themselves with Franco during the Spanish Civil War, and subsequently with their oppressed confrères in communist-dominated eastern Europe. Their embrace of McCarthyism was a logical outcome.[70]

When some of the 2,800 registered delegates and guests arrived in the rain for the opening of the conference, the Park Avenue entrance to the Waldorf Astoria was surrounded by chanting picketers and kneeling nuns.[71] The *Journal-American* recklessly predicted a "mammoth demonstration . . . the biggest parade of pickets in the city's history" under the melodramatic headline "100,000 Due to Ring Hotel," and *The Brooklyn Eagle* and *World-Telegram* each predicted 50,000. In fact, only 35 pickets and 22 policemen attended.[72] A large but shifting crowd, estimated by the police at 10,000, looked on.[73] Fortified by the presence of Veterans of Foreign Wars (some in wheelchairs) and members of the American Legion, the potential for violence was real, but only scuffles occurred. New York's ethnic neighborhoods were home to large numbers of eastern European refugees from communism. Thus, Baltic, Czech, Romanian, and White Russian émigré groups, dressed in traditional costumes, carried national flags (including a Tsarist flag), banners, and placards such as "Join Communism. You Have Nothing to Lose But Your Brains," "Veterans Love Music But Not from Behind an Iron Curtain," and "Ukrainian Insurgents Fight & Die for Democracy & Peace."[74] One placard read "Shostakovich! Jump Thru the Window!," in an allusion to the Russian schoolteacher Oksana Kasenkina's leaping from a third-floor window of the Russian consulate in Manhattan in August 1948.[75] More tolerantly, another sign read, "Shostakovich, We Understand." Less specifically, yet another sign, carried by a disabled veteran, stated, "Russians Breathe the Air of Freedom Here—Take It Home." When Arthur Miller ran the gantlet he encountered a different protestor: "[T]o enter the Waldorf I had to step over the shoulders of a line of kneeling nuns, crying their prayers to heaven of those devil-caught souls bewildered enough to attend." He turned back to look at the sisters' "horrified faces" and sensed a wave of outrage "religious in its depth."[76] The next day, police stopped several fights between picketers and bystanders and physically restrained one woman, carrying a placard reading "Exterminate the Red Rats," who directed a spray gun filled with water on conference delegates.[77] More common, however, were sounds of boos and catcalls, the singing of "God Bless America" and "My Country 'tis of Thee," and the massed recitation of the Lord's Prayer.[78]

At the Waldorf

Inside the spectacular and specially decorated grand ballroom that Friday evening, March 25, 1949, a chain-smoking Shostakovich was, as *Life* put it, the star of the show.[79] The ballroom was filled to capacity, with 1,800 diners. Shostakovich spoke only briefly from a prepared script but received the biggest ovation and was the most photographed. He told the banquet audience that the Russian group was united with the "best" of American intellectuals, the "progressive representatives" of American culture, in the noble task of defending peace against its enemies. He called for the establishment of "firm and friendly" relations between the Soviet Union and the United States based on "trust and mutual respect."[80] A discordant note—a rare one—was struck by Norman Cousins, the editor of the *Saturday Review of Literature*, a liberal, and, as Howard Fast described him, "a man of stature and influence in the publishing industry."[81] Initially, he stunned the audience into silence; by the end it booed him. Turning to the Russians, Cousins said: "Tell the folks at home that the Americans are anti-Communist but not anti-humanitarian and that being anti-Communist does not automatically mean they are pro-war." He continued that Americans wanted peace, but not at any price. He also referred to the American Communist Party as a "small political group" that owed its allegiance not to America but to "an outside Government."[82] His speech was punctuated by hissing and jeering from the diners and received only polite, subdued applause. One enraged young woman at the rear of the ballroom deliberately smashed her plate and yelled, "You hypocrite, you're at the wrong conference!"[83] After Cousins had finished, the playwright Lillian Hellman took the microphone and acidly said: "I would recommend, Mr. Cousins, that when you talk about your hosts at dinner, wait until you go home to do it."[84] Later, Cousins commented: "Lillian Hellman seems to believe that her own political calendar . . . should be the standard by which everyone else is measured."[85] There were allegations that Cousins had been actively encouraged by the State Department.[86] But according to Cousins himself, it was Harlow Shapley, a longtime friend, who, "on his own initiative and authority," invited him to speak. "If the State Department had in fact asked me to speak, I doubt that I would have done so. . . . I acted independently."[87] In an extended interview in 1988, Cousins outlined his position—a position that foreshadowed that of O. John Rogge (the JAFRC lawyer and the focus of Chapter 5) in 1950.

You see, I believed that it was necessary to come to terms with the Soviet Union, and I was terrified by the way any attempts to reduce tensions between the two countries was being tagged as communist activity. My talk at the Waldorf-Astoria tried to define an independent position—one that favored a peaceful settlement of issues with the Soviet Union without accepting communist leadership towards that end. Margaret Mead said that the text of my talk made it clear that I was not doing any red-baiting. But she said the effect of what I said aligned me with those who were.[88]

During the evening a less public drama unfolded. Three delegates at table 7-A were quietly seized by agents from the Bureau of Immigration; the next day they were charged with being members of the Canadian Communist Party, and two of them were deported.[89]

Shostakovich was due to speak again, and at greater length, on the third and final day of the conference, but it was his "chief ringmaster,"[90] Alexander Fadeyev, who was first subjected to hostile questioning. He spoke at a panel session on "Writing and Publishing" on the afternoon of Saturday, March 26.[91] It was attended by more than 800 delegates and chaired by the poet and anthologist Louis Untermeyer.[92] The quixotic journalist, literary critic, and editor of the short-lived quarterly magazine *Politics*, Dwight Macdonald, rose to speak; there was "commotion, subdued booing when I gave my name." He asked "how it serves world peace to accept as the representative of Russian literature at this conference a man who is not primarily a writer, but rather a State functionary?" He pointed out that Fadeyev had produced only three novels, all of them "propagandistic," and that his creative passion had been "reserved for the bureaucratic organizations through which the Soviet state enslaves its writers to its political purposes." He also asked why the conference organizers had not insisted that the Russian representative be a true writer of international reputation, like Boris Pasternak or Anna Akhmetova, and "not a policeman." He asked specifically about the fate of six Soviet writers, including Itzak Feffer. Macdonald then cited from Fadeyev's splenetic speech in Wrocław—referred to earlier—and asked how such a speech furthered world peace. Fadeyev's response was evasive, longwinded, disinguous, and, at times, aggressive, reflecting the polarities of the Cold War: "The point of view of my questioner is familiar: it is that of an enemy of the Soviet Union."[93] He told the "disruptive" questioner that he had personally seen the Yiddish writers referred to and that all were in good health. He lied. Each was already dead or awaiting death in Moscow's Lubyanka prison or on the Siberian tundra. Shostakovich, who was present as an observer, was asked directly by the pacifist poet Robert Lowell, in an allusion to *Zhdanovschchina*, how criticism by the government helped his musical work. Lowell sought an answer from "the only person in the Russian delegation who may be able to understand it, a person for whom I feel the utmost sympathy and pain." Shostakovich was "pale" and "nervous"—his hands were "literally trembling," observed Macdonald—and replied "haltingly" with one sentence in Russian. It was translated by the slick and arrogant Fadeyev as: "The criticism brings me much good—it helps bring my music forward."[94] This exchange fore-shadowed what was soon to come.

Concurrent with this panel at the Waldorf Astoria was a "keynote session" chaired by Harlow Shapley at Carnegie Hall; it was filled to its 2,840-seat capacity, with 150 standees and several hundred turned away. Once again, chanting picketers thronged the entrances.[95] One of those who spoke alongside former presidential candidate Henry A. Wallace was O. John Rogge, who was, *inter alia*, a vice chairman of the NCASP. He commenced by referring to "the lynch spirit that fills the air outside this meeting hall today."[96] His address echoed themes on which he had previously spoken or written: he referred to "this nation's drive to war"; "today a Yankee Doodle fascism has come to town"; and "the billions we spend for Marshall Plans, Truman Doctrines, North Atlantic Pacts . . . bring us nothing but bankruptcy and disaster." For these comments Rogge received generous coverage in *Pravda, Izvestia*, and TASS (the Soviet news agency) dispatches.[97] What was not reported were his bipartisan comments, in which he was edging toward the controversial position he adopted at the Warsaw Peace Congress fifteen months later. He coupled American discrimination against minority groups with the fact that "in the Soviet Union there is not sufficient freedom for political minorities. . . . Injustice on one side is matched by injustice on the other. . . . As the tension increases so do the unjustifiable excess on both sides." Foreshadowing his idealistic proposal in 1950 to form a new Progressive Party, Rogge urged the conference to "call for a united front of all peace-minded people" that would pressure both Stalin and Truman to "talk peace."[98] But the Waldorf conference was marginally more ecumenical than the Warsaw conference, so Rogge was applauded rather than hissed.

This Saturday morning session concluded with the playing of the American national anthem. Glib assumptions that the chairman, Harlow Shapley, was a Kremlin dupe, as Hook and others insisted, are contradicted by this account by the associate editor of *Partisan Review*, William Barrett. Referring to the "very American side" of Shapley's character, Barrett—who was one of Hook's colleagues at NYU's Philosophy Department and who had little sympathy for the Waldorf conference—commented:

> I stood directly in front of Dr. Shapley while the "Star-Spangled Banner" was being sung, and I have rarely seen a face express so much emotion: he looked very much on the verge of tears. When the anthem was finished, he stepped forward to tell the audience that they could not imagine how close to his heart were the feelings expressed in that song.[99]

Not surprisingly, none of this was conveyed to the FBI by the "Confidential Informants" T-5, T-6, or T-8 present at Carnegie Hall that morning.[100] The FBI's incorrect suspicions that Shapley was a dangerous communist persisted until 1953, a year after his retirement from Harvard.[101]

"A ruthless duel"

Shostakovich met his nemesis the next morning, Sunday, March 27. The venue was the fabled Starlight Roof ballroom in the Waldorf Astoria, with its gilt ceiling and crystal chandeliers; the session was the Fine Arts Panel; and the chair was Olin Downes, the music critic for the *New York Times*.[102] After Shostakovich briefly thanked the conference sponsors, an interpreter read, "in a sonorous voice," a 5,200-word prepared speech to the packed crowd of 800 enthusiasts. It took 45 minutes. It was obvious that Shostakovich had not written this speech, which was handcrafted for the occasion. He warned that a "small clique of hatemongers" was preparing a new global war and urged progressive artists to struggle against the new "Fascists" who were seeking world domination. To that end, the United States was "perfecting new kinds of weapons for mass destruction." The attack on American Cold War policies was trenchant but, consistent with the official Soviet political discourse of 1948–49, formulaic. The audience also heard Shostakovich's renunciation of "bourgeois formalism." "In those of my works," the statement continued, "in which I departed from big themes and contemporary issues, I lost my contact with the people—and I failed." However, the "demand of the people," represented by the CPSU, was "extremely important in my creative development." Perhaps the depth of his abasement was reached when he attacked a colleague, another disgraced composer, Sergei Prokofiev, who was in danger of "relapses into formalism" if he, too, failed to "heed the directives" of the

CPSU.[103] Throughout the long speech, Shostakovich remained silent. Indeed, he was decidedly uncomfortable—as evidenced by the observations with which this chapter began—and nervously fidgeted. But the "worst moment in my life" came during question time, and it was another Russian, another composer, who was responsible.

Nicolas Nabokov, first cousin of the writer Vladimir Nabokov and close friend of the composer Igor Stravinsky, was born into a prominent White Russian family that was forced to flee Russia in the wake of the Bolshevik revolution. He moved to the United States in 1933 and became a naturalized citizen in 1939. In 1947, sponsored by the U.S. diplomat George F. Kennan but not cleared by J. Edgar Hoover, he applied for a position with the CIA. As a Russian he understood well the scope and character of Zhdanov's 1948 decree on formalism.[104] Because Shostakovich was scheduled to speak before the Fine Arts Panel at the Waldorf conference, Nabokov decided to attend; this, he wrote, was "strictly within my profession."[105] He noticed that Shostakovich was intensely nervous: "I watched his hands twist the cardboard tips of his cigarettes, his face twitch and his whole posture express intense unease. . . . [H]is sensitive face looked disturbed, hurt and terribly shy. I felt, as I lit his cigarette or passed a record to him from an American admirer, that he wanted it over with as quickly as possible."[106] After the Shostakovich address—and "everybody except me applauded furiously"—Nabokov "sat in his seat petrified by this spectacle of human misery and degradation. . . . This speech of his . . . was part of a punishment, part of a ritual redemption he had to go through before he could be pardoned again."[107] He then recalled:

> The question I wanted to ask Shostakovich was simple and straightforward, but obviously embarrassing to him. I knew in advance what his reply would be, and I also knew that his answer would expose him as not being a free agent. . . . Yet this was in my opinion the only legitimate way to expose the internal mores of Russian communism.

Nabokov's question concerned a recent unsigned *Pravda* article that bore all the hallmarks of an official position. In it, three distinguished composers (Paul Hindemith, Arnold Schoenberg, and Stravinsky) were branded as decadent formalists and lackeys of imperialism. The performance of their music, quoting from the article, should "therefore be banned in the U.S.S.R." The language was vintage Zhdanov. Nabokov then asked Shostakovich whether he personally, as a composer—and not as a delegate of the Soviet government—agreed with this view, as printed in *Pravda*.

One of the Russians on the dais audibly muttered "*Provokatsya!*" (provocation) and the interpreter whispered instructions in Shostakovich's ear. The composer stood up, went to the microphone, looked down at the floor, and, in a thin, uneasy voice, said in Russian, "I fully agree with the statements made in *Pravda*."[108] Solomon Volkov's comment was apt: "What a sad sight: two Russians, two composers, brought together by the Cold War in a ruthless duel."[109]

Forty years later, Arthur Miller was still "haunted" by his memory of Shostakovich that day. "God knows what he was thinking in that room, what splits ran across his spirit, what urge to cry out and what self-control to suppress his outcry. . . ."[110] And thirty years later, Shostakovich was still bitter: "It cost me a great deal, that trip. I had to answer stupid questions and avoid saying too much."[111] But it cost more than that. The publicity given to Nabokov's attack meant that, from that moment, Shostakovich's American reputation was crippled. Irrespective of his inner convictions, painfully suppressed, he was perceived in the West as an acquiescent mouthpiece for the Soviet Union, parroting its propaganda. It was only with the posthumously published *Testimony* that this perception was largely undone.[112]

Hook and the AIF

The significant role that Nabokov played in "exposing" Shostakovich at the Waldorf—a role that Arthur Schlesinger Jr. "especially" remembered[113]—was neither accidental nor unpremeditated. It emanated from a planned campaign to disrupt and discredit the Waldorf meeting by the Americans for Intellectual Freedom (AIF). Nabokov was involved with the formation of the AIF in March 1949,[114] but it was the brainchild of New York University professor of philosophy Sidney Hook, who synthesized the reasons, as he saw them, in a private letter:

> It was I who organized this Committee in opposition to the Communist-controlled Waldorf Astoria peace meeting after its true character was revealed by
> (1) the withdrawal of their acceptance of my submitted outline of a paper—which criticized the concept of national, class, and party truths
> (2) the one sided character of the trusted speakers
> (3) the people or intellectuals *not* invited (anyone critical of the party line [in] the field of the arts and sciences).[115]

Needless to say, a quite different perspective on the vetting of conference speakers emerges from the correspondence from Harlow Shapley. Indeed, on this issue, Shapley called Hook a "prevaricator" and a "liar."[116] A heated confrontation between the two occurred in Shapley's hotel room on the evening of March 25, followed by a sharp and, at times, vitriolic, public exchange of views.[117] Hook's detractors coined a new phrase: "By Hook-ism or crook-ism."[118]

Hook's new group attracted some big names. As well as Nabokov, there was Dwight Macdonald (in whose apartment the first meeting was held); the critic Mary McCarthy (despite her being "not on friendly terms then with Hook"[119]); Professor George S. Counts from Columbia University;[120] the celebrated novelists John Dos Passos and James T. Farrell;[121] the historians Arthur Schlesinger Jr. and Bertram Wolfe (who had recently published *Three Who Made a Revolution*); the Nobel Prize winner, scientist, and academic Professor Hermann Muller; the former leader of the American Socialist Party, Norman Thomas; the former leader of the Russian Provisional Government, Alexander Kerensky; and the editors of *Commentary*, *Partisan Review*, and *The New Leader*. Most of these anti-Stalinist liberal intellectuals had traveled a political path from communism to anticommunism via Trotskyism; many had visited the Soviet Union in the 1930s. Another supporter was the prominent African American (he founded the Council on African Relations) and ex-communist Max Yergan. Ten years before, he had proposed marriage to Helen Bryan, secretary of the JAFRC; now, in 1949, he spoke with the dubious authority of "personal knowledge of Communist treachery and duplicity."[122] The AIF rented a plush three-room suite at the Waldorf Astoria; installed ten telephone lines; obtained funds from David Dubinsky, the anti-Stalinist trade union leader; and "busied themselves with intercepting mail and messages intended for the conference sponsors, and issuing false statements to the press in the peace conference's name."[123] Another key strategy was to organize a separate counter-conference. This, according to Hook, represented "the real triumph of our cause."[124] It was held at Freedom House on West 40th Street, 12 blocks away from the Waldorf Astoria, on March 26, and attended by nearly 1,000 people, most of whom heard the succession of speeches via loudspeakers in nearby Bryant Park. Hook opened the rally by proclaiming, "We are an independent group of scholars, writers and artists who are interested in preserving and extending freedom everywhere in the world."[125] The common theme of the speeches was intellectual freedom, as practiced in the United States, versus intellectual repression, as experienced in the Soviet Union. They were often concerned with "humanizing with names the familiar but vague general picture of writers and scientists in the Soviet Union."[126] Both Hook and AIF co-chairman George Counts offered to help Shostakovich secure asylum should he not wish to return to Russia. This rival rally attracted front-page coverage.[127]

The other strategy pursued by the AIF was to infiltrate the Waldorf conference, fan out among the different panels, and embarrass the speakers. Mary McCarthy, for example, attended the Writing and Publishing Panel, chaired by Howard Fast. On Hook's recommendation, she brought along an umbrella ready to bang loudly on the floor in the expectation of not being recognized by the chair. Hook also recommended that she (and other oppositionists whom he briefed) be prepared to tie herself to her chair so that, when she was expelled, the ushers would have to carry her out, thereby providing valuable publicity to the anticommunist cause.[128] Such overheated precautions were unnecessary. Instead, McCarthy was given the floor and asked the distinguished literary scholar F. O. Matthiessen whether Ralph Waldo Emerson, to whom he had referred, would be permitted to write freely in the Soviet Union.[129] Soon after, as we have seen, a far bigger drama unfolded elsewhere in the hotel. Shostakovich was the primary target, and Nabokov had the ammunition. The result, for Shostakovich, became "the worst moment in my life." But for Hook, the chief ringmaster, it was a triumph: "We had frustrated one of the most ambitious undertakings of the Kremlin."[130]

"The smile of a condemned man"

The Waldorf conference climaxed with a mass rally and concert at Madison Square Garden. A capacity crowd of 19,000 jammed into the cavernous venue. Once again, Shostakovich was the drawcard: we can assume that many New Yorkers had been drawn by the frequent radio announcements during the day that he would play the piano. Once again, noisy pickets were present: 2,000 of them choked the sidewalks of Eighth Avenue at 49th Street (the site of the Garden at that time), and another 5,000 were turned back by the hundreds of police, who formed solid lines and who described the demonstrators as far more pugnacious and boisterous than others had been previously.[131] And once again, Fadeyev received thunderous applause, this time for his denunciation of the Atlantic Pact (later known as NATO) as an attack "on the national sovereignty of peoples. . . . I shall not lower myself to cursing it."[132] But the diffident and publicity-shy Shostakovich drew the greatest ovation of the evening. Earlier, he expressed the hope that his performance would be "more harmonious than my reception" the previous day.[133] He played a transcription of the Second Movement (*scherzo*) of his *Fifth Symphony* on the piano, the "Allegretto," first performed by the Leningrad Philharmonic in 1937. Although he thought, "This is it, this is the last time I'll ever play before an audience this size,"[134] he was, reportedly, "stiff and shy" and "declined firmly to give an encore."[135] The "Madison Square Garden Hootenanny," as one called it, was over.[136]

Shostakovich was scheduled to perform after the Waldorf conference in numerous other cities. He was saved by the U.S. government. The conference organizers intended that the Soviet delegation accompany an "action committee" on a two-week speaking tour and "cultural rallies for peace" that would criss-cross the country.[137] Only hours before Shostakovich was due to play at the huge Mosque Theater in Newark, New Jersey, and speak on "Trends in Modern Music," Attorney General Clark announced that the visas granted to delegates from Russia and Iron Curtain countries were valid only for the New York conference and would not be extended. The Immigration and Naturalization Service (INS) hand-delivered letters to the foreign visitors notifying them of this decision and of their need to arrange immediate departure from the United States. The Justice Department, moreover, would "act against those who failed to abide by the decision."[138] In Baltimore a half-filled Lyric Theater heard a local pianist perform works by Shostakovich; in Chicago's Civic Opera House, a single spotlight shone on a vacant piano stool; in Boston a concert with the Symphony Orchestra was canceled.[139]

At 7:20 on the evening of April 3, the seven Russians departed from La Guardia airport, bound for Stockholm. Shostakovich carried cartons of cigarettes and a bundle of phonograph records. They shook hands, posed for the cameras, and "smiled a good deal."[140] Despite the farewell delegation's expression of "sadness" at the group's early departure, Shostakovich told a reporter, "I am glad to be returning home."[141] Much later, Shostakovich grimly recalled, "Look at the way I'm smiling in the photographs. That was the smile of a condemned man."[142]

Shostakovich was not a condemned man upon his return. Instead, he came in from the cold. His rehabilitation was helped greatly by his ritual atonement at the Waldorf. In 1949 he was placed on the organizing committee for Stalin's seventieth birthday. Photos of him began appearing again in the press. His guilt was further expiated when he composed, in the summer of 1949, the exceptionally bland oratorio *The Song of the Forests*, which glorified Stalin's impractical reafforestation plan.[143] However, his heart was not in it: "I sat down at night and, within a few hours[,] dashed off something haphazardly. When I submitted what I had written, to my amazement and horror, they shook hands and paid me."[144] After it premiered in November 1949, Shostakovich returned to his hotel room, sobbed into a pillow, and took solace in vodka.[145] Nevertheless, *The Song of the Forests* won official favor: in 1950 he was awarded the Stalin Prize (First Class), a *dacha* outside Moscow, and a reinstatement on the editorial board of the scholarly journal *Sovetskaya Muzïka*. What was far more important to Shostakovich—and this is suggestive of the dichotomy between public position and private attitude—was his *String Quartet No. 4 in D, Opus 83*, which he commenced on his return from New York and completed in December 1949. Dedicated to a Jewish friend and artist, Pyotr Vilyams, and influenced by Jewish folk music (the use of Jewish motifs in the fourth movement is, apparently, clear), it was cathartic but consigned to the drawer. Self-censorship was necessary. Stalin's pogrom against "rootless cosmopolitans" was in full flight, and most prominent Jewish artists, scientists, and intellectuals were being purged.[146] The *String Quartet* had its premiere on December 3, 1953, only after Stalin was dead.

Stalin again enlisted Shostakovich in the Soviet quest for international recognition. His high public profile at home and abroad, combined with his apparent meek acquiescence to the dictates of the CPSU, made him an ideal symbol and articulator of Soviet propaganda. In 1950 he joined the Soviet Committee for the Defense of Peace, participated in its National Congresses, and attended the Second World Peace Congress, which had been forced to relocate from Sheffield to Warsaw, in November 1950. Two years later he traveled to Vienna for the Third World Peace Congress, the "Congress of the Peoples for Peace," where he read from a "prepared manuscript."[147] Most likely, these experiences were less traumatic than the Waldorf conference, although, for him, they were an unwelcome distraction from composition. As he confidentially told the Soviet writer Ilya Ehrenburg, these congresses had "torn him away from work and now he was forced to listen."[148] Like most party members he publicly mourned Stalin's death, and his "official" panegyric was widely disseminated. Privately he felt relief more than elation. And his expectations were far from sanguine: "[T]he times are new, but the informers are old."[149] By 1954, he was accorded the title "People's Artist of the U.S.S.R." and received the World Peace Prize. His rehabilitation in the Soviet Union, although not yet in the West, was complete.

Shostakovich's participation in the 1949 Waldorf conference silhouetted sharply the dilemmas facing the intellectual within an authoritarian regime. To refuse Stalin's request to visit the United States was untenable. Isolation or imprisonment was anathema to one so talented and productive as Shostakovich. Stalin required Shostakovich's international reputation to give the Russian delegation respectability and prestige, especially in New York, the home of the United Nations and the very heartland of his Cold War adversary. Shostakovich knew that his role was to be a mouthpiece for Soviet foreign policy, that he would be "a cut-out paper doll on a string,"[150] but his options were limited if his music was to be played while Stalin lived. So this self-effacing, vulnerable man, who eschewed publicity and familiarity, was thrust into the spotlight against his will in order to serve the interests of the state. Deviance was exchanged for conformity. Integrity was traded for survival. The price he paid was public humiliation (mainly at the hands of Nabokov) and private turmoil. Resistance, and a small measure of self-respect, lay in composing nonconforming music and consigning it to the bottom drawer until the political climate changed. It also lay in injecting "subversive" notes and coded tunes, for those able to hear the parody, into a violin concerto. His American detractors knew nothing of these complexities. They perceived his capitulation before Zhdanov, the content of his Kremlin-written speech, and his humiliating answer to Nabokov's question, as proof that he was a party hack or, to use Vasily Grossman's phrase, a "State lackey."[151] But appearing at the Waldorf was his insurance policy. In doing so, he avoided the Gulag, stayed alive, and revived an illustrious professional career.[152]

Police escorting Russian delegation attending the Cultural and Scientific Conference for World Peace. (Photo by Cornell Capa / Time Life Pictures / Getty Images.)

O. John Rogge, 1949.

5
The Lawyer

O. John Rogge

For three long years, a New York lawyer, O. John Rogge, assiduously defended the Joint Anti-Fascist Refugee Committee (JAFRC). Although he could not save its executive board from the federal penitentiary, the reputation of Rogge as a lawyer with a high public profile and an established record of activism in both legal and political circles remained intact. Before Barsky, Bradley, Bryan, and Fast were imprisoned, Rogge was an invited speaker at the Waldorf conference in March 1949, at which Dimitri Shostakovich was the drawcard. After they were imprisoned, he was again on the hustings, invited by the Joint Committee for Aid to Anti-Fascist Emigrants to speak at a New York rally. Yet despite W. E. B. Du Bois' describing him as a "national figure"[1] and two historians' judgment that he was "one of the country's most prominent radical lawyers,"[2] Rogge has been ignored by both biographers and Cold War scholars. Today he remains a forgotten figure in American history. This chapter will therefore rectify a historiographical gap in our understanding of New Yorkers and the Cold War.

However, there is a more compelling reason to include Rogge in our story: unlike all the other New Yorkers examined thus far, this individual was philosophically torn. He and Shostakovich shared not dissimilar dilemmas. Rogge's case was emblematic of the conundrum confronting American liberalism and its attitude toward communism in the Cold War. How anticommunist could a liberal become without jettisoning those bedrock principles of civil liberty? What political space was there for those, like Rogge, who finally chose neither Moscow nor Washington? Was an independent position possible in such a polarized world? In this chapter, I use the lens of O. John Rogge to see how much room for maneuvering existed for those seeking dialogue between East and West during the heyday of McCarthyism.

Rogge, too, warrants our attention for the same reasons that Orwell continues to attract biographers: both repudiated totalitarianism from the left as well as from the right; both condemned Soviet as well as American imperialism; both remained committed social democrats working within but critical of the capitalist system; both attempted to find an independent path, a third way, through the geopolitical and ideological minefields of the Cold War; and both became so disillusioned with, hostile to, or anxious about Stalinism that each was prepared to assist the state: in Rogge's case the U.S. State Department, in Orwell's case the clandestine Information Research Department within the British Foreign Office. And as with Orwell, who remained on the left but was applauded by the right, we can ask of Rogge: where can such an individual be placed on an ideological spectrum that was rapidly being redrawn by Cold War imperatives?

On the Left

Rogge's political trajectory reveals a man full of apparent contradictions. If we take the years 1947–51 as our measure, we could easily conclude that his active record on behalf of progressive causes distinguished him as a man of the left. In 1947, as we shall shortly see, Rogge became the defending attorney for the JAFRC when it was deemed a subversive organization and charged with contempt of Congress by HUAC. He often attended JAFRC executive board meetings to brief members on the legal options available to the organization and was intimately involved with preparing and conducting its legal appeals. He represented the labor leader Harold Christoffel through a series of trials from 1947 to 1950.[3] He served as defense counsel in the Smith Act prosecutions that eventually decapitated the Communist Party of its leadership. Rogge's political commitment in the late 1940s ran far deeper than his choice of legal briefs. In late 1947, he deserted the Democratic Party and took out membership in the increasingly communist-dominated American Labor Party (ALP) led by the charismatic New York congressman Vito Marcantonio and ran on the ALP judicial slate in 1948.[4] He won sufficient votes (97,418) to split the Democratic vote, permitting the narrow election of the Republican candidate, George Frankenthaler. He was an "avowed candidate" for nomination as Henry A. Wallace's running mate in the latter's bid for presidency.[5] Rogge was also both the New York state chairman of the Wallace for President Committee and a National Committee member of the Progressive Party, which was formed in the summer of 1948.[6] Wallace's biographer concluded that the Progressive Party was communist-influenced but not communist-dominated.[7] Yet the label of the latter was firmly fixed early by the Truman administration. However, Rogge stuck by Wallace and the Progressive Party, even when anticommunist propaganda about it, and accusations of Wallace's being a communist dupe, became widespread.[8] It was not until early 1951 that Rogge, like Wallace, warned against the earlier tolerant attitude that embraced communist support.[9]

Fascism in the United States?

In this period, too, Rogge repeatedly and publicly emphasized the dangers of fascism in America: "I am more afraid of fascism than communism in America"; "fascism in America is masquerading under the name of nationalism"; "fascism is not dead in the United States, it is simply reconverting"; "reactionaries are preparing to take the remaining short step to fascism"; "the fascist threat to democracy is greater now than at any time since 1932."[10] In a major article for a weekly New York newsletter in 1947, he outlined in detail the "Blueprint for American Fascism."[11] Later that year, he interpreted Cold War attacks on the Hollywood Ten and American radicals generally as "incipient fascism."[12] In 1949, he claimed that with the Truman administration, "we are getting fascism American style."[13] These are not the words or the perspectives of an ardent anticommunist. Indeed, communists took note of them. His prediction of a "dramatic round-up of dozens of Communist leaders and alleged fellow-travelers"[14] by the Justice Department—similar to the Palmer Raids during the first "Red Scare," in 1919–20—underpinned the Communist Party's fateful decision to go underground in mid-1951.[15] Rogge also assumed leading roles in three organizations that were clearly left-leaning or communist-dominated: the World Committee of Partisans for Peace (vice president),[16] the National Lawyers' Guild (vice president), and the Civil Rights Congress.[17] The last of these picked up Rogge's phrase "Scottsboro—1948" in its championing of the Trenton Six.[18] He regularly attacked conspiracy indictments, Truman's loyalty–security program, the operation of the loyalty boards, the Subversive Activities Control Board, J. Edgar Hoover's FBI, the serious erosion of civil liberties, and the unconstitutionality of HUAC, which he judged as "consistently pushing us in the direction of a fascist police state."[19] He even alleged that Middle Eastern oil, more than anticommunist ideology, was the main motivation for the Truman Doctrine.[20] And he continually alleged that the communist threat was a communist bogey:

> The Communist scare is a tremendous hoax behind which looms the threat of the American police state and the third world war. . . . Insidiously, step by step, the enemies of our civil liberties have advanced behind the poisonous smoke-screen of the "Communist threat."[21]

It was logical that, with the onset of the Cold War, Rogge and the left should embrace each other. As a result of his activities and public statements, Rogge attracted the wrath of the anticommunist crusaders. As one wrote to J. Edgar Hoover, "I hope you will be able to stop this agitator some day for he seems to be only another one of the damnable atheistic and godless Communists, stirring up trouble . . . and arousing hate against Christianity with a pack of lies, lies and more lies."[22]

Switching Sides

From 1951, however, Rogge can be hitched to the *anti*communist wagon. His role in the Rosenberg case exemplifies this. On April 5, 1951, Judge Irving R. Kaufman sentenced Julius and Ethel Rosenberg to death. Crucial to their conviction was the testimony of Ethel's brother, David Greenglass, who had also been arrested for his involvement in espionage at Los Alamos. Unlike the Rosenbergs, Greenglass confessed, turned prosecution witness against his former comrades, and was spared the electric chair. Representing Greenglass—and who, significantly, persuaded him to implicate the Rosenbergs—was Rogge. According to Roy Cohn, "most" of the credit for the convictions rests with Rogge: "Without John Rogge there might not have been a successful prosecution. Indeed, it is not too much to say that Mr. Rogge broke the Rosenberg case."[23] Later that year, Rogge was the key prosecution witness in the Truman government's unsuccessful attempt to prosecute the Peace Information Center for failing to register as agents of a foreign power—namely, the Soviet Union.

But Rogge, it seemed, was not only no longer a radical; he had actually moved to the other side. Accordingly, he was excoriated by the far left. The venerable W. E. B. Du Bois, America's most prominent black intellectual and a leading radical, devoted an entire chapter to Rogge in his autobiographical work. Its title—"Oh! John Rogge"—expressed its tone. He alleged that Rogge "hated Negroes," was "an ambitious man . . . overborne by his sudden rise to notoriety," and "like so many Americans, wanted money and a great deal of it." He saved his most stinging epithet for the final sentence: "to [Henry] Wallace the Weasel I now add, Rogge the Rat."[24] Equally damning was the assessment of Rogge by his former friend Albert Kahn, for whom Rogge wrote the foreword to his polemic *Treason in Congress*.[25] Kahn argued that there was a simple explanation for Rogge's "metamorphosis":

> Turncoats and traitors are not unfamiliar phenomena in our time. Nations have had their Quislings and Lavals, revolutionary parties their Trotskys and Rajks. . . . It was perhaps to be expected the peace movement would have its Rogge. The case of Rogge may be of interest as a study in character degeneration. But its chief significance is not a matter of personality but of politics. Rogge demonstrates the development of a renegade.[26]

Kahn approvingly cited "a Negro woman" who said of Rogge: "There walks a Judas, and a Judas walks alone."[27] Rogge, then, was the quintessential apostate—a man who not only lost his way but who supped with the devil. He was to be condemned, not pitied. Communists were especially vitriolic. To Gus Hall, a secretariat member of the CPUSA, Rogge was "the provocateur and informer" who was found beneath "slimy rocks" from which he was "shoveled up."[28] To Charles Howard, a black lawyer and member of the communist faction within the Progressive Party, Rogge was not only "a paid agent of the Yugoslav government" but also "the advocate of the slaveholder, Jefferson Davis, yes, and even of King George III."[29] To Paul Robeson he was a "tool of fascist aggression,"[30] while to the *Daily Worker* journalist Abner Berry, Rogge was a "stool pigeon" and a "renegade."[31] Yet, until only a few months earlier, the FBI "looked at Rogge and saw only Red."[32] And until then, Rogge was still a member of the Progressive Party's national executive, the American Labor Party, the Civil Rights Congress, and the National Lawyers' Guild, as well as a vice president of the World Committee of Partisans for Peace—all, to varying degrees, left-leaning or communist-dominated.[33]

Rogge Pre–Cold War

Before we explain this apparent metamorphosis, we need to understand his background. Oetje John Rogge was born on a farm in Illinois on October 12, 1903, to two German immigrants.[34] Until he entered school he spoke only Low German. In 1922, this young man of nineteen, now 6′3″ tall, graduated from the University of Illinois. From there he began an exceptional academic career at Harvard Law School, where he earned an LL.B in 1925 and edited the *Harvard Law Review*. He returned to Harvard during the Great Depression and completed a doctor of laws degree (his thesis was "Law and the Social Sciences"). Inspired by professors such as Felix Frankfurter, Rogge moved to Washington and practiced law for FDR's New Deal. After a series of successful cases he was promoted to Assistant Attorney General in the Justice Department's Criminal Division. In 1939, he opened a wide-ranging probe into political corruption directed at the remnants of Huey Long's Louisiana machine. Rogge won indictments and—according to a historian of Louisiana politics— "became a Paul Bunyan of the grand-jury system and the courtrooms of Louisiana . . . [and] cracked apart more fortunes than the genius Huey himself."[35]

In 1940, Rogge gave two addresses—the first to a New England seminar on civil liberties, the second to the New Jersey Civil Liberties Union— that captured the essence of his philosophical position. It needs to be noted that, although the United States had not yet entered World War II, this was the period of the Nazi–Soviet pact, when Western communist parties vehemently opposed any Allied involvement in the war and their legal proscription was either mooted (as in the United States and Great Britain) or realized (as in Australia):

> We can't start suppressing doctrines we despise without suppressing legitimate protest. . . . [I]n dealing with even confessedly subversive elements such as the Reds and militant fascists, as a long as I have anything to say about criminal law policy there, the Department is not going to stretch the existing sedition statutes to fit cases that do not meet the legal test of clear and present danger of revolutionary violence. For the same reason[,] I oppose any proposal for new sedition legislation which does not meet that test.[36]

He also stated that insofar as the Justice Department's Criminal Division had the power to prevent it, "we will not allow the alien or the radical to become [the] victim of persecution; but we will not let such emotionally charged epithets as 'witch hunters,' 'red baiters,' or 'persecutors' to deter us in our efforts to punish communists, fascists and aliens who flout our criminal laws."[37]

In 1943, Rogge became special assistant to Attorney General Francis Biddle and assumed direction of the government's wartime sedition case against thirty American pro-Nazis. This case ended in a mistrial when the presiding judge died but also culminated in Rogge's dismissal by the new Attorney General, Tom Clark, in 1946. Disillusioned with Truman's administration, Rogge left Washington, dropped his Democratic Party affiliation, joined Vito Marcantonio's American Labor Party, and entered private practice (the New York law firm of Rogge, Fabricant, Gordon and Goldman) in mid-1947. This last move prompted the Joint Anti-Fascist Refugee Committee to request that he conduct its legal defence.

Thus, before the Cold War commenced, it would appear that Rogge had developed some recognizable characteristics. He was strong-willed, even stubborn; he was fearless and prepared to speak his mind; his highly successful career was meteoric, but there had been setbacks; he had strongly held principles regarding civil rights and the rule of law; and while politically opposed to both "the Reds" (as he termed them) and the extreme right, he remained committed to their right of free speech if the law was not transgressed. He defended the communist's right to speak because that right "cannot as a matter of practical administration be separated from the right of other people to advocate changes that are necessary to prevent our society from falling into his hands."[38] The abiding impression he gave one interviewer in 1978 was that he was "a strong and independent thinker, a very determined man."[39] This tallies with Harnett Kane's assessment: "forthright, frequently naïve ... [and] had a capacity for indignation."[40] These traits must be recognized when we grapple with his apparent apostasy during the Cold War, especially in regard to his position on Tito and the international peace movement in the early 1950s.

Partisan of Peace

When a historian of the American Communist Party commented that the speech given by O. John Rogge to the Second World Peace Congress in Warsaw in November 1950 "caused a scene of memorable proportions," he was probably underestimating the impact.[41] For Rogge it was his crossing of the Rubicon. For communists and most fellow-travelers within the peace movement, it was heresy. For anti-Soviet officials within the British Foreign Office and the U.S. State Department, it was a watershed. Before we examine his speech, its genesis needs to be traced. According to a highly detailed and comprehensive 166-page HUAC report, there was neither warning nor reason: Rogge "regularly attended and supported international Communist 'peace' gatherings" and until November 1950 (when he was not reelected) was a vice chairman of the

Permanent Committee of the World Congress of Partisans for Peace. Thus, HUAC noted, "for some unexplained reason, Rogge delivered a speech to this 'peace' congress on November 19 in which he made a major break with the Communist Party 'peace' line."[42] The FBI was more dismissive: it commented that Rogge was simply "another 'bumble-head' finally seeing light."[43] The Information Research Department (IRD), located within the British Foreign Office, was more sensitive than HUAC or the FBI to nuances, less blinded by ideological polarities and therefore less surprised. It already had observed that Rogge "has at times taken an independent line and has criticised Moscow."[44]

The IRD was, of course, quite right. Rogge had steadily been moving toward the position he took in Warsaw since, at least, April 1949. Then, he attended a meeting of the World Congress of Partisans for Peace in Paris. According to a *New York Herald Tribune* correspondent present, delegates were "rudely awakened" from their somnolence on the fourth day by O. John Rogge. He drew hisses and boos when he stated that the Soviet Union shared responsibility with the United States for the present state of world tension. In an ecumenical spirit, uncharacteristic of the Soviet-dominated peace movement since the Cominform's "two-camp" thesis,[45] Rogge told the hostile congress that the communist countries "must learn to live with the capitalist countries for each has its virtues and defects and each can learn from the other." Moreover, "injustices and restrictions on the one side are matched by injustices and restrictions on the other." Rogge told the newspaper correspondent that this was the third such congress he had attended. The first was the World Congress of Intellectuals at Wrocław, Poland, in August 1948; the second was the Cultural and Scientific Conference for World Peace at the Waldorf Astoria, New York, in March 1949. Overwhelmingly, he claimed, each conference attacked the United States, and "I don't think that's the way to peace." Rogge had shown the text of his speech to another member of the American delegation who advised him not to make it. But Rogge, being stubborn or defiant, was undaunted: he knew what position he would take before the Congress opened, and "I knew they wouldn't like it." [46]

Although Rogge refrained from using the Waldorf conference as a platform for promoting his unorthodox ideas, he did so on two subsequent occasions. First, at the Continental Congress for Peace in Mexico City on September 9, 1949, he again was critical of the Soviet Union. He also emphasized the suppression of civil liberties by the Truman administration and the path toward fascism he saw the United States taking—

evidenced, he said, by the physical violence displayed by vigilante mobs at Peekskill, New York, the preceding week.[47] For the first three days of the congress, the organizers (who had an advance copy of his speech) bypassed Rogge before he was then permitted to speak.[48] Second, Rogge traveled to the Kremlin and addressed the Presidium of the Supreme Soviet on March 8, 1950. In his "personal plan for peace," he proposed the establishment of a United Nations "watchdog" body that would have the power to conduct unlimited inspection of all atomic energy installations as well as all armed forces and military bases. This body would publish its findings regularly and thereby relieve all nations of the necessity for military intelligence and counterintelligence. This, in turn, would immediately end war tension and pave the way for a general reduction of armaments and the turning of the world to peacetime pursuits.[49] There is no report of the Soviet reaction to this iconoclastic proposal—which, if adopted, would have thwartedthe subsequent Cold War arms race—but judging from the vitriolic anti-American rhetoric of the other American delegate, the artist Rockwell Kent, it likely fell on deaf ears.[50] In the same speech, which Rogge entitled "Moving the Mountains of Fear," he again called for less denunciation and counterdenunciation on both sides.

Ten days later, Rogge was in Stockholm for a meeting of the Permanent Committee of the World Peace Congress. The two-camp line of the Cominform had recently been replaced by the "peace offensive," and in this context the Stockholm Appeal, which called for the outlawing of atomic weapons, was launched.[51] Rogge became one of the original sponsors in what proved to be a major propaganda initiative: an astonishing 473 million signatures were collected internationally within 5 months.[52]

Stockholm was Rogge's third opportunity to remain the pebble in the shoe of the Partisans for Peace.[53] He developed his now-familiar refrain: that America and the Soviet Union must cease blaming each other for the ills of the world; that East and West must become trading partners; and that the United Nations must provide the framework for international cooperation. "Then," he concluded with a rhetorical, if naïve, flourish, "it will be possible for us to transform the face of the world, see our meadows in flower, reach new summits, discover undreamed of horizons and, while still alive, explore paradise as well as the earth."[54] A clear harbinger of the direction in which Rogge was heading, as well as a testament to his fearlessness, was his open dissension at Stockholm with the president of the World Peace Congress, Professor Frederic Joliot-Curie.[55] The latter alleged that the rulers of the United States wanted to wage war; Rogge disputed this and repudiated Joliot-Curie's use of phrases such as "war-mongers" and "bloodthirsty imperialists" to describe American leaders.

The final occasion before the Warsaw Peace Congress at which Rogge contradicted the "party line" was a bureau meeting of the now-renamed Defenders of Peace, held in Prague in mid-August 1950. He submitted three resolutions. One proposed that the Stockholm Peace Appeal be amended to outlaw "all aggression from whatever source and by whatever country"; with the United States in its sights, the existing Appeal condemned as "war criminals" any country that made first use of the atom bomb. Another resolution called on the committee to readmit the Yugoslav delegation, expelled in October 1949 for allegedly preparing for aggression against its communist neighbors; and a third, that a commission be established to report to the UN Security Council and that would mediate between both sides in the Korean War, now two months old.[56] However, none of these resolutions was presented to the executive committee for consideration despite being given to Joliot-Curie by Rogge two days previously. Rogge was being frozen out. Although it was not evident to anyone then or since, or even necessarily from these resolutions, Korea and Yugoslavia were the primary catalysts for Rogge's apparent "transformation" at Warsaw.

"Tool of Titoism"

After the 1948 dispute between Stalin and Tito and the consequent expulsion of Yugoslavia from the Cominform, the ejection of its representatives from the World Peace Congress Permanent Committee, and the imposition of an economic and diplomatic boycott, the Tito government was subjected to a barrage of toxic propaganda from the Soviet Union and its supporters.[57] The term "fascist Tito clique" entered the lexicon of all Western communist parties. A British Communist Party publication, for example, implausibly titled *Tito's Plot Against Europe*, alleged that members of the "Tito clique" were both "fascist" and "agents of Anglo-American imperialism," while the General Secretary of the Spanish Communist Party, Dolores Ibárruri (and, as "La Pasionaria," heroine of the Spanish Civil War), argued that "Tito-ite agents—former Gestapo agents" were assisting preparations "for a new aggressive war against the Soviet Union." The ineptly titled Cominform publication *For a Lasting Peace, for a People's Democracy!* echoed the epithets of the 1930s Stalinist purges and referred to Titoists as "jackals" and a "contemptible gang of spies and assassins."[58]

To independent thinkers on the left, like O. John Rogge, Jean Cassou, and Konni Zilliacus, such invective—quite apart from its inaccuracy—was anathema.[59] The three wrote a remarkably lucid and cogent twelve-page statement in which they defended the right of Yugoslavia to pursue its path of self-determination outside both the Soviet bloc and the West.

> We have all three independently visited Yugoslavia since the out-break of the conflict with the Soviet Union and have seen and heard enough while in that country to enable us to make up our minds on the situation. We have all three independently come to the conclusion that the Soviet-Yugoslav conflict raises issues of principle that go to the heart of the controversy about the cold war and that cannot be neglected in making the case for peace.[60]

They argued that the case of Yugoslavia was of "transcendent importance" to the peace movement because it raised the fundamental issue of interference by a foreign power—in this case, "the power of the Soviet State . . . to coerce Yugoslavia into submission." Just as they were opposed to the American policy of undermining communist parties through interference in the internal affairs of their respective countries, so Soviet policy toward Yugoslavia must be resisted. Without a "live-and-let-live agreement" between East and West, which the Yugoslavia situation epitomized, world peace would be impossible. They described Cominform propaganda—that Yugoslavia had become a military base of Anglo-American imperialism and was receiving arms and officers from the West—as "monstrous inventions" and "sinister" in character. On the other hand, Yugoslavia's stand was "courageous" and deserved praise. Conveniently overlooking its role within the Cominform prior to its ex-communication, when it set the pace (with Soviet blessing) for intolerance and intransigence, Rogge, Cassou, and Zilliacus stated:

> In international affairs the Yugoslavia Government are opposed to blocs and alliances and take their stand on the U.N. Charter, particularly on the fundamental principles of equality, non-interference in internal affairs, and peaceful settlement of all differences. They have not entered into any political or military commitments . . . [and] have pursued an independent policy at the United Nations, frequently making proposals of their own.[61]

These were precisely the values that Rogge stood for. It is not surprising, therefore, that he should embrace Yugoslavia. Nor was it surprising that, when he did, the full, unqualified venom of the pro-Soviet left would be aimed at him.[62] There was, for example, "a lively scene," according to a MI6 report, when, in London on June 1, 1950, Paul Robeson became "embroiled" with a Yugoslav press representative. Rogge intervened on behalf of the Yugoslav, whereupon Robeson, "in great anger," declared both to be the "tools of fascist aggressors."[63] Such wrath confirmed Rogge in the righteousness of his judgment, and such attacks pushed him into a harder, more anti-Soviet position. His close relationship with Yugoslavia was variously exemplified. First, he agreed to serve as legal counsel for Yugoslavia in the United States—hence the epithet "Tito's paid agent." On January 26, 1950, the Yugoslav delegation to the United Nations paid Rogge's law firm a retainer of $10,000. Rogge had frequently visited the chairman of the Yugoslav delegation, Dr. Ales Bebler, throughout February 1950.[64] Second, when he visited the country and met with Tito in April 1950, he was awarded an honorary degree of Doctor of Law. Third, on November 1 prior to the Second World Peace Congress, he visited his confidant in the State Department, Jesse MacKnight, the Deputy Assistant Secretary for Public Affairs. The basis of their friendship—correspondence was addressed "Dear Mac" and "Dear John"—remains obscure, but given Rogge's increasing isolation and the Truman administration's "growing anxiety" in late 1950 about "a dangerous escalation of the Cold War,"[65] it is perhaps not surprising that each was willing to assist the other. According to the confidential "Memorandum of Conversation," "Mr. Rogge indicated that the Yugoslavs had urged him to attend the Sheffield meeting [of the World Peace Congress] and speak out on the National independence line. . . . Mr. Rogge said that this was what Tito wanted."[66] It is also what Rogge thought. At a press conference in London after the Warsaw conference, he urged the organization of a new peace movement on the initiative of Yugoslavia, which "did not participate in any of the blocs."[67]

The other catalyst was Korea. In Rogge's view, the invasion of South Korea by North Korean and Chinese troops in June 1950 was wrong, and the response by the United States and the United Nations was right. But if the conflict was to avoid escalating into a third world war, it "must be settled through the United Nations, with the active participation of the Soviet Union and China as well as the Western powers." Furthermore, Korea could become "the beginning of the end of the cold war by negotiations for a general settlement."[68] He was therefore dismayed when the Soviet press, the American Communist Party, the communist factions in both the Progressive Party and the American Labor Party, and—significantly—his own Permanent Committee of the Partisans of Peace all condemned one side only: the United States. Such organizations also frequently implied that the South had invaded the North, not vice-versa, and that North Korea bore no responsibility for the invasion. In all of Rogge's numerous writings in 1949–50, which analyzed the sources of Cold War tension and/or provided a variety of solutions to conflict, whether in Yugoslavia, Korea, or East–West relations generally, he always strove to be even-handed and critical of aspects of both the United States and the Soviet Union. For instance, in his "Appeal to Moderates," he stated: "The present power struggle is further complicated by a new wave of authoritarianism which is sweeping the earth. There is considerably more of it in the East than in the West, but under the influence of our own McCarthys and McCarrans we have started to develop our own brand of it."[69] Thus, to Rogge the moral myopia of Stalin's supporters, in which one side is absolved and the other is condemned, was abhorrent.

In addition to the role of Yugoslavia and Korea in Rogge's embrace of anti-Stalinism, there was also the alarming issue of atomic espionage. Given Rogge's intense interest in the atom bomb since 1945,[70] as well as his defense of David Greenglass since June 1950, Rogge would not have been immune to this issue. There had already been several episodes in this interlocking story of actual or suspected espionage: the defection and sensational revelations of Igor Gouzenko in 1945; the arrest of Allen Nunn May in 1946; HUAC and the Condon case in 1947–48; and the congressional investigation of the Atomic Energy Commission in 1949. All pointed to the possibility of scientists' disloyalty and atomic espionage. But it was not until the Soviets' successful nuclear detonation in September 1949 that anxiety became alarm. America may have possessed ideological righteousness, but it no longer had technological superiority: it had lost its atomic monopoly. Worse, some American and British scientists working on the Manhattan Project knowingly assisted this development. Incontrovertible evidence of a successful Soviet atomic spy ring at Los Alamos became apparent with the confession and arrest of Klaus Fuchs on February 2, 1950. As is well known, Fuchs' confession led to the arrest of his American courier, Harry Gold, who in turn implicated David Greenglass. After a lengthy interrogation by the FBI, Greenglass confessed to espionage and was arrested on June 16, 1950. As his attorney, Rogge persuaded Greenglass to turn prosecution witness against his sister and brother-in-law, Ethel and Julius Rosenberg. Thus Rogge was very familiar with that defining landmark of the early Cold War, espionage, which contributed so decisively to the rising tide of domestic anticommunism.

Such were the influences and events that shaped Rogge's thinking as he crossed the Atlantic in November 1950. There were clear signs, already, that he was a maverick within the peace movement and, with his defense of Yugoslavia, his position on Korea, his repudiation of one-sidedness, and his awareness of Soviet espionage, it was becoming apparent that his address to delegates in Warsaw would be certain to cause offense. As a State Department official later commented on this pre-Warsaw period, "Mr. Rogge conducted a one-man campaign inside the Partisans of Peace movement."[71] Soon, however, as we shall see, Rogge became disillusioned. As he told MacKnight, "[I]t was a pretty hopeless situation since the organization [Partisans of Peace] had become . . . a hard-core Stalinist enterprise."[72]

"A Trojan Dove"

The Second World Peace Congress, scheduled for November 13–19, 1950, was originally to be held in London before the British Peace Committee, unable to secure a suitable venue, switched it to Sheffield.[73] It needs to be emphasized that this congress, far more than the first (held in Paris in April 1949), was of immense political significance in the developing Cold War. In order to appreciate why Clement Attlee's Labour government subverted the congress, we must understand how it was perceived—a perception that, increasingly, Rogge shared.

Opposition to the congress hinged on the connection that existed between it, the Partisans of Peace, and the Cominform. This link had been extensively researched and documented by the Foreign Office (and, in particular, by the IRD) with much of the *prima facie* evidence being provided by documents emanating from the Cominform itself.[74]

> Frankly the position from the Foreign Office is this. The World Peace Campaign [*sic*]is nothing more than a Communist stunt, an instrument of Soviet foreign policy designed to stir up resistance to the Western defence programme and to the Atlantic Pact. It is run by Communists under direction from Moscow and is not to be regarded as a genuinely international peace movement of a democratic kind.[75]

That the early postwar peace movement was a creature of the Cominform was regarded as axiomatic; it was "a fact not needing further proof."[76] This view, when stripped of some of its Cold War clothing, is essentially correct. With the exception of Rogge, the Partisans of Peace (later reformulated as the World Peace Council) *did* desire peace, but on Soviet terms. And it is a view shared by the preeminent historian of the peace movement of this period.[77] So the Sheffield congress was, to use the colorful phrase of Denis Healey, "a Trojan Dove."[78]

The British government believed the staging of the Peace Congress was a crucial dimension of the Soviet-sponsored "peace offensive" that, because of the Stockholm Appeal, the debate over German re-armament, and the war in Korea, was burgeoning. And because that offensive "has absorbed all other Communist activities and is now regarded by the Soviet leaders as the most important and active task of World Communism, embracing all the main objectives of Soviet foreign policy,"[79] it must be confronted. If the Soviets' peace campaign was now "a propagandist weapon of war,"[80] as an MI6 assessment argued, and the World Peace Congress a means of "weakening the determination of the Western powers to build up their defences against Soviet pressure,"[81] then the West must react aggressively. Importantly, this response would combat the projection of the World Peace Council as an effective rival, a political alternative, to the United Nations. With the outbreak of the Korean War, to which the UN was militarily committed, such a projection assumed immense significance. The fact that the timing of the congress coincided (deliberately, in the view of the Foreign Office) with the meeting of the General Assembly of the United Nations, and that resolutions of the congress were expected to synchronize with proposals put forward by the Soviet delegation on atomic disarmament, was a source of particular concern.[82] This concern cannot be underestimated, for that vexed question— with whom should the responsibility for preventing war and preserving peace reside: the fledgling United Nations or the embryonic World Peace Council?—then went to the core of Cold War geo-strategic politics. This question would be raised and answered by several speakers at the Warsaw congress; Rogge, an ardent believer in the UN, had an opposite answer. From both sides of the ideological divide, therefore, the congress was full of propaganda potential and political significance. In an important sense it was a crucible of what the Cold War was primarily about: the control and mobilization of public opinion, at home and abroad.

In this context the Labour government decided to cripple the congress. It did this mainly by closing Britain's doors. Through an enlarged definition of *persona non grata*, which provided the quasi-legal basis for withholding visas, more than two-thirds of the foreign delegates and almost the entire foreign leadership of the Partisans for Peace were excluded. The congress was thereby decapitated. This was accomplished through duplicity, shrewd timing, and effective execution. It meant that at the last minute, the British Peace Committee was forced to cancel the congress.[83] The dove of peace (drawn by Pablo Picasso specifically for the occasion) flew east, to Warsaw. However, there was one rather desultory meeting, on the first scheduled day, November 12, attended by a group of local delegates and the small number of foreign delegates permitted entry. Rogge was one of these and he addressed that meeting.[84]

The only report of his speech was in the *Sheffield Telegraph*, whose "special correspondent" noted that "delegates shuffled in their seats" when Rogge claimed that all the threats to world peace stemmed from two concentrations of power—a political concentration in the Soviet Union and an economic concentration in the United States. When he stated that he was "more disturbed" by the former than by the latter, the audience was "shocked" but "decided to treat it as a lapse which was best overlooked."[85] No such forbearance was extended in Warsaw. Actually, Rogge went much further at Sheffield. We know this only because the text of his speech was cabled to the Voice of America in New York. A copy of that cable is now located in State Department files. Part of it read:

> A second difficulty which flows from the fanatical zeal of Communists is that it tempts the Soviet Union, by equating progress with its policies, to seek to control progressive movements in other parts of the world with the result that progressive forces everywhere are being divided and destroyed.... The Progressive Party in the United States, to which I still belong and which I tried to help build, has been committing political suicide because progressives do not feel as free to criticize relevant mistakes of the Soviet Union as those of their own country.[86]

It is little wonder that delegates, most of whom would have been more sympathetic to the communist position, should shuffle in their seats. Discomfort was relieved by sardonic humor when a Soviet delegate, Boris Polevoy, stated that "everyone knows the Soviet people want peace. Anyone who doesn't ought to be locked in a lunatic asylum." According to the local press correspondent, Polevoy looked along the row toward Rogge with the result that "laughter and applause swept the hall."[87] The next day the delegates left for Warsaw.

Fighting for Peace?

For Mrs. Nan Green, an organizing secretary of the Sheffield congress, going to Warsaw was "like changing worlds, like stepping into the sun after being in the rain."[88] Flags, streamers, and multicolored posters displaying Picasso's peace dove decorated streets, shops, ports, and railway stations. Large welcoming committees greeted the arriving delegates in Warsaw, where, according to the British *Daily Worker*, "tremendous enthusiasm reigns."[89] The *New York Times* correspondent described how "girls of 18 to 25 swarmed onto the platform as each train pulled in and handed bouquets to the delegates while army bands played."[90] The warm welcome was not the only reason for delegates' gratitude. They also each received 500 z/loty pocket money, cigarettes by their bedside every night, and all travel, dining, entertainment, and accommodation costs met by the Polish government. Whether this was beneficence or bribery is difficult to tell but, to the British Foreign Office, "it made clear for all the world to see that the thing was a Cominform racket."[91] At least one communist, from Australia, spent most of his 500 z/loty, equivalent then to the average monthly wage of a Polish worker, on vokda and dinner-dances at the Bristol Hotel "while telling Poles who asked if I could help them escape that they should be ashamed to run away from socialism."[92]

The congress was declared open by Frederic Joliot-Curie at 7:00 P.M. on November 16 in front of 1,756 delegates representing 81 countries and 309 guests and observers.[93] All the luminaries barred by the Attlee government—Dimitri Shostakovich, Ilya Ehrenburg, Pietro Nenni—were there. But none of the Yugoslav delegates was credentialed. The venue was the unoccupied vast hall of the state printing works, which had been transformed by the prodigious, 'round-the-clock efforts over four days by hundreds of Polish workmen.[94] Huge pictures of Stalin, Bolesław Bierut (the Polish President), Joliot-Curie, and the now-ubiquitous white dove adorned the low hall. The slogan "Stalin is with us" was displayed but, diplomatically perhaps, only in Polish. To those delegates from Western countries who were for the first time "[experiencing] a real people's democracy,"[95] the rituals, quite different from those in Sheffield, would be a surprise. Between speeches, the congress organizers regularly brought into the hall groups of dancing boys and girls dressed in peasant costumes who showered the delegates with posies. Members of the Polish communist youth organization gave leading speakers gifts such as the head of Stalin rendered in coal. After certain speeches, *pokoj*, the Polish word for peace, was repeated rhythmically to clapping for many minutes. When Pak Den-Ai, the North Korean delegate, spoke—in Russian—delegates "rose as one man" and cheered for a full ten minutes; when Mao Zedong and Kim Il Sung were toasted, "again they rose to cheer until they could cheer no more."[96]

This, then, was the triumphalist, quasi-revivalist atmosphere that Rogge faced when he took the lectern. In contrast to the ecumenical spirit of the first congress he attended—at Wrocław in August 1948, where "the representation was wide and there was much good will"[97]—here, he was about to experience narrowness and intolerance. In part, this was a reflection of the increasing chilliness and polarization of the Cold War, but Rogge—as we have seen—had also changed. What had not altered was his refusal to accept the "party line," his single-minded determination to speak, as he saw it, the truth, no matter how unpalatable, no matter how hostile the audience. Rogge was scheduled to speak on the third day of the congress, in the morning session of November 19. There had already been innumerable rousing speeches denouncing the American and British "warmongers" and the "aggressive" role of the UN—the "tool of the imperialists"—in Korea. The perspectives, policies, and peace initiatives of the "mighty bastion of peace," the Soviet Union, were applauded. Nearly all received standing ovations. These were widely reported and reprinted and will not be summarized here.[98] Rogge was the first and only dissentient. The concern expressed by one British delegate, Elinor Burns, that "this was meant to be a peace conference not a communist conference," was voiced two weeks after, not during, the congress.[99]

Unlike his Sheffield speech, a copy of the full text of his Warsaw speech is unavailable. The following, therefore, is pieced together from various press reports.[100] After accusing communists of "displaying a fanatical missionary zeal," Rogge declared: "Today I would not sign the Stockholm Appeal." He spelled out the policy of the Yugoslav government in refusing to join either the Western or Soviet power blocs. He directly addressed the Chinese delegates, to whom he expressed his hope that communist China would follow Yugoslavia's example of independence. It is not clear whether he reiterated his statement at Sheffield that he "long felt" that the "New China" should be recognized and become a member of the UN Security Council. However, he certainly referred to the "traditional American–Chinese friendship" that would endure, and this produced "general merriment in the hall." He asserted that the communist belief in the use of force was "a roadblock in the path of human progress." Cominform communists had already resorted to violence to convert the world to their point of view. In this context he alluded not only to Korea but also to the Chinese invasion of Tibet, the only speaker to do so. This invasion, he stated, called into question the sincerity of the principal supporters of the peace campaign. He denounced North Korean aggression and denied that the United States desired war. He also argued that the communist domination of the peace movement would lead to its complete failure: "If we are truly partisans of peace, we cannot be the partisans of one nation alone." He would not accept the Cominform position that progress must be identified with the policies of the Soviet Union. He attributed the decline of the American Progressive Party to its unwillingness to criticize mistakes of the Soviet Union as freely as those of the United States. Finally, he urged the congress to incorporate in its final recommendations a policy of broad exchange of ideas between the Soviets and the Americans.

Rogge's address struck the audience like a thunderbolt. Many of the 2,000 delegates loudly booed, jeered, scoffed, and interrupted throughout his forty minutes on the platform. The Czech chairperson, Mme. Anezka Hodinova-Spurna, was obliged to "shush the delegates to silence several times." When Rogge sat down, he received only a subdued "smattering of applause."[101] Such antipathy was echoed by Moscow radio, which described Rogge as a money seeker with a "divided soul" and his speech as "provocative"; *Pravda* simply denounced him as a "tool of Titoism."[102] Despite this response, Rogge remained sanguine. He told a reporter that some French, Danish, British, and Irish delegates had approached him sympathetically after his address.[103] Moreover, according to a Foreign Office report, using uncharacteristic hyperbole, "although his speech was distorted in the Polish press, its real content spread through Warsaw like wildfire. . . ." It noted that "Mr. Rogge had more support than was manifest and this was his own view."[104] The final phrase points to the fact that Rogge had communicated with the British Embassy in Warsaw.[105] Similarly, Rogge had contacted his friend in the U.S. State Department, Jesse MacKnight, and provided him with a draft of his Sheffield speech for comment. MacKnight made four suggestions. Their gist was that Rogge avoid "factional rhetoric" and "provocative words": "[Y]ou do not have to talk about 'aggression,' 'crimes,' 'atrocities,' etc." Instead, Rogge should direct his proposals to both sides, not favor one against the other, and uphold the role of the UN in both Korea and the Indo-China "squabble." MacKnight also recommended that Rogge introduce a resolution that "the Partisans of Peace . . . call on the U.S.S.R. and the U.S. to take all necessary steps to increase human intercourse between them. . . ."[106] This is precisely what Rogge did at Warsaw. He also, according to a *New York Times* journalist present, "spoke with restraint in language that bore little resemblance to that used by the fiery Russian speakers to the [Warsaw] congress"[107]—suggesting, again, that he took note of MacKnight's advice, which was also, most likely, congruent with his own predisposition.

"The end of the road"?

After Rogge returned to the United States he met, at his own request, with MacKnight in Washington. The consequent memorandum of conversation, stamped "Restricted," reveals Rogge's own assessment of reactions to his Sheffield and Warsaw speeches. On the one hand, he judged his contributions to have been "useful." He believed "the news about what he had to say got around Warsaw and described various indications of its content being known." On the other hand, security precautions at Warsaw were "extremely strict," which acted as a deterrent to potential supporters of his independent position: he had "no chance to talk with any of the Chinese delegates" who were "instructed to stay away from him." As noted earlier, Rogge hoped especially to steer them toward Yugoslavia and away from the Soviet Union. He noted that he had "no support" from members of the American delegation, Dimitri Shostakovich "avoided him completely," Ilya Ehrenburg was "very unfriendly," and he (Rogge) was "very heavily attacked" for his support of Tito. The extent of Rogge's isolation was underscored by MacKnight's asking him whether he intended to participate in a report-back meeting in New York by American delegates from Warsaw. Rogge answered that "he had heard nothing about the meeting."[108] Such deliberate marginalization also had an administrative dimension. After the Warsaw congress, the new Bureau (formerly Permanent Committee) of the World Peace Council (formerly Partisans of Peace) was elected. Rogge was not "elected"—the outcomes of such elections were predetermined—either as a vice president or as a member.[109] Of the fifteen Americans elected to the Bureau, one was Howard Fast, whom, as an executive member of the Joint Anti-Fascist Refugee Committee, Rogge had earlier defended. According to Rogge, he had reached "the end of the road."[110]

But not yet. Freezing out O. John Rogge from the "official" peace movement did little to dampen his ardor for searching out alternative paths. He told MacKnight that he intended to write an article on Warsaw for the *New York Times Magazine*. Once again, he sought MacKnight's advice and, once again, the importance of communist China can be discerned. MacKnight told Rogge that

> he might stress the long record of friendship by America so far as the Chinese people were concerned. I thought it might be useful if he spent some time on this and raised the question as to how

much the new masters of China and their Kremlin friends were doing and had done for the Chinese people. I agreed to see if I could get a round-up of U.S. activity in assisting and sending it along to him.[111]

Unfortunately for Rogge, the *New York Times* rejected his article on the grounds that "it contained nothing new."[112] However, an abridged version was published by *The New Leader* under the title "My New Plan for Peace." He proposed a new, non-communist, inclusive, and broad-ranging peace organization, Independent Americans for Peace, which would organize peace meetings devoid of invective. He also proposed cultural exchange "of people, ideas and news" between the Soviet bloc and the United States that would build a series of bridges straddling East and West. The article featured a photo of Rogge conferring with Tito and captioned "Can there really be a middle ground?"[113] *The New Leader* seems a curious outlet for Rogge. Aligned with the small Social Democratic Federation after the 1936 split in the American Socialist Party, it drifted to the right in the 1940s.[114] Ex-Trotskyists, such as Melvyn J. Lasky, joined its ranks, and it became active in both opposing the Waldorf conference in New York in 1949 and in supporting the Congress for Cultural Freedom in Berlin in 1950. While Albert Kahn's assessment of *The New Leader* as a "red-baiting journal"[115] may have underestimated its social-democratic (but not anti-Stalinist) leanings, the fact that Rogge sent his piece to a relatively obscure and peripheral journal highlighted how limited his choices were. After no fewer than six iterations, Rogge's short article was eventually transformed into a major twenty-six-page document entitled "An Appeal to Moderates." However, within the Policy Planning Staff of the State Department, the reception was not favorable, and it was never published.[116] Parallel with his proposed Independent Americans for Peace organization, he also initiated a financial drive to form a new political party, a "Third Party that doesn't admit Communists." Having forsaken the Progressive Party, he met with anticommunist union leaders and CIA collaborators Jay Lovestone, David Dubinsky, and Walter Reuther but received no financial assistance or encouragement.[117] By attempting to occupy "the middle ground" between left and right, East and West, in the early 1950s Rogge stood in an ideological no-man's land: isolated, lonely, and vulnerable. The paucity of allies had to be matched by a surfeit of resilience.

Otherwise Engaged

Absence of self-doubt, as well as abundant resilience, was necessary for Rogge's final foray into the politics of the peace movement. On February 7, 1951, the esteemed eighty-two-year-old W. E. B. Du Bois—who had moved steadily to the extreme left, partly under the influence of his Communist Party lover, Shirley Graham[118]—was indicted and arraigned for "failure to register as an agent of a foreign principal." In other words, the Department of Justice sought to link the Peace Information Center (PIC), of which Du Bois had been the chairman until it was dissolved in October 1950, with the World Peace Council and thereby with the foreign policy of the Soviet Union.[119] Du Bois and four co-defendants faced a possible fine of $10,000 each and five years' imprisonment. The PIC had been responsible for circulating the Stockholm Appeal in 1950, and O. John Rogge was a foundation member and driving force. Now, controversially, he was to be the prosecution's star witness or, less charitably, the "Star Stoolie."[120]

In the interregnum between the indictment and trial of W. E. B. Du Bois and the PIC, Rogge, in his characteristic manner, was extremely active. He was still representing his client David Greenglass in appealing Judge Kaufman's fifteen-year jail sentence in April; he addressed the International Association of Democratic Lawyers—against which Rogge was "conducting a Tito operation against its Moscow line"[121]—in East Berlin in September; he attended the Yugoslav Peace Congress in Zagreb in October; and he commenced negotiations to represent Dr. Elsie Field, whose brothers, Noel and Hermann Field, had mysteriously disappeared in eastern Europe in 1949.[122] He also worked on two lengthy manuscripts: "In the Courts and in the Streets," a copy of which he later sent to the wife of David Greenglass, Ruth,[123] and "The Accusatorial Versus the Inquisitional Method," which was primarily a 220-page study of show trials in the Soviet Union and eastern Europe from 1933 to 1951.[124] Neither was published.

The trial, which commenced in November after several protest demonstrations,[125] was a heated affair. Rogge and ex-Congressman Vito Marcantonio, with whom Rogge has been closely associated in the American Labor Party and who worked without fee as co–defense attorney for Du Bois,[126] clashed frequently. On one occasion, Rogge shouted over a Marcantonio objection: "Its [PIC's] stated objective was to work for world peace . . . actually it was an agency of a foreign power." Marcantonio cogently replied: "Two people may have parallel views. . . . That does not establish agency." Ultimately, the judge, Matthew F. McGuire, dismissed the case, telling jurors that "we are not trying the foreign policy of the Soviet Union."[127] Rogge's detractors were triumphant. The outcome of the trial was hailed as a "break-through victory for peace and civil liberties"[128]— precisely those causes that Rogge had previously championed—and, in the words of I. F. Stone, the first "stunning defeat" for the Truman government since its commencement in 1947 of "the greatest witch-hunt in modern times."[129] It was now open season for spraying venom toward Rogge. In the left-wing press he was labeled a stool pigeon, a paid agent, a provocateur, and a renegade, and accused of betrayal.

If his accusers had known of his unsolicited approaches to the FBI director, Du Bois' epithet, "Rogge the Rat," would have been more firmly affixed. On several visits to Washington between June and August 1950, when he was working closely with the Greenglasses, he called in at the FBI headquarters. On one occasion it was to "merely advise" that his clients were continuing to cooperate with the Bureau. On another occasion he wanted the absent Hoover "to know personally that if he [Rogge] could be of any assistance that he would be happy to do so."[130] On a subsequent occasion, he "just stopped by to say hello to the Director. . . . He said he didn't care to see anyone else as he no business to discuss."[131] Despite these approaches and despite Hoover's addressing him in correspondence as "Dear John,"[132] Hoover never trusted Rogge. He warned an associate to "be most circumspect in any conversation with Rogge"; he required his secretary to use standard FBI stationery, not his personal letterhead, when corresponding with Rogge; and he instructed that Rogge "is not to be contacted without prior Bureau authority."[133] The FBI's institutional memory was long. A memorandum referred to "Bureau files" that contained Rogge's public speeches and writings; these "made attacks on the Bureau alleging racial discrimination and violation of civil liberties." It also referred to his past membership in the National Lawyers' Guild, a Communist Party "front" organization, and his work on behalf of Tito.[134] Persuading David and Ruth Greenglass to cooperate with the Justice Department, or testifying against the Peace Information Center, did not—in the view of the FBI—expiate Rogge of his past sins.

By the early 1950s Rogge had ceased being the Lone Ranger conducting his "one-man campaign," as MacKnight put it, against communist domination of the international peace movement. In April 1957 he informed the FBI that he would, if subpoened, act as "a cooperative witness" and testify against the National Lawyers' Guild, to which he had once belonged. However, he stated, this was not his desire because of "the extreme pressure of his legal business."[135] Indeed, his law firm was flourishing. Along with his New York legal partner Herbert J. Fabricant, he immersed himself in a plethora of lawsuits, many concerned with defending freedom of expression. During the 1960s and 1970s Rogge filed numerous legal briefs on behalf of the poor and minority groups. He campaigned for equal rights for women and argued passionately in favor of the absolute right to freedom of speech. And he kept writing: *Why Men Confess* (in which his most famous client, Greenglass, was not mentioned) appeared in 1959; *The First and the Fifth: With Some Excursions into Others* in 1960; *The Official German Report: Nazi Penetration, 1924–1942* in 1961; and *Obscenity Litigation in Ten American Jurisprudence Trials* in 1965. He was also a prolific contributor to edited books and to law journals. He continued to adhere to the main tenets of his most significant work, *Our Vanishing Civil Liberties*. But his days of paddling upstream, usually without assistance, against the strong political currents of the early Cold War years, were over. Those tempestuous years provide a stark reminder of the difficulties, for individuals such as Rogge, in answering "which side are you on?"

Conclusion

"The Un-American hearings were held last week," wrote Jessica Mitford on December 10, 1953. "You can't imagine how revolting they are. They dragged about 100 people into it . . . just about every kind of person you can imagine."[1] Mitford, a member of the Communist Party in California who had already appeared before HUAC in September 1951, says little more in her letters about the direct impact of McCarthyism. Each of the Americans whose stories are told in this book had previously confronted HUAC, and it was no less "revolting." Unlike Mitford, most lost their jobs. But as with Mitford, the radical activism that brought them before the Committee was forged in the 1930s. The economic depression, the rise of fascism, and the Spanish Civil War directly or indirectly colored their outlook and shaped their commitment. They embraced communism because it appeared to be the best instrument for transforming America into a more egalitarian society free from racism, injustice, and the threat of war. This embrace continued into the postwar years, but now they were no longer on the "right" side of history. *They* had not shifted, but the external environment had. The interregnum of cordial East–West relations during World War II was over and, with the onset of the Cold War, defense of political freedoms at home became tainted by Stalin's actions abroad.

Yet being a devoted communist involved an unquestioning attachment to Stalin's policies. Blinded by the Soviet myth, as Orwell termed it, they had an ideological myopia that made it easy for anticommunists to ascribe allegiance to a foreign power and, *ipso facto*, impute disloyalty

159

to the United States. The inherent nature of international communism required conformity and loss of local autonomy. The wartime flirtation with Browderism—when the Communist Party of the United States of America (CPUSA) followed the lead of its General Secretary, Earl Browder, and sought a more independent, national path to socialism— was extinguished by the victory of the hardliners, the reassertion of Soviet control, and the formation of the Cominform. Now, one followed the party "line," however sectarian or self-defeating it may have seemed. The stricture to adhere to this rigid orthodoxy was intense just as the pressure to close eyes or mouths, when confronted with evidence of Stalin's crimes, was overwhelming. So the CPUSA was not an innocent victim. It did far more than faithfully follow Moscow's instructions or zigzagging foreign policy: it collaborated willingly and extensively in Soviet espionage operations, sent members to the Lenin School for training, and, along with a dozen other Western communist parties over many years, received considerable sums of "Moscow Gold."

But what of our individuals? Where did they stand? How did they respond? Those involved with the Joint Anti-Fascist Refugee Committee (JAFRC) did not seek the overthrow of the U.S. government. Although defined as "subversive," the organization had limited objectives and specific activities. Helping the casualties of the Spanish Civil War was paramount. For Barsky, Burgum, and Fast, all communists, resisting HUAC was axiomatic. None could be called a sentimental idealist. But none saw themselves as "unpatriotic" Americans, nor would they countenance—if they knew of it—espionage activity. So we must delineate the clandestine "nonlegal" party apparatus from the open, daily struggles waged by communists for social justice and "a better world." The existence of the first does not invalidate the legitimacy or sincerity of the second. Barsky, Burgum, and Fast were convinced, wrongly, that the United States was inexorably drifting toward fascism, but the onslaught of the state against communists, actual and suspected, seemed to provide abundant evidence of that direction and the correctness of their diagnosis. By the mid-1950s, Barsky and Burgum had withdrawn from political activity. By then Fast had crossed his Rubicon. It was only after his God had failed that he may have seen how the blacklist from which he had suffered straddled both sides of the Cold War: just as his *Citizen Tom Paine* had been banned in New York public schools, so Shostakovich's symphonies were banned in the Soviet Union.

For the non-communists in the JAFRC, Bradley and Bryan, defense of civil liberties and taking a stand on principle were paramount. There was loyalty, too: one could not desert an organization one worked for and believed in, or "rat" on fellow members. Both displayed integrity and courage. In this political environment, when so many retreated into timidity and exercised self-censorship, the penalty for such a display was harsh. Not only were both jailed, but Bradley became a pariah to his NYU colleagues and never returned to the classroom. Bryan quietly constructed a life in rural America. Neither was ever a "security risk." And surveillance did not stop when their professional lives were mutilated and their activism withered. Both cases illustrate, in rather brutal fashion, how the safeguarding of American freedoms threatens those same freedoms; how the quest to eliminate the influence of the Communist Party—a legal political party—and its actual or perceived sympathizers undermined the fundamental rights of dissident citizens to speak or act freely.

Many of the civil liberties jeopardized by McCarthyism were notably absent in the Soviet Union. Even choice was circumscribed: despite his unwillingness, Dimitri Shostakovich complied with Stalin's instruction to visit New York. His Waldorf speech implied sycophancy to Stalin, but he was no mindless mouthpiece. His anguish found expression in music for a silenced voice: secret compositions that contained proscribed Jewish folk music. It was not just his Soviet handlers who caused his humiliation in New York; local Cold War liberals were also responsible. The Americans for Intellectual Freedom (AIF), especially Nicolas Nabokov, sought to expose Soviet duplicity, and the high-profile Shostakovich became the unfortunate target. The AIF's combat with the totalitarians (as Hook termed them) dovetailed with McCarthyism, notwithstanding any distaste for the demagogue from Wisconsin. The Waldorf conference gave anti-Stalinism a sturdy public platform and helped spawn the Congress for Cultural Freedom. Shostakovich, meanwhile, returned to Moscow fearful for his life but saw his career revive after Stalin's death. Unlike our American protagonists, Shostakovich tried to duck beneath the parapet and favored circumvention over confrontation. Because he was forced to negotiate the minefields of Cold War politics, this effort was doomed. But as with our American protagonists, any hope of separating personal life from professional career was illusory. Neither Stalinism nor McCarthyism allowed such duality.

Despite an enduring commitment to the protection of civil liberties, O. John Rogge switched sides and was attacked by both. In the late 1940s he denounced fascist tendencies in America and defended the JAFRC; in the 1950s, he sought meetings with J. Edgar Hoover and the prosecution of W. E. B. Du Bois. He was joined by Howard Fast in campaigning for the Progressive Party but parted company when the party was critical of the Soviet Union. Hoover still distrusted him, and his erstwhile allies repudiated him. Although his legal career continued—and in that sense was never a "victim"—his search for a "third way" failed. Rogge's independence, if not iconoclasm, could not be accommodated by the polarities of Cold War politics. In contrast to Rogge, our other Americans were more stalwart. None yielded to their opponents and, as a result, incurred their wrath and their sanction. They paid a heavy price for clinging to their ideals. All suffered loss of income; all had to relinquish their former lives; all had to struggle to survive.

The persecutors who populate this book, and who were responsible for what Justice William O. Douglas called "the neurosis that has possessed us," were the victors, although their victory later proved pyrrhic. Congressional committees, university administrators, FBI special agents, professional witnesses, publishers, journalists, city councils, federal government bureaucracies, and red-baiting private organizations were not a cabal, but, collectively, their actions crippled the left and stifled the forces of change. As Ellen Schrecker has noted, the success of their assault must be measured, in part, by what they prevented: "reforms that were never implemented, unions that were never organized, movements that never started, books that were never published, films that were never produced."[2] The persecutors believed they also prevented a subversive communist conspiracy that endangered national security. What they stopped was far more prosaic: Spanish refugees' receiving aid from the JAFRC, NYU students' learning from two distinguished professors, Beth Israel patients' receiving expert medical help. To those victimized, it mattered little whether Democrat or Republican was in the White House: those Southern Democrats who conducted HUAC investigations were no less vigilant in their red-hunting than their Republican colleagues. Nor did it matter if a university, such as NYU, or a publishing house, such as Little, Brown, had liberal credentials because most institutions were infected with some form of the anticommunist virus. Fear of the taint of communism being attached by Cold War crusaders was so pervasive that defense of academic freedom or First Amendment rights became a risky act of defiance.

Through our case histories we have witnessed the ways in which Cold War anticommunism reshaped daily lives. By delving beneath formal politics and examining the lived experience at the "ground level," we can see how six individuals—and there were countless thousands more—experienced and responded to one of the most savage assaults on civil liberties in American history. From the blacklist to the Attorney General's list, from being declared unfit to teach or to practice medicine to juggling public persona with private belief, the impact of McCarthyism was both traumatic and enduring. We have also seen how some of the central political questions of the late 1940s and 1950s were handled: what were the limits of constitutional rights; how far should academic freedom be protected; who controlled the peace movement; how should the Soviet Union and Stalin's crimes be viewed; how should alleged disloyalty and subversion be met. The answers depended on whether one was a communist or a non-communist, true believer or apostate, prosecutor or persecuted, citizen or foreigner. But the upshot was that the reforming zeal associated with the New Deal period of the 1930s was, more often than not, shelved during the 1950s. Popular Front–type activism was pushed aside by paranoia and red-hunting. This changed with the emergence of the New Left and Great Society reforms in the 1960s, but by then the subjects of this book were demoralized, embittered, or no longer politically active. Their collective stories illuminate the personal costs of holding dissident political beliefs in the face of intolerance and moral panic, and this is as relevant today as it was seventy years ago.

Notes

Introduction

1. E. B. White, *Here Is New York* (New York: Warner Books, 1949), 54.

2. Sidney Hook, "The Future of Socialism," *Partisan Review* 14:1 (1947), 29.

3. "CPUSA Membership," FBI New York Field File 100-80638, Domestic Intelligence Division Inspection Report by R. T. Harbo, 3 June 1955. At the beginning of 1956, the total party membership was approximately 20,000, 8,800 of them in New York; David Shannon, *The Decline of American Communism: A History of the Communist Party of the United States Since 1945* (New York: Harcourt, Brace, 1959), 360.

4. *U.S. News and World Report*, 1 April 1955 (speech by Attorney General Herbert Brownell, 21 March 1955).

1. The Doctor: Edward Barsky

1. Herbert Arthur Philbrick, *I Led Three Lives: Citizen, "Communist," Counterspy* (New York: McGraw-Hill, 1952), 251.

2. The new HUAC was not merely a reactivation of the Dies Committee; it was, uniquely, a permanent committee. It was approved by the House by 207 votes to 186 with 40 (including Lyndon B. Johnson) abstaining. As the initiator of the motion, John E. Rankin, rejoiced: "I caught 'em flat-footed and flat-headed." Cited in Walter Goodman, *The Committee* (London: Secker & Warburg, 1969), 169.

3. Two examples are Robert Justin Goldstein, *Political Repression in Modern America* (Cambridge, Mass.: Schenkman, 1978); and William Preston, *Aliens and*

Dissenters: Federal Suppression of Radicals, 1903–1933 (Chicago: University of Illinois Press, 1995).

4. "Statement issued by Honorable John S. Wood, of Georgia, Chairman, House Committee on Un-American Activities," 24 January 1946, in Charlotte Todes Stern Papers, 1925–1956, #70, Box 2, Folder 1, Tamiment Library and Robert F. Wagner Archives, New York University (henceforth Stern Papers).

5. Medicine was in the marrow: his father was also a surgeon at Beth Israel, and his two brothers, George and Arthur, also became doctors. (Arthur was a pioneering plastic surgeon who treated Vietnamese children during the Vietnam War.) Barsky's private practice focused on industrial injuries (i.e., workers' compensation cases) that required surgery.

6. Joseph North, "A Case for the Doctor," *New Masses*, 19 August 1947, 7.

7. Peter N. Carroll, "Introduction," in Peter N. Carroll and James D. Fernandez (eds.), *Facing Fascism: New York and the Spanish Civil War* (New York: Museum of the City of New York and New York University Press, 2007), 15–16.

8. Edward Barsky, "The Surgeon Goes to War," 12–13 (from chapter 1, "Someone Had to Help"), undated and unpublished manuscript, Edward K. Barsky Papers, 1936–1970, Abraham Lincoln Brigade Archives (ALBA), 125, Box 5, Folder 4, Tamiment Library and Robert F. Wagner Archives, New York University (henceforth Barsky Papers).

9. See Nelson's eulogistic recollections of Barsky in Spain in *New Masses*, 19 August 1947. Nelson joined the Communist Party in 1925, Barsky in November 1935.

10. Barsky, "The Surgeon Goes to War," 214–15, Barsky Papers, Box 5, Folder 4; *New York Journal*, 19 July 1937; *New York Post*, 19 July 1937: *New York World-Telegram*, 19 July 1937 (clippings in Barsky Papers, Box 2, Folder 13).

11. See James Neugass, *War Is Beautiful: An American Ambulance Driver in the Spanish Civil War* (New York: The New Press, 2008), frontispiece; this book is dedicated to Barsky. The 1937 tour allegedly raised "hundreds of thousands of dollars" for more medical equipment. *New York Times*, 13 February 1975 (obituary).

12. Howard Fast, *Being Red: A Memoir* (Boston: Houghton Mifflin, 1990), 143. In 1945, too, a reporter described him as "a tall . . . youngish-looking man of not quite fifty, with thick dark straight hair and a clipped, graying moustache." Mary Braggiotti, "For a Forgotten People," *New York Post*, 13 March 1945.

13. Howard Fast, "Why We Were Sent to Prison," *New Times*, No. 26, 1950, 10.

14. Ernest Hemingway to Milton Wolff, 7 May 1950, cited in Peter N. Carroll, *The Odyssey of the Abraham Lincoln Brigade: Americans in the Spanish Civil War* (Stanford, Calif.: Stanford University Press, 1994), 316; *New York Times*, 13 February 1975. (Hemingway met Barsky in Spain; Wolff was the last commander of the Abraham Lincoln Brigade.) For glowing character references from JAFRC staff, see Joseph North, "A Case for the Doctor," *New Masses*, 19 August 1947, 8–9. North judged Barsky to be "great in heart as in talent" and "totally absorbed with the pain of mankind" (7).

15. See Veterans of Abraham Lincoln Brigade Records, ALBA 0.19, Box 10, Folders 15 and 25, Tamiment Library and Robert F. Wagner Archives, New York University.

16. The British Consul in Madrid conservatively estimated that 10,000 Republicans were shot in the first five months after the war; the killings continued well into the 1940s. Paul Preston, *The Spanish Civil War 1936–39* (London: Weidenfeld & Nicolson, 1986), 167–68.

17. Sebastiaan Faber, *Exile and Cultural Hegemony: Spanish Intellectuals in Mexico, 1939–1975* (Nashville: Vanderbilt University Press, 2002), 154; Preston, *The Spanish Civil War*, 167.

18. For a detailed report of its operations and finances for its first two years, see "Joint Anti-Fascist Refugee Committee," May 1944, in Barsky Papers, Box 1, Folder 31. By then, it had raised $295,000, 25 percent of which came from trade unions and 75 percent from 75,000 individual contributions.

19. Typescript of address given by Barsky [1, 5], 21 April 1945, Barsky Papers, Box 3, Folder 3. At this dinner at the Hotel Astor in New York, Lillian Hellman was the guest of honor. A far larger audience attended the huge JAFRC-sponsored rally at Madison Square Garden, the brainchild of Helen Bryan, on September 24, 1945. Its slogan was "Break off Relations With Franco," and its goal was to inaugurate the "Fall drive" to raise $300,000 for the rest of the year. The transcript of Barsky's stirring speech is located in Barsky Papers, Box 1, Folder 13. The fact that the rally was supported by the CPUSA and advertised in the *Daily Worker* was regarded as *prima facie* evidence of the JAFRC's being a "front" for the Communist Party. See *Congressional Record–House*, 28 March 1946, 2802.

20. See Joint Anti-Fascist Refugee Committee, Correspondence, 1941–1945, bMS 16031/2 (1–3) and Joint Anti-Fascist Refugee Committee, Evidence of Communist affiliation and responses, 1941–1943, bMS 16031/2 (4), Unitarian Service Committee, Administrative Records, 1941–1957, Andover–Harvard Theological Library, Harvard Divinity School, Cambridge, Mass.

21. *New York Compass*, 7 June 1950, 3.

22. The total amount raised in 1945 was $318,293. This dropped to $306,695 in 1946 and to $254,430 in 1947. Financial Statement, National Office, JAFRC, attached to correspondence, 27 February 1948, Department of Justice, Federal Bureau of Investigation files, "Joint Anti-Fascist Refugee Committee" (henceforth FBI JAFRC files).

23. Already, on December 1, HUAC had requested that the President's War Control Board cancel the JAFRC's license to collect and distribute funds for the relief of Spanish refugees in Europe.

24. Minutes, Executive Board meeting, 14 December 1945, Stern Papers, Box 2, Folder 1. A copy of the December 14 resolution was sent to all JAFRC sponsors. Barsky also invoked HUAC's charter (concerning overthrow of the U.S. government and subversive and/or un-American activities) when he testified

before it; see HUAC, *Executive Session, Testimony of Dr. Edward K. Barsky*, 13 February 1946, 161.

25. Letter, Barsky to contributors, 2 January 1946, Stern papers, Box 2, Folder 1.

26. See his *Secret Battalion: An Examination of the Communist Attitude to the Labour Party* (London: Labour Publications Department, 1946).

27. *Congressional Record. Proceedings and Debates of the 79th Congress, second session*, 28 March 1946, 2801–2 (henceforth *Congressional Record–House*). Four years later, in January 1949, Laski's visit to the University of California, sponsored by its Political Science Department, was canceled after the UCLA Board of Regents expressed its opposition to the "ultra left" Laski. Bob Blauner, *Resisting McCarthyism: To Sign or Not to Sign California's Loyalty Oath* (Stanford, Calif.: Stanford University Press, 2009), 60–61.

28. Eric Bentley, *Thirty Years of Treason: Excerpts from Hearings before the House Committee on Un-American Activities, 1938–1968* (New York: Viking, 1971), 413.

29. *New York Times*, 28 December 1945. In fact, Adamson personally wrote to various contributors in January 1946, advising them that they were "misinformed" about the true nature of the JAFRC. See copies of correspondence in Barsky Papers, Box 1, Folder 28.

30. *Congressional Record–House*, 28 March 1946, 2801. Wood became chairman in July 1945.

31. Carroll, *The Odyssey of the Abraham Lincoln Brigade*, 268–69; Carroll and Fernandez, *Facing Fascism*, 182, n.7. See also Kenneth O'Reilly, *Hoover and the Un-Americans: The FBI, HUAC and the Red Menace* (Philadelphia: Temple University Press, 1983), 119.

32. Stephen J. Whitfield, *The Culture of the Cold War* (Baltimore: Johns Hopkins University Press, 1991), 91–96; David Caute, *The Great Fear: The Anti-Communist Purge Under Truman and Eisenhower* (New York: Simon & Schuster, 1978), 108–10.

33. *Congressional Record–House*, 16 April 1946, 3840.

34. J. Edgar Hoover, Memorandum for the Attorney General, 27 January 1938, reprinted in *Science & Society*, vol. 68, no. 3, Fall 2004, 363.

35. Correspondence, J. T. Bissell, Colonel, General Staff, Military Intelligence Service, Washington, to J. Edgar Hoover, 14 April 1944, No. 5918/R, FBI JAFRC files.

36. In February 1946, a conference of senior FBI officials decided to provide covert support to HUAC; O'Reilly, *Hoover and the Un-Americans*, 76, 98. By 1947, assisting HUAC became "an FBI priority." Athan Theoharis, *Chasing Spies* (Chicago: Ivan R. Dee, 2002), 161. See also Ellen Schrecker, *Many Are the Crimes: McCarthyism in America* (Boston: Little, Brown, 1998), 214–15.

37. Longstanding, because it had commenced in 1919, when Attorney General A. Mitchell Palmer appointed Hoover to head the General Intelligence Division of the Justice Department; this involved, *inter alia*, the compilation of index files on leading radical "agitators" and organizations.

38. Minutes, Executive Board meeting, 1 February 1946, Stern papers, Box 2, Folder 1.

39. Fast, *Being Red*, 144, 151.

40. Henry Cadbury, "Introduction," Helen Bryan, *Inside* (Boston: Houghton Mifflin, 1953), ix.

41. Executive Session, HUAC, 24 January 1946, Testimony of Helen R. Bryan. Congressional Hearings Digital Collection, HRG-1946-UAH-0020: 601–5. See also her similar testimony to an open session on April 4, 1946, in *Investigation of Un-American Propaganda Activities in the United States. Executive Board Joint Anti-Fascist Refugee Committee*. HUAC Hearings, 79th Congress, 2nd session, 4 April 1946, 96–103.

42. Lily Kingsley, "She Wouldn't Let Them Down," *PM*, 1 July 1947; Fast, *Being Red*, 144; Cadbury, "Introduction," ix–x.

43. Confidential report, 12 July 1950, FBI New York File No. 100–45542, Helen Reid Bryan (henceforth FBI Bryan file), 3–4. FOIA No. 1129600-001.

44. *New York Times*, 2 August 1953 (review by Lucy Freeman).

45. Estelle B. Freedman, *Maternal Justice: Miriam Van Waters and the Female Reform Tradition* (Chicago: University of Chicago Press, 1996), 325–88. Freedman was superintendent of Framingham from 1932 to 1957 and a leading prison reformer; she also read, and was profoundly affected by, Bryan's *Inside* and reviewed it for *The Nation*.

46. Her father, Reverend W. S. Plummer Bryan, who died in 1925, had been an eminent Presbyterian minister in Chicago.

47. Report, Albany office, 31 March 1958, 5–6, FBI Bryan file.

48. Memorandum, SAC, Albany to Director, FBI, 29 May 1958, 2, FBI Bryan file.

49. Report, New York office, 22 February 1945, 7–8, FBI Bryan file.

50. Yergan's apostasy is discussed in David H. Anthony, *Max Yergan: Race Man, Internationalist, Cold Warrior* (New York: New York University Press, 2006), 231–42.

51. Glenda Elizabeth Gilmore, *Defying Dixie: The Radical Roots of Civil Rights, 1919–1950* (New York: Norton, 2008), 437.

52. *New York Times*, 22 July 1947. In fact, in the summer of 1946 Treasury Department investigators spent more than two weeks in the JAFRC office examining financial records. Minutes, Executive Board meeting, 20 June 1946, Stern Papers, Box 2, Folder 1.

53. "Statement with regards to the present investigation of the [JAFRC] by [HUAC]," n.d. [1946], Barsky Papers, Box 1, Folder 28. Bryan's FBI file reveals that the FBI also had such records.

54. The JAFRC's legal counsel also advised Bryan that the subpoena itself was invalid; see the unread "Statement made by Helen R. Bryan to the House Committee on Un-American Activities, 1/23/46," 3, Stern Papers, Box 2, Folder 1. It was subsequently incorporated into "Investigation of Un-American Propaganda

Activities in the United States. Executive Board Joint Anti-Fascist Refugee Committee." HUAC Hearings, 79th Congress, 2nd session, 4 April 1946, 103–5.

55. For example, Henry Steele Commager, "Who Is Loyal to America?," *Harper's Magazine*, 9 September 1947. (Commager was a professor of history at Columbia University.) For the sheer volume of protests and petitions against HUAC for just October–November 1947, see M. Stanton Evans, "The Campaign Against HUAC," in William F. Buckley Jr. (ed.), *The Committee and Its Critics* (New York: Putnam, 1962), 212–13.

56. Elizabeth Edwards Spalding, *The First Cold Warrior: Harry Truman, Containment, and the Remaking of Liberal Internationalism* (Lexington: University Press of Kentucky, 2006), 175.

57. Civil Rights Congress, *America's "Thought Police": Record of the Un-American Activities Committee* (New York, October 1947), i–ii (foreword by Wallace entitled "Strike Back").

58. Fast, *Being Red*, 148.

59. Minutes, Executive Board meeting, 1 February 1946, Stern papers, Box 2, Folder 1.

60. Minutes, Executive Board special meeting, 11 February 1946, Stern papers, Box 2, Folder 1.

61. See Executive Session, HUAC, 13 February 1946, Testimony of Dr. Edward K. Barsky, Congressional Hearings Digital Collection, HRG-1946-UAH-0020: 776–808. For the edited (and sanitized) version, see HUAC, *Report. Proceeding Against Dr. Edward K. Barsky and Others*, 28 March 1946, 79th Congress, 2nd Session, Report No. 1829, 1–4.

62. *New Masses*, 19 August 1947.

63. *The Nation* (19 January 1946) editorialized that HUAC was on "a fishing expedition in the hope of finding something that looks like evidence to back the verdict it has already reached." There was some truth to this.

64. Such activities were intensified and widened in scope, evidenced by the regular "Developments on Pressure Campaign" reports to the executive board meetings throughout 1946.

65. *Congressional Record–House*, 27 February 1946, 1763. What he may have had in mind was this: on March 28, Thomas reported that an "intensive" investigation had revealed that Gusavo Duran, who had been a major in the Spanish Republican Army during the civil war and a communist, arrived in the United States in 1940 and worked (1943–45) as an assistant to Assistant Secretary of State Spruille Braden, in the U.S. State Department. According to Thomas, Duran was an NKVD (Soviet secret police) agent and "the directing genius" behind the JAFRC. *Congressional Record–House*, 28 March 1946, 2802. On March 14, 1950, Duran, now a UN employee, was one of the first targets of Senator Joseph McCarthy; after five hearings before the Tydings Subcommittee and the Loyalty Board, he was finally cleared of all charges in January 1955. Caute, *The Great Fear*, 331–38.

66. Goodman, *The Committee*, 269–70. He was joined in Danbury by two of the Hollywood Ten and one JAFRC member (Dr. Jacob Auslander).

67. Minutes, Executive Board meeting, 8 March 1946, 2, Stern papers, Box 2, Folder 1.

68. *Congressional Record–House*, 28 March 1946, 2085.

69. *Ibid.*, 2803, 2806, 2808. The four opponents were Marcantonio, Adam Clayton Powell Jr. (New York), Edward Izac (California), and Matthew Neely (West Virginia). A copy of this citation can be found in the Stern papers, Box 2, Folder 1.

70. Minutes, Executive Board meeting, 28 March 1946, Stern papers, Box 2, Folder 1. Self-delusion must have been infectious: at the same meeting, members were "in full agreement" that "one of the most effective ways" of fighting the Wood–Rankin Committee was to "raise larger funds for the Spanish republican exiles than have been raised in the past."

71. *Investigation of Un-American Propaganda Activities in the United States. Executive Board Joint Anti-Fascist Refugee Committee.* HUAC Hearings, 79th Congress, 2nd session, 4 April 1946, 1–105; *House Report No. 1936—Proceedings Against the Joint Anti-Fascist Refugee Committee*, April 16, 1946.

72. [Association of American University Professors], "Report of Investigating Committee" [1957], 5, n. 2, in RG 3.0.6. Records of the Office of President / Chancellor New York University, 1951–1965, Administrative Subject Files, Box 15, Folder 1, NYU Archives. The confidential report continued that Bradley "was not allowed to bring his counsel into the hearing room, he was not allowed to leave the room with his counsel during the questioning, and he was not allowed to read his written statement."

73. "Investigation of Un-American Propaganda Activities in the United States. Executive Board Joint Anti-Fascist Refugee Committee." HUAC Hearings, 79th Congress, 2nd session, 4 April 1946, 9–10. By 1946, John Rankin was renowned for his virulent racism and anti-Semitism as well as his anticommunism.

74. See Samuel H. Hofstadter, *The Fifth Amendment and the Immunity Act of 1954* (New York: n.p., n.d. [1956]), 26–30 ("Immunity in Congressional Investigation").

75. Fast, *Being Red*, 149, 176. But see Schrecker, *Many Are the Crimes*, 323, for the perceived risks of "taking the Fifth" in 1947.

76. In fact, five constitutional challenges were made against HUAC between December 1947 and April 1950; three emanated from HUAC's investigation of the JAFRC. For Rogge's sanguine challenges to HUAC and his repeated (thirty-three times) "We are going to show . . ." gauntlet-throwing, see his fifteen-page draft statement to the Federal District Court, 16 June 1947, Stern Papers, Box 2, Folder 1.

77. As we shall see in Chapter 5, Rogge was experienced, high profile, and a committed civil libertarian. He wrote *Our Vanishing Civil Liberties* (New York: Gaer, 1949), which was serialized in the left-wing *Daily Compass*.

78. *Congressional Record–House*, 16 April 1946, 3844.

79. Ibid., 3848.

80. Ibid., 3939.

81. See *New York Times* report, "17 Foes of Franco Voted in Contempt," 17 April 1946. For a fuller discussion of this debate, see Carl Beck, *Contempt of Congress: A Study of the Prosecutions Initiated by the Committee on Un-American Activities, 1945–1957* (New York: Da Capo Press, 1974), 29–31.

82. "Memorandum of Legal Procedure and Legal Status" [n.d. April 1947], Barsky Papers, Box 1, Folder 28; *New York Times*, 4 April 1947.

83. Minutes, Executive Board meeting, 9 April 1947, Stern Papers, Box 2, Folder 1. On April 16, Barsky requested that executive board members raise $900 each for their own expenses within fifteen days (Letter, Barsky to Charlotte Stern, 16 April 1947; Minutes, 30 April 1947, Stern Papers, Box 2, Folder 1). There was neither "Moscow gold," nor free legal representation: Rogge, the chief defense attorney, did not work *pro bono*.

84. Correspondence, Edward K. Barsky to Charlotte Stern, 16 April 1947, Stern Papers, Box 2, Folder 1.

85. *Washington Post*, 12 June 1947.

86. *New York Times*, 9 September 1948.

87. Fast was again critical: "instead of arguing the legality of the charge, Rogge was engaging in a political attack against [HUAC]. It left me bewildered. . . ." Fast, *Being Red*, 176.

88. The five were Leverett Gleason (publisher of *Reader's Scope* and the comic *Crime Does Not Pay*), Louise Kamsley, Herman Shumlin (a theatrical producer), Jesse Tolmach, and Bobbie Weinstein. It is not known what the others thought of this five. No discussion of this action was recorded in the JAFRC minutes when, in absentia, their resignations were formally accepted. Minutes, Executive Board meeting, 15 September 1947, Stern Papers, Box 2, Folder 1. Efforts were made to secure additional executive board members, but none was successful. In February 1949, Dr. Louis Miller, in whose home Barsky first formed the American Medical Bureau to Aid Spanish Democracy in 1936, also resigned; but his resignation was accepted with "real regret." Minutes, Executive Board Meeting, 18 February 1948.

89. Cited in *New Masses*, 19 August 1947.

90. Minutes, Executive Board meeting, 15 September 1947, Stern Papers, Box 2, Folder 1. Vincent Sheehan, the chairman of the "Citizens to Safeguard the JAFRC," sent a letter on September 30, 1947, appealing for financial contributions to help "bear the costs of another trial"—that of Helen Bryan, on October 27. It was accompanied by a Howard Fast brochure, "Three Names for Anti-Fascists," of which 100,000 were printed to sell at one cent each. A major fundraising "Court of Public Opinion Dinner" at the Astor Roof was held on October 30, 1947, and raised $29,055 in cash and pledges. Letter, Helen Bryan to Executive Board members, 6 November 1947, Stern Papers, Box 2, Folder 2.

91. Robert Justin Goldstein, *American Blacklist: The Attorney General's List of Subversive Organizations* (Lawrence: University Press of Kansas, 2008), 62.

92. Samuel Walker, *In Defense of American Liberties: A History of the ACLU* (New York: Oxford University Press, 1990), 179. However, the ACLU did not petition the Supreme Court to rule on the constitutionality of the List, which remained in use until 1974.

93. *New Masses*, 11 February 1948. Indicative was this FBI report: "Edward L. Parsons, Episcopal Bishop of Northern California, has formally resigned as Honorary Chairman of the JAFRC in SF [San Francisco]. Bishop Parsons has indicated that because the JAFRC has been designated as a subversive organization he can no longer ask his friends and supporters to support the JAFRC. This has caused a financial crisis with the local chapter of the JAFRC . . . and [he] is considering discontinuing maintenance of offices in SF." FBI JAFRC files, Telex, "Whelan" to J. Edgar Hoover, 7 October 1953 (FOIPA No. 1056236).

94. Letter, Barsky to "Dear Friend," 3 February 1948, Stern Papers, Box 2, Folder 1. At the December 1948 meeting, Helen Bryan reported the "serious decline" in funds and noted that projected financial aid was not sent to Mexico or were outstanding legal bills met. Minutes, Executive Board Meeting, 17 December 1948, 2–3, Stern Papers, Box 2, Folder 1.

95. [Reports and Proceedings], National Conference of the Joint Anti-Fascist Refugee Committee, 27–28 August 1948 [1–21], Stern Papers, Box 2, Folder 1.

96. *United States v. Barsky*, 72 F. Supp. 165 (1947); *Barsky v. the United States*, 167 F. 2d 241 (1948); *Barsky v. the United States*, 334 U.S. 843 (1948); *Bryan v. United States*, 174 F. 2d 525 (1949); *United States v. Bryan*, 339 U.S. 323 (1949); *Bryan v. United States*, 183 F. 2d 996 (1950); *Bryan v. United States*, 340 U.S. 866 (1950). The full text of *Appeal from the District Court of the United States for the District of Columbia, United States Court of Appeals, Barsky et al., v. United States of America*, No. 9602, Vol. 1 (1–288) and Vol. 2 (289–631), is located in Barsky Papers, Box 3, Folder 1.

97. Nor will the myriad public relations and fundraising activities undertaken by the JAFRC in 1948–49 be discussed. These are outlined in the Executive Board Minutes; it is remarkable that Barsky had any time or energy left for surgery.

98. *Barsky v. the United States*, 164 F. 2d 241 (1948), 254; *New York Times*, 19 March 1948.

99. The right of witnesses to refuse to testify before congressional committees and state agencies was upheld by the Supreme Court in the late 1950s; see *Slochower v. Board of Higher Education*, 350 U.S. 551 (1956); *Watkins v. United States*, 354 U.S. 178 (1957); *Sweezy v. State of New Hampshire*, 354 U.S. 234 (1957).

100. Press release, 18 March 1948, Stern Papers, Box 2, Folder 4.

101. "US 'Gestapo' Forseen," *New York Times*, 31 October 1947.

102. FBI file, "O. John Rogge," Report of meeting, Boston, Massachusetts, 8 December 1948 in Memorandum, D. M. Ladd to J. Edgar Hoover, 23 December 1948 (FOIPA Request No. 1035916, "O. John Rogge"). An earlier FBI report in the same file (December 29, 1947) noted that Rogge had stated: "We are

almost exactly following the Nazi blueprint, and the threat to Democracy from Fascism is greater now than at any time since 1932."

103. See Rogge's article "Courts Contradictory in Contempt Case," *Daily Compass*, 17 November 1949.

104. *United States v. Bryan*, 339 U.S. 323 (1950); *Bryan v. United States*, 340 U.S. 866 (1950). Justices Black and Frankfurter dissented.

105. *New York Times*, 8 June 1950; JAFRC, *Campaign Bulletin*, 3, 16 June 1950, 1, Barsky Papers, Box 1, Folder 16.

106. Copy of letter, Kane to Truman, 26 June 1950, Barsky Papers, Box 4, Folder 16. At a more organized level the battered remnants of the JAFRC still mobilized more than 3,000 letter-writers urging the President to use his executive power to free the JAFRC board members. JAFRC, *Campaign Bulletin*, 3, 16 June 1950, 1, Barsky Papers, Box 1, Folder 16; letter from Dorothy Parker to Charlotte Stern, 5 July 1950, Stern Papers, Box 2, Folder 1.

107. Prison Records, Receipt of Property, Barsky Papers, Box 5, Folder 3.

108. As a result of his conviction in 1947, Bradley was dismissed by NYU in 1951. Fast resigned from the Communist Party in the wake of Nikita Krushchev's "secret speech" in February 1956; see Howard Fast, "On Leaving the Communist Party," *The Saturday Review*, 16 November 1957.

109. "Three Anti-Franco Women at West Virginia Prison," *Daily Worker*, 20 June 1950. It was claimed that they were "America's first three women political prisoners."

110. Leon Edel, "'Premature Anti-Fascists' Go to Jail Today," *New York Compass*, 7 June 1950.

111. Transcript, Hearing on Charges against Professor Lyman R. Bradley, [January 5, 1951], 308, Lyman Bradley Papers, New York University Archives, Box 1, Folder 1.

112. According to his lawyer, they "suffered extreme hardship during the five months of his incarceration." Abraham Fishbein to Committee on Licenses of the Board of Regents of the University of the State of New York, 18 June 1954, 2, Barsky Papers, Box 4, Folder 8. During that five months he had to maintain his office and secretary to prevent his practice from collapsing, imposing a further a financial burden on the family's resources. Because of his regular and substantial donations to the Spanish Refugee Appeal (which operated under the JAFRC rubric), Barsky had no reservoir of savings on which to draw.

113. Anderman to Barsky, 23 June 1950; C. C. Nicholson (Warden, Petersburg Penitentiary) to Anderman, 3 July 1950. The original was then sent to Vita Barsky. Barsky Papers, Box 4, Folder 16. The same occurred with the letter to Barsky, 25 August 1950, from Dave and Ester Greene, whose "outrage at your forced confinement hasn't abated a single bit."

114. Barsky Papers, Box 4, Folder 16.

115. JAFRC, *Campaign Bulletin*, [no. 12], 1 December 1950, 2, Barsky Papers, Box 1, Folder 16.

116. Circular, "New Officers of the Joint Anti-Fascist Refugee Committee" [n.d.], Barsky Papers, Box 1, Folder 32. The new chairman was another physician, Dr. Mark Strauss. Bryan was also replaced; the new executive secretary was Milton Kaufman.

117. *New Masses*, 19 August 1947.

118. Ibid.

119. Maxwell Frank to Board of Regents, State of New York, 27 November 1950, Barsky Papers, Box 5, Folder 1.

120. Barsky Papers, Box 4, Folder 12.

121. *Petitioner's Brief to New York State Department of Education, Committee on Grievances*, February 1951, Barsky Papers, Box 4, Folder 2.

122. *New York State Department of Education, Committee on Grievances. Minutes of Formal Hearing*, 15 February 1951, 463, Barsky Papers, Box 4, Folder 1.

123. *Joint Anti-Fascist Refugee Committee v. McGrath*, 341 U.S. 123 (1951); Goldstein, *American Blacklist*, 158–61.

124. *New York State Department of Education, Committee on Grievances. Minutes of Formal Hearing*, 15 February 1951, 457, Barsky Papers, Box 4, Folder 1.

125. New York State Department of Education, *Report of the Regents' Committee on Discipline*, 31 July 1951, 28, Barsky Papers, Box 4, Folder 3. Its detailed report was later praised by the Supreme Court (majority opinion) for its "high degree of unbiased objectivity." *Barsky v. Board of Regents*, 347 U.S. 442 (1954), 455.

126. *Re Barsky*, 305 N.Y. 89, 111 N.E. 2d.

127. *Brown v. Board of Education*, 347 U.S. 483 (1954).

128. *Barsky v. Board of Regents*, 347 U.S. 442 (1954), 69–Dissent (A), 4. Without such dissenting opinions, there may been a little truth in I. F. Stone's comment that "the Cold War hysteria has now completely enveloped the judiciary." *Daily Compass*, 30 May 1950, 3.

129. *New Masses*, 19 August 1947, 7.

130. Correspondence, Angela Barksy Mortarotti to author, 18 March 2009.

131. Barsky to Committee on Licenses, Board of Regents, 12 June 1954, Barsky Papers, Box 4, Folder 9. Barsky did not write alone. Also appealing for clemency on his behalf were 621 New York physicians who petitioned the Board to mitigate its disciplinary action. Letter, 14 June 1954, signatories to Board of Regents, Barsky Papers Box 4, Folder 8.

132. Charles A. Brind to Barsky, 21 June 1954, Barsky Papers, Box 4, Folder 10.

133. This phrase was used to describe the jailing of Helen Bryan but is also applicable here. *Campaign Bulletin*, no. 10, 2 November 1950, Barsky Papers, Box 1, Folder 16.

134. "Many of my patients are of moderate to poor circumstances . . ." Barsky to Angela Parisi, Chairman, Workers' Compensation Board, 28 August 1955, Barsky Papers, Box 5, Folder 1.

135. Barsky to Parisi, 28 April 1955, Barsky Papers, Box 5, Folder 1.

136. This was the case with Dr. Jacob Auslander, one of the JAFRC eleven jailed in 1950.

137. Barsky to Chester L. Davidson, Medical Practice Committee, 31 May 1955, Barsky Papers, Box 5, Folder 1.

138. Catherine C. Hafele, Executive Secretary, Medical Registration Office, to Barsky, 22 July 1955, Barsky Papers, Box 5, Folder 1.

139. Barsky to Medical Appeals Unit, 16 August 1955; Barsky to Parisi, 24 August 1955; Haven Emerson ("Provisional Committee") to Parisi [n.d.], Barsky Papers, Box 5, Folder 1.

140. *New York Times*, 16 February 1955. See also undated [fall, 1954?] correspondence to "Friends" of the JAFRC from Mark Strauss (chairman), Ralph H. Gundlach (chairman, Citizens to Defend JAFRC), and Karen Morley (on behalf of the treasurer, Citizens to Defend JAFRC), Barsky Papers, Box 1, Folder 19.

141. FOIA No. 1056236-002.

142. Correspondence, J. T. Bissell, Colonel, General Staff, Military Intelligence Service, Washington, to J. Edgar Hoover, 16 March 1943. The fact that Kusman was a close friend of Gerhart Eisler, whom we have already met, intensified suspicion.

143. Correspondence, 14 April 1944, No. 5918/R.

144. Personal and Confidential Memorandum to Director, "Joint Anti-Fascist Refugee Committee—use of technical equipment on surveillance of Felix Kusman in Seattle Field Division," 26 February 1945.

145. Schrecker, *Many Are the Crimes*, 226–27. In its anticommunist zeal, the FBI engaged in various forms of lawbreaking, including burglaries.

146. Kusman's keys were sent by courier to the FBI's New York office; if they were his office keys they were possibly used for further illegal activity.

147. He managed this through his contacts in the National Maritime Union. The FBI learned of his six-week absence in Lisbon through its bugging of Louise Bransten's San Francisco home: "Louise: No! Felix. FELIX! I didn't know you were out of the country Felix! KUSMAN: Nobody knew." SAC NJL Pieper to Hoover, 17 February 1945, with Attachment, "Conversation between Felix Kusman and Louise Bransten at Latter's Home—February 11, 1945" (emphasis in original transcript).

148. Confidential Security Information, Warren Olney III (Assistant Attorney General, Criminal Division) to Director, FBI, 6 July 1953, (file 100-7061). Kusman had been interviewed by the FBI on three previous occasions under TOPLEV (under which FBI agents sought to persuade high-ranking communists to become informants). It was noted that "[u]ndoubtedly Kusman could furnish information of interest to the U.S. Government if he would cooperate." No details of the final interview, on July 10, 1953, were located, but in a memo to Hoover concerning another matter, dated October 12, 1953, it was noted that Kusman had "declined to cooperate." Not contained in the FBI-JAFRC files but in the FBI-Kusman file (FOIPA 0975848) in ALBA 178, Box 1, Folder 3, Tami-

ment, is a thirty-six-page Report on Kusman, dated February 1, 1954. It sheds no further light on this issue.

149. For revealing portraits of both, see John E. Haynes, *Red Scare or Red Menace? American Communism and Anticommunism in the Cold War Era* (Chicago: Ivan R. Dee, 1996), 180–83. For an excellent analysis of how informers like Matusow operated, see Robert M. Lichtman and Ronald D. Cohen, *Deadly Farce: Harvey Matusow and the Informer System in the McCarthy Era* (Urbana and Chicago: University of Illinois Press, 2004).

150. Ruth Davidow subsequently featured in the documentary film *The Good Fight: The Abraham Lincoln Brigade in the Spanish Civil War* (Abraham Lincoln Brigade Film Project, 1984).

151. FBI Report, Cleveland (file 100-11805), 16 February 1953, "Joint Anti-Fascist Refugee Committee: Internal Security Act, 1950," Section V: Appendix-Witnesses, 10. Evidence of overlapping membership was the main subject of a detailed twenty-three-page file, "Interrelationship of CPA and JAFRC," compiled by the San Francisco Bureau (file 100-10486). What a historian might think dubious, the FBI judged damning: "[T]he CPA [Communist Party of America] has often helped the JAFRC by distributing much of the JAFRC literature through the medium of their various clubs" (5).

152. FBI Report, San Francisco (100-10486), 30 October 1953, "Section IV: General Activities," 4–11; FBI Report, Los Angeles (100-3514), 2 June 1953, "Joint Anti-Fascist Refugee Committee—Prosecutive Summary Report," 9.

153. See, for example, memoranda dated May 11, May 26, June 4, 1953 (file 100-7061).

154. Correspondence with author, 18 March 2009, Angela Barksy Mortarotti; John Dittmer, *The Good Doctors: The Medical Committee for Human Rights and the Struggle for Social Justice in Health Care* (London: Bloomsbury, 2009).

2. The Writer: Howard Fast

1. He also wrote 23 plays, 13 lengthy pamphlets, 19 film and television scripts, 115 feature articles for the *Daily Worker*, and innumerable short stories. Fast died in Greenwich, Connecticut, in 2003. Since the completion of this chapter, the first comprehensive biography of Fast, by Gerald Sorin, *Howard Fast: Life and Literature in the Left Lane* (Bloomington: Indiana University Press), has appeared (November 2012); notable are the extensive interviews with numerous family members, who paint a highly unflattering portrait of Fast.

2. Daniel Traister, "Noticing Howard Fast," *Prospects: An Annual of American Cultural Studies* 20 (1995), 528.

3. Deming Brown, *Soviet Attitudes Toward American Writing* (Princeton, N.J.: Princeton University Press, 1962), 281–82. Brown estimated that in the Soviet Union alone, 2.5 million copies in twelve Soviet languages were printed between 1948 and 1957, easily outstripping all other American writers of this period. See

also Rossen Djagalov, "'I Don't Boast About It, but I'm the Most Widely Read Author of This Century': Howard Fast and International Leftist Literary Culture, ca. Mid–Twentieth Century," *Anthropology of East Europe Review* 27:2 (Fall 2009), 40–55.

4. Djagalov, "I Don't Boast About It," 49. Emphasis in original.

5. Cited in Traister, "Noticing Howard Fast," 534. The individual was Walter Felscher (1931–2000), a noted German mathematician and scholar.

6. In 1957, *Spartacus* was banned in East Germany; thereafter, sales were strong in West Germany, where previously it had been banned. *New York Post*, 22 May 1959, 39.

7. *The New Leader*, 12 February 1951.

8. *New York Times*, 7 February 1947.

9. *Daily Worker*, 7 February 1947.

10. *New York Times*, 7 February 1947.

11. *Publishers Weekly*, vol. 5, 15 February 1947, 1134–35.

12. *Daily Worker*, 12 February 1947; *New York Times*, 20 February 1947; *New York Herald Tribune*, 26 February 1947. The publishers (including Doubleday; Little, Brown; Random House; and Scribner's) stood by Fast on this occasion; in four years' time, as we shall see, they did not.

13. *New York Times*, 26 February 1947.

14. Minutes of Meeting, City of New York Board of Education Records, Series 116, Municipal Archives, New York (also published in *Journal of the Board of Education of the City of New York, 1947*, vol. 1, 489–93, City Hall Library).

15. Cited in unidentified article in James Marshall Papers, Series 354, Box 23, Folder 7 (scrapbook), Municipal Archives, City of New York. Timone was a far-right, pro-Francoist, anti-Semitic Catholic who was soon to become "the vigilante, the leading spirit behind the purge" of New York teachers. David Caute, *The Great Fear: The Anti-Communist Purge Under Truman and Eisenhower* (New York: Simon & Schuster, 1978), 433.

16. *Journal of the Board of Education of the City of New York, 1947*, vol. 1, 492–93.

17. Howard Fast, *Citizen Tom Paine* (New York: Duell, Sloan & Pearce, 1943), 22–23.

18. According to Ann Lyon Haight, it was banned "because it was written by a spokesman of [*sic*] a totalitarian movement." Haight, *Banned Books: Informal Notes on Some Books Banned for Various Reasons at Various Times and in Various Places* (New York: Bowker, 1955), 111.

19. *Daily Worker*, 6 February 1947.

20. *Daily Worker*, 8 February 1947. Emphasis in original.

21. Haight, *Banned Books*, 112. Ironically, Hughes was also the author of the magisterial three-volume biography of George Washington that Fast explicitly acknowledged as a major source for his 1942 novel *The Unvanquished*.

22. Lonigan to Untermeyer, 7 February 1947. Untermeyer read the full letter over the phone to Howard Fast and then sent it to him with an accompanying note that the letter "would be filthy if it were not so farcical" and that Untermeyer's reply "should wither Miss Lonigan and her superiors." Howard Fast Papers, correspondence files, Manuscript Library, University of Pennsylvania (henceforth Fast Papers). These papers, acquired in 2010, have yet to be catalogued; thus there are no series, box, or folder numbers.

23. Paradoxically, as we shall see, this foreshadowed his post-1956 presence in the Soviet Union: "I not only was not but had never been." Howard Fast, *The Naked God: The Writer and the Communist Party* (New York: Praeger, 1957), 32.

24. *New York Times*, 12 March 1947. Two years later, members of the American Legion burned his books in a bonfire at Peekskill; see Fast, *Being Red: A Memoir* (Boston: Houghton Mifflin, 1990), 234.

25. Fast himself used the same rallying cry at a meeting in Boston on December 9, 1951. Speaking on "cultural freedom" under the auspices of the Progressive Party, he allegedly claimed that "thousands of his books had been burned in a burning of the books at some place in New York." Reported by "Confidential Informant T-51, of known reliability," FAST, Howard Melvin, File 100-HQ-327116, 1953 dossier, pp. 58–9, FOIPA No 1130357-000 (henceforth Fast FBI file). A Security Card Index was first activated on May 27, 1946; his FBI reference number throughout the 1,603 pages of his file remained NY 100-61206.

26. *New York Times*, 5–6 December 1947; *Daily Worker*, 17 December 1947.

27. *New York Herald Tribune*, 21 November 1950; the associate provost stated the ban "speaks for itself." The Yale University Political Union withdrew its invitation to Fast on altogether different grounds: simply that his appearance would cause "friction." *New York Times*, 13 February 1952; *Daily Worker*, 18 February 1952.

28. *New York Herald Tribune*, 11 December 1947; *World Telegram*, 11 December 1947; *New York Times*, 11–13 December.

29. *ALA Bulletin*, vol. 42, no. 9 (15 September 1948), 75, located in American Library Association Archives, Record Series 13/5/10, Box 5a, University Archives, University of Illinois at Urbana–Champaign. Some librarians had themselves been blacklisted; see Caute, *The Great Fear*, 454–55.

30. *Daily Worker*, 29 September 1947.

31. Fast, *Being Red*, 276. Curiously, he mentioned nothing of his literary plans for *Spartacus* in the many detailed letters he wrote to his wife, Bette (see Fast Papers).

32. Fast, *The Naked God*, 147.

33. He later wrote, "I was flushed with the gratification of having licked the hardest job I had ever undertaken as a writer and also produced something of worth." Ibid.

34. Little, Brown published *My Glorious Brothers* in 1948 and *The Proud and the Free* in 1950.

35. Copies of both the Little, Brown report and Angus Cameron's personal letter can be found in Kenneth Cameron Papers, TAM 186, Box 2, Folder 20, Tamiment Library, NYU. Much later, Cameron reflected, "I wasn't quite as enthusiastic over it as Howard thinks I was." Cited in Natalie Robins, *Alien Ink: The FBI's War on Freedom of Expression* (New York: Morrow, 1992), 242.

36. Fast FBI file, (updated) 1953 dossier, 83–85.

37. *Time*, 1 October 1951.

38. John Simon, interview with the author, New York, February 9, 2011. Simon was a protégé and then close friend of Cameron's until his death in November 2002. On April 8, 1952, Schlesinger debated Fast for two hours at Yale University on the status of the United States as a protector of cultural freedom. Fast FBI file. There was no love lost between the two: As early as 1946, Fast called Schlesinger "a hack historian" employed by Henry Luce's *Life* magazine for the ignoble "task of red-baiting." See Arthur Schlesinger Jr., "The U.S. Communist Party," *Life*, 29 July 1946; *Daily Worker*, 6 October 1946. For illumination of the strident and polemical nature of Schlesinger's Cold War activism, see Michael Wreszin, "Arthur Schlesinger, Jr., Scholar-Activist in Cold War America: 1946–1956," *Salmagundi* 63/64 (Spring/Summer 1984), 255–85. As we shall see, he was actively involved in opposing the Waldorf conference in 1949.

39. Notes of an interview between Angus Cameron and Ellen Schrecker, 30 December 1976 (henceforth Schrecker interview). According to John Simon, Cameron had "complicated" views about the Soviet Union but never took an active anti-Soviet position. Simon, interview with the author, 9 February 2011.

40. It became best-known for its *Red Channels: The Report of Communist Influence in Radio and Television* (New York: Counterattack, 1950). For its dossier on Howard Fast, see American Business Consultants, Inc. Counterattack: Research Files, TAM 148, Box 28, F 14–152, Tamiment Library, NYU.

41. *Counterattack*, no. 223, 31 August 1951.

42. Ibid., 6.

43. Schrecker interview, 30 December 1976.

44. Fast FBI file, Report SAC John J. Sullivan, 12 August 1955, 9. Herbert A. Philbrick also stated this to the same committee on May 8, 1953. By then Cameron himself had appeared before HUAC in Boston in May 1952. The adroit Cameron outfoxed the inquisitors by, at different times, switching between the First, Fifth, and Ninth amendments; "[I]t was scary . . . [but] I was determined to oppose the sons of bitches." Schrecker interview, 30 December 1976.

45. This had previously not been an issue even when, in 1950, he publicly spoke against the Korean War, although a friend believed that, in doing this, he "took a step too far." John Simon, interview with the author, 9 February 2011.

46. The above is drawn from Schrecker's second interview with Cameron, 5 April 1977; Simon interview, 9 February 2011; Robins interview, cited in *Alien Ink*, 242; *New York Compass*, 19 September 1951.

47. This ended in late 1959 when Alfred Knopf offered him a job as a senior editor. Before then he had formed Cameron and Kahn, then Cameron Associates, and had taken over the ailing Liberty Book Company. None of these ventures was financially successful. Their authors were mainly blacklisted writers, although one, Harvey Matusow, a former FBI agent, had been (like Budenz) a professional anticommunist witness who lied. Cameron published his controversial *False Witness* in 1955. For Cameron's account of the FBI's attempts to stop publication of *False Witness*, see Griffen Fariello, *Red Scare: Memories of the American Inquisition. An Oral History* (New York: Norton, 1995), 352–55; for Matusow's account, see ibid., 97–108; for a historian's account, see Robert M. Lichtman and Ronald D. Cohen, *Deadly Farce: Harvey Matusow and the Informer System in the McCarthy Era* (Urbana and Chicago: University of Illinois Press, 2004), chs. 8–9.

48. Salmen was himself "forced out" of Little, Brown in 1956. No reasons were given. Angus Cameron to Howard Fast, 17 August 1956, Carl Aldo Marzani Papers, TAM 154, Box 22, Folder 6, Tamiment Library, NYU (henceforth Marzani Papers).

49. In a letter to his friend at the *New York Post*, Max Lerner, who specifically asked him to list all the publishers who turned him down, "for the satisfaction of my mind," Fast wrote a three-page reply—"a full explanation"—detailing the sequence, the publisher, the editors with whom he had communicated, and their precise responses. He listed Macmillan, Random House, World Publishing Company, Viking, and Doubleday. Lerner to Fast, 13 March 1952; Fast to Lerner, 14 March 1952, Fast Papers. This is consistent with what he recalled in 1967 (Oral History Transcripts, 1 December 1967, Campenni Papers). However, in his 1990 autobiography, he added Harper; Scribner's; Knopf; Duell, Sloan & Pearce; and Simon & Schuster (he actually wrote to Lerner that "the foregoing explains why I did not give it to Jack [Goodman]" at Simon & Schuster). Fast, *Being Red*, 289–90. For some inexplicable reason, Macmillan, which he first contacted (not Viking, as claimed in *Being Red*) and whose letter from its vice president, J. Randall Williams, Fast quoted to Lerner (the original letter, dated 12 September 1951, is in Fast's papers), has been omitted. On Lerner, previously a columnist for *PM*, see William L. O'Neill, *A Better World. The Great Schism: Stalinism and the American Intellectuals* (New York: Simon & Schuster, 1983), 170–72.

50. Williams to Fast, 12 September 1951, Fast Papers. This highlights the difficulty of examining blacklisting in publishing compared with the more tangible, less elusive evidence of blacklisting in television or film or radio.

51. Fast to Lerner, 14 March 1952, Fast papers.

52. Ibid. Albert Maltz had similar experiences; see Maltz to Fast, 19 August 1955, Fast Papers.

53. Memorandum, SAC, Boston to Director, FBI, 29 December 1951. Once again, Fast claimed that the FBI was responsible. According to the informant's report to SA Richard Clancy on December 18, Fast stated that all the publishers

to which he sent *Spartacus* "first received it with enthusiasm but subsequently turned it down because the F.B.I. had intimidated the publishers to prevent the publication of this book." Once again, if his private letter to Max Lerner is a guide, Fast was being cavalier with the truth.

54. "A Book for Our Times," *Compass*, 6 January 1952; also reproduced in *National Guardian*, 9 January 1952 and *The Nation*, 19 January 1952. See also Fast, *Being Red*, 294–95.

55. *Compass*, 6 January 1952.

56. Cameron to Fast, 28 October 1951, Kenneth Cameron Papers, TAM 186, Box 2, Folder 20, Tamiment Library, NYU.

57. Personal letter to J. Edgar Hoover, 23 October 1951. The librarian, whose identity (and more) is redacted, enclosed Fast's letter to her/him and her/his reply to him, both dated October 23, 1951. The librarian hoped that an FBI agent from the Louisville office would "drop in to see me about the Fast pamphlets I have received." The same librarian also contacted Hoover ("You will probably want this for your Fast file") again on September 29, 1952. Fast FBI file.

58. *Compass*, 6 January 1952.

59. FBI Legal Attaché, American Embassy, London to Director, FBI, 3 September 1952, Fast FBI file.

60. In *Being Red* (298), Fast wrote that "the name arose from the caustic suggestion of a friend that I call it the Red Herring Press." In fact, it was named after the Blue Heron Inn, where a Jewish patriot, Haym Salomon, hid from his British pursuers during the American Revolution; see Howard Fast, *Haym Salomon: Son of Liberty* (New York: Messner, 1941).

61. He had bought the contractual rights, the plates, the dies, and the remaining stock for these and another ten of his books from Little, Brown (which acquired them from the original publisher, Duell, Sloan & Pearce) in 1952 for a bargain sum ($4,683), enabling, in his retrospective and probably erroneous view, to get Little, Brown "off the hook" and the FBI "out of their editorial chambers." *Seeing Red*, 298; correspondence Stanley Salmen (Little, Brown) to Fast, 12 March 1952; Fast to Salmen, 15 March 1952, Fast Papers.

62. In addition, the fact that it was Du Bois who presented Fast with his Peace Prize, that Fast was a close friend (until 1956) of Paul Robeson's, and that he spoke on radio about the "Negro" question in his 1952 congressional campaign all suggest the strength of his relationship with the African American Left.

63. Fast to Cameron, 18 June 1956, Box 22, Folder 6, Marzani Papers.

64. Kahn to Fast, 13 October 1952, Fast Papers.

65. Fast to Maltz, 20 September 1955, Fast Papers.

66. Oral History Transcripts, 1 December 1967, Box 8, Folder 11, Frank Campenni Papers, UWM MSS 213 University of Wisconsin–Milwaukee Archives, Milwaukee (henceforth Campenni Papers). When he wrote to Gertrude Heym (wife of East German writer Stefan), his tone became self-pitying: "My own pathetic attempts with the Blue Heron Press has left me triumphantly poor and

minus some 26 or 27,000 dollars . . . Liberty Book Club is the only thing we have managed to keep going." Fast to Heym, 14 December 1955, Fast Papers.

67. Fast, *Being Red*, 299.

68. Oral History Transcripts, 19 August 1974, 3, Box 9, Folder 1, Campenni Papers.

69. On his health problems, see correspondence, Albert Maltz to Fast, 13 April 1954, 15 September 1954, and 18 August 1955; Fast to Maltz, 20 September 1955, Fast Papers. On May 26, 1955, he told Steve Nelson, "My health is so bad that I don't dare leave for even a weekend." Steve Nelson Papers, ALBA 008, Box 1, Folder 48, Tamiment Library, NYU. His daughter (personal conversation, 28 April 2011) confirmed that Fast's recurring cluster headaches immobilized him, sometimes for days on end.

70. On the silence that greeted *The Proud and the Free*, see Joseph North, "Papers Try to Keep People from Reading Fast's Novel," *Daily Worker*, 19 October 1950, and Fast's consequent vitriolic letter, *Daily Worker*, 30 October 1950.

71. FBI Memorandum, M. A. Jones to Mr. Nichols, "Book Review, 'Clarkton' by Howard Fast," 21 November 1947, Fast FBI file. At the other end of the spectrum, see review in *Daily Worker*, 24 September 1947. Even the *New York Times* published a review, albeit critical, of *Clarkton*; see C. V. Terry, "Mr. Fast's Defense of the American Communist," *New York Times*, 28 September 1947.

72. Maltz to Fast, 7 May 1951, Fast Papers.

73. Maltz to Fast, 24 December 1951, Fast Papers.

74. The May 1956 issue (17–22) of *Masses & Mainstream* published an entire chapter from *Lola Gregg*. *Liberty Book Club News* (June 1956) also reviewed it.

75. Fast to Angus Cameron, 24 May 1956, Box 22, Folder 6, Marzani Papers.

76. *Daily Worker*, 2 March 1953.

77. David F. Krugler, *The Voice of America and the Domestic Propaganda Battles, 1945–1953* (Columbia: University of Missouri Press, 2000), 185.

78. Willard Edwards, "Uncover Plot in 'Voice' to sabotage U.S.," *Chicago Daily Tribune*, 13 February 1953.

79. *Seeing Red*, 8–15.

80. This suggests greater sophistication in the understanding of the value of Fast's anticommunist propaganda, closer to the approaches of the Information Research Department in the UK. McCarthy, the fundamentalist, would not have seen this. There are therefore uneven dimensions in the "geography of the blacklist."

81. *New York Times*, 22 February 1953. This directive was rescinded on February 18 by the Secretary of State, John Foster Dulles, after it was "brought to his attention" by the McCarthy committee. *Christian Science Monitor*, 19 February 1953.

82. Unless otherwise stated, the following is drawn from Senate Committee on Government Operations, *Hearings before the Permanent Subcommittee on Investigations of the Committee on Government Operations*, 83rd Congress, 1st session, 19 February 1953, Part 2, 96–112, U.S. Government Printing Office, Washington,

1953. Fast also appeared before an executive (closed) session on February 13, but the hearing was desultory; see *Executive Sessions of the Senate before the Permanent Subcommittee on Investigations of the Committee on Government Operations*, 83rd Congress, 1st session, 13 February 1953, Part 1, 484–98.

83. He had been subpoenaed on February 12, along with approximately 100 of the 1,500 VOA employees. The subpoenas were delivered en masse at the VOA headquarters at 57th Street and Broadway. Fast's was hand delivered at 9:00 A.M.; a copy is in MSS 213, Box 7, Folder 6, UWM Archives.

84. This is confirmed by television footage of the hearing. Fast's daughter clearly remembered watching "Father on our first television set, ridicule, sneer at, shame Joseph McCarthy before his Senate subcommittee. Father's eloquence, his nerve awed me." Rachel Ben-Avi Fast, "A Memoir," in Judy Kaplan and Linn Shapiro (eds.), *Red Diapers: Growing Up in the Communist Left* (Urbana and Chicago: University of Illinois Press, 1998), 131.

85. It was this exchange that was given prominence in the press; see *New York Herald Tribune*, 19 February 1953; *New York Daily News*, 19 February 1953 (its article was headlined "Asked if He's a Commie, Fast Won't Tell Probers"); *Washington Post*, 19 February 1953. Potter later chaired a Senate subcommittee investigating alleged communist atrocities in Korea.

86. "Fast's testimony represented no new or unverified pertinent information which requires further investigation at this time." Internal FBI Memorandum, A. H. Belmont to D. M. Ladd, 6 July 1953, Fast FBI file.

87. The American High Commissioner in Germany and former president of Harvard University, James B. Conant, mildly rebuked the State Department in Washington in a cryptic cable: "Please define etcetera." *Washington Post*, 14 June 1953.

88. *New York Times*, 4,11 June 1953.

89. A partial list of titles, including six of Fast's books, was published in the *New York Times*, 22 June 1953.

90. Eisenhower stated: "Don't join the book burners. . . . Don't be afraid to go in your library and read every book, as long as that document does not offend our own ideas of decency. That should be the only censorship. How will we defeat communism unless we know what it is, and what it teaches . . . ?" *New York Times*, 15 June 1953. On the same day, coincidentally, the columnists Joseph and Stewart Alsop went much further, courageously referring to this "book-burning program undertaken in craven fear of Senator Joseph R. McCarthy" as an example of "cowardly knuckling-under to the political yahoos." *Washington Post*, 14 June 1953.

91. Cable, 14 December 1953, Fast FBI file. A memorandum dated November 3, 1954, refers to "attached excerpts" from the transcripts of interviews with returned American POWs from Korea. These excerpts, which may have confirmed Abbott's allegation, given they were in Fast's file, were not released under the FOIA.

92. Fast, *Being Red*, 174.

93. Fast to Maltz, 20 September 1955, Fast Papers.

94. For the transcripts (each twelve pages in length) of two of his wireless programs in September and October 1948, see Box 7, Folder 3, Campenni Papers.

95. He was reduced to writing an "open letter to the American people" in a magazine published in Moscow, *Literaturnaya Gazeta*, because "the pages of the American press have been completely closed to him." *Washington Evening Star*, 7 July 1948. It can be assumed that very few of "the American people" subscribed to *Literaturnaya Gazeta*.

96. See *New York Times*, 8 November 1950; *Daily Worker*, 11 November 1950, 6 April 1951, 4 February 1952, 22 June 1955.

97. Fast gives a full account of this trip in *Seeing Red*, 207–21. For a contrasting account, see *Washington Times Herald*, 20 April 1949; its headline, "Stalin's Favorite U.S. Author Rolls in Ease to Pinko Gabfest," suggests its tenor.

98. At least he could attend the premiere of his work *The Hammer* on September 8, 1951; he had emerged from jail, twenty-eight pounds lighter, only a week before.

99. *Daily Worker*, 27 December 1953. Fast was presented the prize by W. E. B. Du Bois on April 22, 1954, at New York's McAlpin Hotel. Bette and Rachel Fast were pictured on the platform (*Daily Worker*, 9 May 1954). Also present was Paul Robeson, also denied a passport and to whom Fast had presented the same prize on September 23, 1953 (*New York Times*, 24 September 1953, 38). Robeson and Fast were the only two Americans to receive this prize.

100. *New York Times*, 9 September 1952. By 1952, the controlling force within the American Labor Party was the Communist Party.

101. So did the Communist Party, if the report of confidential informant T-16, "of known reliability," is to be believed. 1952 Dossier, 13, Fast FBI file. The decisive defeat of ALP Congressman Vito Marcantonio in 1950 should have held a salutary lesson; it didn't. Nor did Henry Wallace's disastrous presidential run in 1948, for which Fast (as a member of "Writers for Wallace") campaigned actively.

102. Radio Broadcast, Agreement and Transcripts, Box 7, Folder 3, Campenni Papers. All scripts had to be submitted to WMCC prior to broadcast time; the cost of this airtime was $1,280.

103. See Fast, *Being Red*, 305–13. For example, he campaigned 3 hours per night and 10 hours on Saturdays on a sound truck (see photo between pages 184 and 185). He spoke at 125 election rallies, 85 of which were street meetings (*Daily Worker*, 3 November 1952). He often took his daughter with him on the sound truck; she "was always frightened." Ben-Avi Fast, "A Memoir," 132.

104. Fast to Maltz, 28 October 1952, Fast Papers.

105. Oral History Transcripts, 1 December 1967, 5, Box 3, Folder 11, 5, Campenni Papers.

106. Indicative is the folder in the Fast Papers containing correspondence to and from the Civil Rights Congress regarding Fast's speaking engagements on

its behalf. All these activities were dutifully recorded by the FBI. For example, five separate informants reported that until 1955, Fast was active in "23 front groups." Summary Report, SA John J. Sullivan, New York, 25 April 1956, 2. It is little wonder that his file was so thick and that it cost an estimated $10 million to compile; Andrew Macdonald, *Howard Fast: A Critical Companion* (Westport, Conn.: Greenwood Press, 1996), 21.

107. Maltz to Fast, 24 April 1951, 17 July 1951, 11 September 1952, Fast Papers. Maltz had long forgiven Fast for his disgraceful role in the party's brutal denunciation of Maltz in 1946. Maltz had called for greater artistic latitude for communist writers; exemplifying cultural Stalinism, Fast called him "the formal apostle of literary liquidation . . . of all creative writing." Fast, *The Naked God*, 110. For accounts of the "Maltz Affair," see Daniel Aaron, *Writers on the Left: Episodes in American Literary Communism* (New York: Harcourt, Brace & World, 1961), 386–90; Jack Salzman, *Albert Maltz* (Boston: Twayne, 1978), 90–95.

108. Howard Fast, *Literature and Reality* (New York: International Publishers, 1950), 91, 98.

109. Brown, *Soviet Attitudes*, 287. It was published, in abridged form, in the Soviet magazine *Novy Mir*, no. 12, 1951 (reported in the *Daily Worker*, 29 January 1951, 11). See also the long, laudatory reviews in *Masses & Mainstream*, March 1950, 76–79, although, as Daniel Aaron (*Writers on the Left*, 390) noted, "only its readers know of the Left Wing books it reviews, books published by obscure firms and unjustly ignored by the bourgeois press."

110. In later years Fast himself regretted writing the book: It was "not an act of sensible criticism. It was a reaction . . . to the literary establishment which never lifted its voice to protest. . . . [It] was directed much too much against the establishment." Oral History Transcripts, 1 December 1967, 5, Box 3, Folder 11, Campenni Papers. There is no mention of the book in his memoirs, and it was quietly dropped from flyleaf lists of previous books published by the author.

111. His old friend Albert Maltz was bluntly critical ("I have too much admiration for the body of your work to go in for polite deception") of *Lola Gregg*, which, he wrote, lacked depth, passion, and reflection. Maltz to Fast, 30 July 1956, Fast Papers.

112. Oral History Transcripts, 15 April 1968, Box 8, Folder 13, Campenni Papers. He also said they lacked the "repose, reflection and thoughtfulness" that a good book required. Ibid., 1 December 1967, 5, Box 3, Folder 11.

113. Fast, *Literature and Reality*, 57.

114. Oral History Transcripts, 15 April 1968, 12, Box 8, Folder 13, Campenni Papers. This was preceded by a protracted debate over "progressive Jewish consciousness"; this became the "Fast Controversy" after *Jewish Life* published *An Epitaph for Sidney* in January 1947. See Morris Schappes Papers, TAM 179, Box 25, Folder 19, Tamiment Library, NYU.

115. Fast, *The Naked God*, 22. He also claimed (99) that charges of expulsion were brought against him twelve times. According to Fast, one bone of

contention, separate from his writing, was his devotion to the peace issue. "I was one of the people who started, founded and developed the American peace movement, and this was in antagonism to the main thinking of the Communist Party.... I was opposed by the entire leadership in the Party; they all disagreed with me." Oral History Transcripts, 16 April 1968, 12, Box 8, Folder 14, Campenni Papers.

116. This incident, indicative of the depth of humiliation, occupied five pages in Fast's memoir (*Being Red*, 270–74).

117. Bette to Howard, 23 August 1950, Fast Papers. The FBI was also aware of his "renewal of activity"; Memorandum, SAC, New York, to Director, FBI, 13 September 1950, Fast FBI file. Correspondingly, his Security Card Index was reinstituted.

118. Fast, *Being Red*, 303.

119. Howard to Bette, 8 June 1950, Fast Papers. Fast's FBI file contains numerous informants' reports of their marital difficulties; see, for example Memorandum, SAC NY to Director, FBI, 25 May 1949; Report, SA John W. Dooley, New York, 20 March 1953; Report, SA John E. Clark, New York, 5 November 1953. Fast's daughter recalled that, in this period, "my parents drank too much, fought a good deal." Ben-Avi Fast, "A Memoir," 129.

120. Maltz to Fast, 19 January 1956, Fast Papers.

121. Decoded cablegrams, Mexico City to State Department, 9,11 June 1954; Legation, Mexico to Director, FBI, 21 July 1954. According to Fast's memoir (*Being Red*, 329–41), the sojourn in Mexico was to seek temporary refuge from FBI harassment and the "unceasing witch hunt." According to his daughter, Dr. Amann was treating his cluster headaches. Personal conversation with Rachel Ben-Avi, 28 April 2011.

122. Legation, Mexico to Director, FBI, 21 July 1954.

123. Maltz to Fast, 19 January 1956, Fast Papers. Already he had written no fewer than 115 feature articles for the paper ("Confidential" Report, J. J. Sullivan, 4 April 1956, 2, Fast FBI File).

124. Fast, *The Naked God*, 115. Similarly, "denying a man the right to continue in a creative effort he has spent his life to perfect is an awful thing." Fast, *Being Red*, 344–45.

125. It is probable Fast was already broadly aware: Johnny Gates (*Daily Worker* editor, with whom Fast was friendly) attended the party's National Committee meeting in New York on April 28–May 1, at which Khrushchev's speech was read.

126. *New York Times*, 1 February 1957. The article was written by Harry Schwartz, whose criticisms of the Soviet Union Fast had previously attacked; see *Daily Worker*, 24 June 1956.

127. Fast, *The Naked God*; Fast, *Being Red*.

128. James R. Barrett, *William Z. Foster and the Tragedy of American Radicalism* (Urbana: University of Illinois Press, 1999), 267; David Shannon, *The Decline of*

American Communism: A History of the Communist Party of the United States since 1945 (New York: Harcourt, Brace, 1959), 354–60.

129. Caute, *The Great Fear*, 114.

130. Zhores A. Medvedev and Roy A. Medvedev, *The Unknown Stalin* (London: J. B. Tauris, 2006), 98.

131. "Leaving the Party," 3, Steve Nelson Papers, ALBA 008, Box 9, Folder 4, Tamiment Library, New York University (henceforth Tamiment); Steve Nelson, James R. Barrett, and Rob Ruck, *Steve Nelson: American Radical* (Pittsburgh: University of Pittsburgh Press, 1981), 387.

132. Dorothy Healey and Maurice Isserman, *Dorothy Healey Remembers* (New York: Oxford University Press, 1990), 152, 154.

133. George Charney, *A Long Journey* (Chicago: Quadrangle, 1968), 270.

134. Peggy Dennis, *The Autobiography of an American Communist: A Personal View of a Political Life, 1925–1975* (Westport, Conn.: L. Hill, 1977), 225.

135. Al Richmond, *A Long View from the Left: Memoirs of an American Revolutionary* (Boston: Houghton Mifflin, 1973), 369.

136. Generally they (and Fast) fitted Shannon's description of those who left the party in 1956–57: In contrast with Foster (born 1881), they were "younger people . . . whose contacts with non-Communists had been wide, and . . . [inhabited] the mainstream of American culture." Shannon, *Decline*, 319.

137. *Daily Worker*, 5 June 1956; the headline, stretched across two pages, read "Stalin's Repressions Spelled Out in Khrushchev Speech Made Public Here." The paper printed a condensed version of 4,000 words.

138. *Daily Worker*, 5 June 1956.

139. John Gates, *The Story of an American Communist* (New York: Nelson, 1958), 161.

140. He previously wrote a column, "As I Please," which belies its adherence to the party line. According to Fast's FBI file, the number of feature articles he wrote for the *Daily Worker* up until March 1, 1956, amounted to 115.

141. *Daily Worker*, 17 May 1956.

142. Barsky to Fast, 14 May 1956, Fast Papers.

143. Howard Fast, "My Decision," *Masses & Mainstream* 10:3 (March 1957), 32. A condensed version of this twelve-page article in this left-wing literary magazine was published in *I. F. Stone's Weekly*, 25 March 1957, 2. It was also cited extensively by the *New York Times*, 7 March 1957, and, critically, by the Trotskyist *Militant*, 21:15 (15 April 1957), 3–4 ("Where Howard Fast Goes Astray on Stalinism").

144. Fast, *Naked God*, 39.

145. *Daily Worker*, 12 June 1956. The column was widely cited in the mainstream press; one report, captioned "Fast is Loose," noted—correctly—that this was published only because the *Daily Worker* was under the control of a faction within the CPUSA (John Gates, Alan Max, Joe Clark) that drew inspiration not from Moscow but from Warsaw (where the Polish communist leader Władysław Gomułka was pursuing his Polish road to socialism in the face of

Soviet opposition). *Washington Post*, 5 February 1957, 20. After Fast formally left the party in early 1957, the *Daily Worker*, in sharp contrast, as we shall see, to the Soviet press and orthodox CPUSA leaders, refrained from labeling him a "traitor" or "renegade" or "deserter under fire." See, for example, A. B. Magill, "He Affirms Socialist Beliefs But Severs Communist Ties," *Daily Worker*, 10 March 1957, 4.

146. Magill, "He Affirms Socialist Beliefs," 16 June 1956, 4. In a similar vein, Charney recounts that he was present at a meeting in 1956 when "I heard charges made, first by Ben Davis, that had we had state power we would, like Stalin, have executed dissident comrades." Charney, *Long Journey*, 270. The African American Benjamin J. Davis, a close ally of Foster and a member of the New York City Council for Harlem until jailed in the "second string" Smith Act prosecutions in 1951, told a meeting in 1949 that he "would rather be a lamppost in Moscow than president of the United States." Cited in Gates, *Story of an American Communist*, 165.

147. Cited in Robins, *Alien Ink*, 236.

148. Michael Walzer, "The Travail of the U.S. Communists," *Dissent* 3:4 (Fall 1956), 407.

149. The Fast family relocated to Teaneck both for family reasons and in the hope that the move might help Fast's health. Since his imprisonment in 1950, he suffered from crippling cluster headaches. They were still afflicting him badly in 1956; see Fast to Albert Maltz, 7 February 1956, Fast Papers.

150. Personal conversation with Fast's daughter, Rachel Ben-Avi, New York City, 28 April 2011.

151. Gates, *Story of an American Communist*, 169.

152. Confidential Report, John J. Sullivan, New York Office, 26 October 1956, 2, Fast FBI file.

153. Shannon, *Decline*, 283.

154. *New York Times*, 19 January 1957. The Ukrainian-born Steuben was the author of *Strike Strategy* (New York: Gaer Associates, 1950) and editor of *March of Labor* (1950–54). The reporter referred to his "acute" "spiritual pain."

155. Marzani was an Italian American communist and union organizer, imprisoned from 1949 to 1951, editor of a union paper until 1954, and then, with Angus Cameron (another close friend of Fast's), ran the Liberty Book Club (established 1948), of which Fast was a director until 1955.

156. Edith Marzani to Howard Fast, 3 February 1957, Fast Papers. Harry Schwartz was the Soviet specialist for the *New York Times* who broke the story of Fast's departure from the CPUSA.

157. Private letter, Howard Fast to Mr. Marcus, 8 July 1957, Box 54.5, Folder 3, Fales Manuscript Collection, MSS 001, Fales Library, NYU.

158. Irving Abella, "Portrait of a Jewish Professional Revolutionary: The Recollections of Joshua Gershman," *Labour / Le Travail: Journal of Canadian Labour Studies* 2 (1977), 204. For his defense of Israel, see Fast, "My Decision," 32–33.

159. Oral History Transcripts, 15 April 1968, 12, Box 8, Folder 13, Campenni Papers.

160. There is a parallel between Fast and the British intellectual Hyman Levy, who made unyielding allegations of Soviet anti-Semitism throughout 1956 and 1957 and published *Jews and the National Question* in 1957. Levy was expelled in April 1958 after twenty-six years in the British Communist Party.

161. Eight years later Novick angrily accused Fast of misrepresenting Fadeyev's fabricated statement concerning the Jewish poet Itzik Feffer in an interview with the conservative New York Jewish daily, *Forward*, published 3 August 1957. ("You were present . . . why didn't you tell this story . . . ?") Paul Novick to Fast, 30 August 1957, 1–3. Fast Papers.

162. Fast, *Being Red*, 206–7, 218–19.

163. "Review and Reappraisal," *Jewish Life*, June 1956, 3–7. New York Jewish communists, who published *Jewish Life*, also published the daily Yiddish paper *Morgn-frayhayt*, which had started reporting on the destruction of Jewish cultural institutions in the Soviet Union. See Gennady Estraikh, "Metamorphoses of Morgn-frayhayt," in Gennady Estraikh and Mikhail Krutikov (eds.), *Yiddish and the Left* (Oxford: European Humanities Research Centre, 2001), 150.

164. Shannon, *Decline*, 284.

165. Gates, *Story of an American Communist*, 163. It was this that prompted party leader Eugene Dennis to comment ("Sorrow and Perspective") on anti-Semitism in the Soviet Union; see *Daily Worker*, 16 April 1956.

166. *I. F. Stone's Weekly*, 11 February 1957.

167. Martin Duberman, *Paul Robeson: A Biography* (New York: Knopf, 1988), 352–54. By then, he had already been charged with treason. In a bugged hotel room he gestured to Robeson that there was little hope and dramatically drew his finger across his throat.

168. Feffer was executed on August 12, 1952, seven months before Stalin's death.

169. Fast, *Naked God*, 128–29; Fast, *Being Red*, 330.

170. Republished in the *New York Times Magazine*, 9 June 1957.

171. From eastern Europe, a group of diplomats, "shaken as they were," gave him further information "even more monstrous" than Khrushchev's original revelations. *New York Times*, 26 August 1957; *New York Post*, 26 August 1957. Fast refused to identify these "diplomats," in whose identity the FBI took a keen interest; see Memorandum, L. B. Nichols to Mr. Tolson, 27 August 1956, Fast FBI File.

172. Fast to Heym, 24 October 1956, Fast Papers.

173. Heym to Fast, 24 November 1956, Fast Papers.

174. Comment by Todd Gitlin in *Arguing the World* (New York, 1997), a documentary film on Howe and New York intellectuals (dir. Joseph Dorman).

175. Jeremy Larner, "Remembering Irving Howe," *Dissent* 40 (Fall 1993), 540; Irving Howe, *A Margin of Hope: An Intellectual Autobiography* (San Diego: Harcourt

Brace Jovanovich, 1982), 188; John Rodden and Ethan Goffman (eds.), *Politics and the Intellectual: Conversations with Irving Howe* (West Lafayette, Ind.: Purdue University Press, 2010), 182–83 (Irving Howe, interview with Todd Gitlin, April 1985).

176. According to the *New York Daily News*, 25 August 1957, 27, it was "actually" during the Budapest uprising that Fast resigned, which, if true, makes his willingness to debate Howe soon after even more incomprehensible.

177. Four months later, Fast would write that dissident Russian writers "would have either been disgraced, jailed or even put to death." Cited in *Commonweal* 65 (22 March 1957), 629.

178. The wording was simple and unambiguous: "Howard Fast, the novelist, who is no longer a member of the party. . . ." *Fortune*, January 1957, 238.

179. This chain of events is detailed in Howard Fast, "The Writer and the Commissar," *Prospectus* 1:1 (1957), 32.

180. The communist writer Mike Gold (see Richmond, *Long View*, 382) implied that Fast consciously chose Schwartz and the *New York Times*—"I find something repulsive about such a choice"—when he could have announced his resignation in a left-wing paper; *The Worker* (the weekend edition of the *Daily Worker*), 18 August 1957. This view was echoed by some rank-and-file members; see letters published in the *Daily Worker*, 5 February 1957, 11 February 1957, 14 February 1957, 21 February 1957. Typical was the comment from "A.S." that Fast "knows very well (or should know) that turning to the New York Times, one of the chief spokesmen [*sic*] of capitalist power and reaction, is not going to provide him with the balm his wounds need." For an attack on the *New York Times* (but not Fast) by the managing editor of the *Daily Worker*, see Alan Max, "Howard Fast and the N.Y. Times," *Daily Worker*, 12 June 1957.

181. It was published, with a foreword by Salisbury, under the byline "Writers in the Shadow of Communism" in the *New York Times Magazine*, 9 June 1957, 10.

182. This appeared in the non-communist Jewish daily paper *Forward*, 3 August 1957.

183. *Daily Worker*, 21, 28 April 1957, which in turned provoked a series of letters in the weekend *Worker*, 31 March 1957; *Hartford Times*, 24, 26 September 1957.

184. Oral History Transcripts, 19 August 1974, 4, Box 9, Folder 1, Campenni Papers. Milovan Djilas, *The New Class: An Analysis of the Communist System* (New York: Praeger, 1957).

185. *New York World Telegram*, 21 November 1957.

186. Upton Sinclair to Fast, 22 September 1957, Fast Papers.

187. Wolfe to Fast, 30 September 1957, Fast Papers. Praeger had just published Wolfe's *Khrushchev and Stalin's Ghost: Text, Background and Meaning of Khrushchev's Secret Report to the Twentieth Congress, 1956*. Wolfe's political trajectory, from communist to anticommunist via Trotskyism, was not dissimilar from that of Eugene Lyons and those of a host of other Cold War anti-Stalinists who grouped around *The New Leader*.

188. Letter, "L.A.C.," *Daily Worker*, 11 February 1957.

189. Unnamed Los Angeles worker, cited in *Daily Worker*, 18 August 1957.

190. Edward Johanningsmeier, *Forging American Communism: The Life of William Z. Foster* (Princeton, N.J.: Princeton University Press, 1994), 347–66.

191. Healey and Isserman, *Dorothy Healey Remembers*, 164.

192. Walzer, "Travail of U.S. Communists," 407.

193. Mac G. (surname indecipherable) to Fast, 1 February 1957, Box 1, Folder 1, Campenni Papers. Despite disagreeing with Fast's decision, he hoped to continue their friendship.

194. Gates, *Story of an American Communist*, 169.

195. William Z. Foster, "Howard Fast's Call to Surrender," *Daily Worker*, 17 June 1957.

196. Alfred Greenberg to Fast, 10 April 1957, Fast Papers. Eastman (1883–1969) was an early member of the CPUSA; a close friend of John Reed, editor of *The Masses*; and a visitor to the Soviet Union. In the 1930s he embraced Trotskyism but by the 1950s had become a pronounced anticommunist and, initially, a supporter of Joe McCarthy.

197. Joseph Freeman to Daniel Aaron, 16 June 1958, in Alan Wald, *Exiles from a Future Time: The Forging of the Mid-Twentieth-Century Literary Left* (Chapel Hill: University of North Carolina Press, 2002), 187. On Freeman, see Aaron, *Writers on the Left*, 68–72.

198. V. J. Jerome, "A Letter to Howard Fast," *Political Affairs*, 39:1 (January 1959), 60.

199. Letter (undated, March 1957), Jim Jackson to Milton Howard, James Jackson Papers, TAM 347, Box 17, Folder 21, Tamiment. There was only silence from another African American, Paul Robeson, to whom Fast had been very close; see letter, Robeson to Fast, 14 November 1955, Fast Papers.

200. Alfred Greenberg to Fast, 10,22 April 1957, Fast Papers.

201. Howard Fast, "My Decision," *Masses & Mainstream* 10:3 (March 1957), 31.

202. Memorandum, COINTELPRO to Director, FBI and SAC, New York, 2 April 1957. Neither this memo nor the two memoranda approving the operation appear in Fast's FBI file. COINTELPRO closed in 1971 after more than 2,000 operations.

203. Djagalov, "I Don't Boast About It," 49. Emphasis in original. Or, as *The New Leader* (12 February 1951) put it, "From Bratislava to Pyongyang his name is a banner and a byword."

204. Fast, *Being Red*, 356.

205. He was awarded it in 1953, but a passport ban prevented his visit to the Soviet Union to collect it. It was finally presented to him by W. E. B. Du Bois in New York in April 1954 (*Daily Worker*, 9 May 1954). In 1958 the Internal Revenue Service attempted to extract income tax from Fast on this $25,000. *New York Post*, 30 October 1958, M6.

206. After he defected, these were never transferred. *New York Times*, 14 October 1957, 8; *New York Post*, 3 December 1957, 40. He collected only 5 percent of his Soviet royalties.

207. Brown, *Soviet Attitudes*, 295. Brown also commented that, as a writer, Fast "was not worthy of the extreme praise which Soviet critics heaped upon him." Ibid.

208. Fast, *Naked God*, 32.

209. Translation of article, 24 August 1957, Box 1, Folder 9, Campenni Papers. For Fast's reply (he likened his Soviet detractors to "petulant children"), see *New York World Telegram*, 26 August 1957; *Daily Worker*, 26 August 1957; *Washington Post*, 27 August 1957.

210. This was reported by the same "yellow" Schwartz, *New York Times*, 31 January 1957.

211. Translation of article, 30 January 1958, 1–22, Box 6, Folder 8, Campenni Papers.

212. Fast hit back the next day at the "maniacal castigation" of him by "this most ominous document," which contained a "disgraceful display of bad taste and hooliganlike obscenity." *New York Times*, 1 February 1958, 4. In contrast, see the marvelously measured open letter to *Literaturnaya Gazeta* by Dorothy Thompson, president of the U.S. branch of the International PEN Club: "Who made Mr. Fast . . . You did." *Washington Star*, 10 February 1958, 13.

213. Arthur Koestler's seminal recantation of communism. The title (and the themes) of his famous 1945 essay "The Yogi and the Commissar" may have influenced Fast's "The Writer and the Commissar." Coincidentally, like Fast's *Spartacus*, Koestler's first novel, *The Gladiators* (1939), was also about the Spartacus slave revolt in Rome.

214. Richard Crossman, ed., *The God That Failed: Six Studies in Communism* (London: Hamilton, 1949).

215. Alan Wald and Alan Filreis, "A Conversation with Howard Fast, March 23, 1994," *Prospects: An Annual of American Cultural Studies* 20 (1995), 511, 512, 516.

216. Hershel D. Meyer, *History and Conscience: The Case of Howard Fast* (New York: Anvil-Atlas, 1958), 43.

217. George Sokolsky, *Washington Post*, 22 April 1958 (he also added: "an enormously significant book . . . a better analysis of inside the party techniques than I have yet seen"). *The Naked God* received an astonishing number of reviews in both the daily press and weekly magazines. For the former see, for example, *New York Times*, 1 December 1957 (Harry Schwartz was ambivalent about the book but claimed Fast's defection was "one of the biggest propaganda defeats Moscow received in 1957"), and *Christian Science Monitor*, 5 December 1957. For the latter, see Arthur Schlesinger Jr.'s generally favorable "Life with an Illusion," *The Saturday Review*, 21 December 1957, 17, 43, and Irving Howe's highly critical "A Captive Not Quite Freed," *The New Republic*, 16 December 1957, 18–19. When

the book was published in England (by Bodley Head) in mid-1958, it was also extensively reviewed.

218. A rare copy is located in the Tamiment Library, NYU. It was the brainchild of, and bankrolled by, Gabriel Gladstone, a highly successful New York investment banker and son of a Yiddish poet and writer, Jacob Glatstein; see *New York Times*, 30 August 1957.

219. Fast, "On Leaving the Communist Party," *The Saturday Review*, 16 November 1957, 15–17, 57–58.

220. "Transcript," 29 August 1957, Fast Papers.

221. "Transcript of NBC interview," 13 October 1957, Fast Papers. The transcript of this lengthy interview was also reproduced in *Progressive* 22 (March 1958), 35–38.

222. Bruce L. Melvin to Fast, 18 October 1957, Fast Papers.

223. However, George Sokolsky hoped that "now that Fast has overthrown Marx, he may, in time, and after considerable struggle, come around to God," *New York Journal-American*, 16 May 1957. Similarly, Mary Hornaday believed that Fast's confession would be the forerunner of "absolution and penance." *Christian Science Monitor*, 20 June 1956.

224. *New York Times*, 1 February 1957.

225. Memoranda, SAC, New York to Director, FBI, 22 March 1957, 2 April 1957, Fast FBI file. The FBI was also concerned that as a writer, Fast could "turn a contact with him by the FBI into an embarrassing situation." However, a marginal handwritten comment signed by "J. Edgar" recommended that "we should follow this and reconsider" if the situation changed. The FBI had a long wait. In an interview in 1959, Fast remarked that the concept of the professional anticommunist was "terrible." *New York Post*, 6 September 1959.

226. Cited in Louis Budenz, "The Reds—What Now?," *Catholic News*, 11 May 1957. In an irregular practice, the identical article was published on the same day but, ostensibly, written by his wife; see Margaret Budenz, "The Reds—What Now?," *Tablet* (Brooklyn, N.Y.), 11 May 1957.

227. *Daily Worker*, 8 December 1957. See Shields' autobiographical *On the Battle Lines, 1919–1939* (New York: International Publishers, 1986). Shields concluded his letter with: "it is sad to think that the author of 'Peekskill' has come to this." Like its counterpart Radio Free Europe, Radio Liberation (which targeted only the Soviet Union, not the satellite countries) was funded by the CIA.

228. *New York World Telegram & Sun*, 16 November 1957. Fast knew one of those imprisoned, Tibor Dery, who was then a contender for the Nobel Prize in literature.

229. *New York Herald Tribune*, 1 November 1958. *Doctor Zhivago* was banned in the Soviet Union but was a bestseller in the West. For an outline of the "Pasternak drama," see *Publishers Weekly*, 10 November 1958, 29–30.

230. Copy of Western Union telegram, Fast to Pasternak, 25 October 1958, Box 6, Folder 8, Campenni Papers. What Fast did not know was that Olga Ivin-

skaya, Pasternak's mistress and muse (and on whom Lara was modeled), was in this same period informing on him to the KGB. *New York Times*, 27 November 1997.

231. Vivian Gornick, *The Romance of American Communism* (New York: Basic Books, 1977), 13.

232. Oral History Transcripts, 1 December 1967, 6, Box 8, Folder 11, Campenni Papers.

233. Memoranda SAC, New York to Director, FBI, 13 April, 24 April 1957, Fast FBI file.

234. Fast's daughter wrote: "His is the only death I remember celebrating." Ben-Avi Fast, "A Memoir," 133.

235. *New York Times*, 27 December 1957. The film, on which Fast was contracted to collaborate, was never completed. Instead, Kramer made the star-studded, award-winning, post-apocalyptic drama (set in Melbourne, Australia) *On the Beach*. Fast was adamant that he wrote the bulk of the screenplay but that Dalton Trumbo (one of the "Hollywood Ten") refused to share any of the credit and is still, now, wrongly credited as the screenwriter. Oral History Transcripts, 1977 (no precise date given), 4–5, Box 9, Folder 2, Campenni Papers.

236. *New York Times*, 4 November 1958.

237. "Author Interview—Howard Fast," *The Library* 1:1 (October 1973), 6; J. Hoberman, *The Dream Life: Movies, Media, and the Mythology of the Sixties* (New York: New Press, 2003), 36.

3. The Professors: Bradley and Burgum

1. Telegram, Madden to Bradley, 16 April 1951, Records of the Lyman R. Bradley Academic Freedom Case 1947–1961, RG 19.2 (henceforth Bradley Papers), Box 3, Folder 4, New York University Archives.

2. Telegram, Heald to Burgum, 13 October 1952, Records of the Edwin Berry Burgum Academic Freedom Case, 1934–1961, RG 19 (henceforth Burgum Papers), New York University Archives, Box 3, Folder 2. News of his suspension was carried the next day in the *Daily Compass*, the *New York Times*, and the *New York Herald Tribune*.

3. See Ellen Schrecker, *No Ivory Tower: McCarthyism and the Universities* (New York: Oxford University Press, 1986).

4. Born on October 20, 1898, in Spencer, near Ithaca, New York, Bradley served briefly in World War I and was educated at the Hartford Public High School (Connecticut), Harvard University (A.B., 1921; M.A., 1922), and NYU (Ph.D., 1930).

5. The MLA was not entirely venerable. One of its executive members was also an FBI informant. He advised the FBI that Bradley, whom he had known for more than twenty years, was "leftist" in his views but "very well regarded as a teacher and as a research man." FBI report, New York (100-69110), 3 March

1945, Federal Bureau of Investigation, Department of Justice, Headquarters Files 100-HQ-340005 and 100-HQ-260819, FOIPA No. 115281-000 (henceforth FBI Bradley files).

6. Judging from the attendees at executive board meetings, Bradley was not an especially active member. Until a special meeting on February 11, 1946, he had attended only one meeting since 1944. See JAFRC Minutes, Charlotte Todes Stern Papers, Collection 70, Box 2, Folder 1, Tamiment Library and Robert Wagner Archives, New York University (henceforth Stern Papers).

7. *New York Times*, 20 December 1945; "Proceeding Against Dr. Edward K. Barsky and Others," HUAC, 79th Congress, 2nd Session, Report No. 1829, 28 March 1946, 1.

8. [Lyman Bradley], *Professor Bradley States His Case*, 3 (undated pamphlet, Bradley Papers, Box 2, Folder 14). An exception was Professor Harlow Shapley, who organized the Waldorf conference in March 1949, but he was at Harvard, not NYU. He wrote that "the disciplining of a heroic, gentle and highly altruistic professor is simply a disgrace." *In Fact*, 17 November 1947, cited in *The Evening News*, 24 November 1947, in Bradley Papers, Box 2, Folder 14. See also his similarly heartfelt letter to Chancellor Chase, 18 August 1847, in Bradley Papers, Box 2, Folder 11. For FBI surveillance of Shapley, see Peter L. Steinberg, *The Great "Red Menace": United States Prosecution of American Communists, 1947–1952* (Westport, Conn.: Greenwood Press, 1984), 35–36.

9. A year later, this was still substantially the case. Bradley "deplored the fact that the WSC [Washington Square College] faculty either individually or collectively had done nothing." *The Evening News*, 22 November 1948.

10. See five-page letter from William Parker (Secretary, MLA) to executive council members, 4 November 1950, Bradley Papers, Box 2, Folder 9.

11. However, from the late 1940s until 1955, under the moribund leadership of Ralph Himstead, the AAUP was ineffective and dysfunctional. See Schrecker, *No Ivory Tower*, 319–32.

12. Cited in ibid., 312. Nor did the American Civil Liberties Union, which was deeply divided and weakly led; see Samuel Walker, *In Defense of American Liberties: A History of the ACLU* (New York: Oxford University Press, 1990), 175–76. It was not until the mid-1950s that it published *Academic Freedom and Academic Responsibilities* (ACLU, New York: 1956) in RG 3.0.6. Records of the Office of President/Chancellor New York University, 1951–1965, Administrative Subject Files, Box 15, Folder 1, NYU Archives.

13. Minutes of the Council of New York University, 27 October 1947, Bradley Papers, Box 3, Folder 5.

14. "NYU Cracks Down on Bradley," *PM*, 23 July 1947; *New York Times*, 23 July 1947.

15. *New York Herald Tribune*, 19 December 1947. Fast's visit also aroused intense opposition: A. J. Thompson, for example, found it "shocking and disgusting" that Fast was allowed to "spread Anti-American Propaganda" and recommended that

"the place be fumigated" after he had given his "Hate America speech." Bradley Papers, Box 2, Folder 2.

16. See leaflet, "Professor Bradley Banned," Bradley Papers, Box 2, Folder 14.

17. See "Memorandum on sequence of events which led up to the conviction of Professor Bradley for contempt of Congress" [n.d.], 6–8, Bradley Papers, Box 1, Folder 10. Bradley's future wife, Ruth Leider, was also linked to Eisler through her signature on Eisler's application for an "alien departure permit" in January 1942. FBI report, "Ruth Leider," 13 April 1951, FBI Bradley files.

18. Herbert Romerstein and Stanislav Levchenko, *The KGB Against the "Main Enemy": How the Soviet Intelligence Service Operates against the United States* (Lexington and Toronto: Lexington Books, 1989), 238–39. The FBI's demonization of Eisler relied in part on the testimony of an ex-communist apostate who described Eisler as "Stalin's chief agent here." Louis Francis Budenz, *Men Without Faces: The Communist Conspiracy in the USA* (New York: Harper & Bros., 1948), 4.

19. House Committee on Un-American Activities, *Hearings on Gerhardt Eisler: Investigation of Un-American Propaganda Activities in the United States*, 6 February 1947, 11–12.

20. Bradley Papers, Box 1, Folder 2. Photocopies of twenty-seven checks to Eisler, many signed by Bradley in 1943, 1945, and 1946, became Exhibit 35. Bradley Papers, Box 1, Folder 3.

21. Cited in Maurice Isserman, *Which Side Were You On?: The American Communist Party During the Second World War* (Middletown, Conn.: Wesleyan University Press, 1982), 171.

22. Minutes, executive board meeting, 21 November 1946, Stern Papers, Box 2, Folder 1. Schrecker's account of Eisler also counters the conspiratorial interpretation of Eisler's post-war activities in the United States; Ellen Schrecker, *Many Are the Crimes: McCarthyism in America* (Boston: Little, Brown, 1998), 122–30.

23. He was cited on February 18, 1947, and convicted by the Court of Appeals, 170 F. 2d 273 (1948). For the consequences of his action, see Ellen Schrecker, "Immigration and Internal Security: Political Deportations During the McCarthy Era," *Science & Society*, 60:4 (Winter 1997), 409–10.

24. Chase to John Gerdes, 24 March 1948, Bradley Papers, Box 2, Folder 5. There were, of course, precedents for purges of radical academics and college teachers (especially by the New York–based Rapp-Coudert committee), but not at NYU, whose commitment to academic freedom was stronger. See Schrecker, *No Ivory Tower*, ch. 3. Bradley's dismissal was soon paralleled by events at the University of Washington in 1948–49; see Raymond B. Allen, *Communism and Academic Freedom: The Record of the Tenure Cases at the University of Washington* (Seattle: University of Washington Press, 1949).

25. See *Barsky et al. v. United States* 334 US 843.

26. Correspondence, Chase to Bradley, 21 June 1948, Bradley Papers, Box 1, Folder 10; press release, New York University Bureau of Public Information, 25 June 1948, Bradley Papers, Box 2, Folder 15. This decision was confirmed

by the Council on October 25, 1948, which in turn was conveyed by the vice chancellor to Bradley the following day. See correspondence, Harold O. Voorhis to Bradley, 26 October 1948, Bradley Papers, Box 1, Folder 10.

27. According to Bradley's FBI files, Bradley married Francine Brustein, who was eight years older than he, on May 31, 1934; they divorced on July 12, 1948. He married Ruth Leider, née Rosie Marshak (born in 1904 to Russian parents), an activist lawyer and widow with three children (her husband, Daniel, a Romanian-born labor attorney, died suddenly in 1944 at the age of forty) on August 2, 1948. Daniel Leider's brother, Ben, a *New York Post* reporter, was the first American to be killed in the Spanish Civil War. Like Bradley, Ruth was involved with the JAFRC from the outset and was one of those imprisoned in 1950. After his divorce, Bradley moved into Ruth's home at 60 Sidney Place, Brooklyn.

28. Bradley to Chase, 28 June 1948, Bradley Papers, Box 1, Folder 10.

29. Chase to Pollock, 2 July 1948, Bradley Papers, Box 2, Folder 1.

30. See, for example, correspondence, Chase to Clyde R. Miller, chairman, Bureau on Academic Freedom, National Council of the Arts, Sciences and Professions, 7 December 1948, Bradley Papers, Box 2, Folder 14.

31. Minutes of Meeting of the Council of New York University, 25 October 1948, Bradley Papers, Box 3, Folder 5. Exhibit G was a petition signed by students calling for Bradley's reinstatement.

32. Bradley Papers, Box 1, Folder 2; Box 2, Folder 15.

33. A copy of the tape recording is located in NYU Archives and titled "Exhibit 1, Bradley 1/4/51."

34. Chase to Pollock, 9 November 1948, Bradley Papers, Box 2, Folder 1.

35. Transcript of interview with Bradley by Paul Tillett; original tape in Paul Tillett Files, Seeley G. Mudd Library, Princeton University (henceforth Tillett files). My thanks to Ellen Schrecker for this source.

36. There was also an orchestrated postcard campaign: literally hundreds of pre-typed and pre-paid postcards were sent to Chancellor Chase; all were retained.

37. Letter, [first name illegible] Elkin to Chase, 23 June 1948, Bradley Papers, Box 2, Folder 16. Emphasis in original.

38. Voorhis to Chase, 4 September 1947, Harry W. Chase Papers, RG 3.0.5. Box 61, Folder 5, NYU Archives.

39. Pollock to Chase, 14 December 1948; Clyde R. Miller to Chase, 10 December 1948, Bradley Papers, Box 2, Folder 14.

40. The director of the American Civil Liberties Union of New York wrote that "the record of New York University in matters of academic freedom has over the years given us almost no cause for intervention," Roger N. Baldwin to Pollock, 18 December 1947, Bradley Papers, Box 1, Folder 9.

41. A close friend of Pollock's, the dean of the College of Arts and Sciences at Ohio's Oberlin College, wrote to "Dear Tom": "These are difficult days for liberals like you and me. Sometimes I think there are not many of us left." Carl Wittke to Pollock, 20 December 1947, Bradley Papers, Box 1, Folder 9. When Chase

was chancellor of the University of North Carolina in the 1920s, he publicly defended the teaching of evolution within the specific framework of academic freedom; see Louis R.Wilson, "Chase, Harry Woodburn," *Dictionary of North Carolina Biography, Vol. 1* (Chapel Hill: University of North Carolina Press, 1979).

42. See Howard Fast, *Being Red: A Memoir* (Boston: Houghton Mifflin, 1990), 246.

43. Bradley to Chase, 29 January 1949, Bradley Papers, Box 1, Folder 10.

44. *The Evening News*, 22 November 1948.

45. Bradley and other JAFRC board members had been buoyed by the confident conviction of O. John Rogge that the Supreme Court would decide in their favor.

46.Voorhis to Chase, 2 February 1949, Bradley Papers, Box 3, Folder 2.

47. Chase to Bradley, 8 February 1948, Bradley Papers, Box 1, Folder 10.

48. See *Barsky et al. v. United States* 339 US 971. The decision was 5-2, with dissenting Justices Hugo Black and William O. Douglas supporting the petition for rehearing.

49. *New York Herald Tribune*, 30 May 1950.

50. Confidential Report, 12 December 1949, FBI New York File 100-455542, Helen Reid Bryan, p. 5. The report was written by Special Agent John J. Doermer, using information supplied by Informant T-1, who, it appears, worked in the JAFRC offices.

51. See "Three Anti-Franco Women at West Virginia Prison," *Daily Worker*, 20 June 1950. Helen Bryan was imprisoned on November 13 after a final appeal failed.

52. See Fast, *Being Red*, 174, 248, and, more generally, 247–68.

53. Correspondence, William Leider (stepson) to author, 19 March 2009.

54. SAC, Pittsburg to Director, FBI, 5 September 1950. FBI Bradley file.

55. Bradley to Chase, 23 September 1950, Bradley Papers, Box 2, Folder 4.

56.Voorhis to Chase, 8 June 1950, Bradley Papers, Box 2, Folder 14. Nor were Bradley's NYU supporters inactive. On the same day, June 8, 1950, the "Bradley Committee" announced that an organizational meeting was planned for June 16 to plan for "summer action" and to complete fundraising for Bradley's $500 fine. But there is no further record of any "summer action"; the forces were not evenly matched. Untitled leaflet, 8 June 1950 ("intercepted" by Dean Pollock's office), Bradley Papers, Box 2, Folder 14.

57. Pollock to Chase, 7 June 1950, Bradley Papers, Box 2, Folder 1.

58. Rather patronizingly, Voorhis had earlier remarked to Chase that "the way in which Pollock is handling himself [in the Bradley case] is altogether to his credit." Voorhis to Chase, 4 September 1947, Harry W. Chase Papers, RG 3.0.5. Box 61, Folder 5, NYU Archives.

59. For reference to Chase's postwar anticommunism, see Thomas T. Frusciano and Marilyn H. Pettit, *New York University and the City* (New Brunswick, N.J.: Rutgers University Press, 1997), 178.

60. See Sidney Hook, "What Shall We Do about Communist Teachers?," *Saturday Evening Post*, 10 September 1949: 164–68; "Academic Integrity and Academic Freedom," *Commentary* 8 (October 1949): 329–39.

61. Pollock to Chase, 23 October 1950, marked "Confidential—for discussion only," Bradley Papers, Box 2, Folder 1.

62. Madden, who was also university treasurer and a businessman, was appointed on January 1, 1951, after Harry Woodburn Chase, chancellor since 1933, retired at the age of sixty-seven (and died in 1955). Madden was replaced by Henry T. Heald at the end of 1952. In July 1956, under the incoming Carroll V. Newsom, the title "chancellor" was changed to "president."

63. Arad McCutchan Riggs was a 6′4″ law professor at NYU (appointed 1937; retired 1964) and partner in the Madison Avenue law firm of Allin, Riggs & Shaughnessy.

64. Riggs to Madden, 1 March 1951, 5–8, Bradley Papers, Box 2, Folder 10.

65. Message, 5 March 1951, Office of Director, FBI Bradley files. Although Madden's name was deleted, there is conclusive internal evidence that it was he who visited the FBI. For example, both [BLANK] and Madden were directors of the Metropolitan Life Insurance Company of New York, and both [BLANK] and Madden were in an acting position "until someone else could be appointed."

66. "Memorandum to Mr. Tolson," 8 March 1951, FBI Bradley files. Clyde Tolson was an FBI assistant director.

67. Ibid. Quite possibly, this action was part of the FBI's highly confidential project that commenced in 1951, the "Responsibilities Program"; see "The FBI Responsibilities Program File and the Dissemination of Information File [1951–1955]," microfilm copy (#9703), New York University.

68. "Statements Made Before Meeting of Council," 26 March 1951, 29–30, Bradley Papers, Box 1, Folder 7.

69. Ibid., 34–45.

70. Thus, Madden was disingenuous when he told Harper that action had been deferred because of the congested condition of the calendar of the Council. Madden to Harper, 30 April 1951, Bradley Papers, Box 3, Folder 4.

71. The sole dissenter was opposed only to the "form" of the resolution; he, too, favored making the suspension permanent.

72. The foregoing is based on the University Council Minutes for 26 March, 23 April, 28 May, and 20 June 1951. Bradley Papers, Box 3, Folder 5.

73. Harper replied that he could find "no statement of the basis for the dismissal" of Bradley and requested such a statement "of the grounds on which Council's action was taken." Harper to Voorhis, 3 July 1951, Bradley Papers, Box 3, Folder 3. No subsequent letter from Voorhis to Harper could be located.

74. Excerpt from Minutes of Executive Committee, 13 April 1952, ibid.

75. This offer was made before Bradley, Pollock, and Harper on January 3, 1951. It formed part of the testimony made by Bradley under oath at a pre-trial

hearing in November 1953. Robert Reagan of Townley, Updike & Carter was present and telephoned Pollock with this information. Notes of telephone call, 4 November 1953, Bradley Papers, Box 2, Folder 12. Pollock also recommended in his October 23, 1950, report to Chancellor Chase that Bradley be paid a total of $4,900 for the twelve months following his original dismissal. This, too, never publicly surfaced.

76. Riggs to Pollock, 23 July 1951, Bradley Papers, Box 2, Folder 10. Riggs was paid $5,177.91 for his services as counsel to Pollock.

77. It was a midsized Manhattan law firm that commenced in 1937 and closed in 1995.

78. See judgment by Mr. Justice Cohen (Supreme Court) in *New York Law Journal*, 27 July 1953, and *Bradley v. New York University*, 124 N.Y.S. 2d 238 (Sup. Ct. 1953). See also *New York Times*, 26 January 1954 and 21 May 1954. In naïve hope more than realistic expectation, France wrote to the president, Carroll V. Newsom, in 1960 seeking to review the case and recover some of this salary. The response was negative. France to Newsom, 12 April 1960; Dudley Miller (NYU legal counsel) to France, 2 May 1960, Bradley Papers, Box 2, Folder 4.

79. Reagan to Pollock, 31 March 1951, Bradley Papers, Box 2, Folder 12.

80. Reagan to Pollock, 4 June 1953, 31 July 1953, ibid.; Reagan to Voorhis, 4 June 1953, Bradley Papers, Box 3, Folder 4.

81. Memorandum, 6 November 1946, Director to SAC New York; SAC New York, to Director, 19 March 1947; "Correlation Summary," 5 February 1973, File Nos. 100–34005 and 100–69110.

82. SAC New York to Director, 14 September 1966, FBI Bradley files.

83. SAC New York to Director, 15 September 1955, "Succinct Resume of Case," 1. In this document, Yergan's name was not redacted; in other documents he is identified as "Confidential Informant T-23." For Yergan's apostasy, see David H. Anthony, *Max Yergan: Race Man, Internationalist, Cold Warrior* (New York: New York University Press, 2006), 231–42.

84. SAC New York to Director, 15 September 1955, "Succinct Resume of Case," 12; FBI Report, NY 100–69110, [n.d. 1959], p. 6; SAC New York to Director, 12 September 1960, 1–2. FBI Bradley files.

85. Cited in Schrecker, *No Ivory Tower*, 268.

86. Correspondence, Irene Solomon to author, 9 March 2009.

87. There were 933 FBI informants inside the Communist Party (948 in 1956), 420 confidential sources (578 in 1956), and 12 active double agents (23 in 1956), Inspection Report, R. T. Harbo, and Memorandum, Inspection Summary Report, H. L. Edwards to John P. Mohr, 11 October 1956, "CPSU Membership," FBI New York Field File 100-80638. https://sites.google.com/site/ernie124102/cpusa.

88. SAC New York to Director, J. Edgar Hoover, and Assistant Director, A. H. Belmont, 6 October 1954, FBI Bradley files.

89. Ibid.

90. When asked the next day, "What are your immediate plans?" Burgum replied, "The whole affair has taken me too much by surprise to make any definite plans." *The Education Sun*, 15 October 1952.

91. Despite this American pedigree, an FBI informant (NY T-1) noted forty years later that Burgum "speaks with thick English accent, typical English type appearance resembling the late actor W. C. Fields." US Department of Justice, Federal Bureau of Investigation, FOIPA No. 115280-000 (henceforth FBI Burgum file), Report, "Edwin Berry Burgum," 17 October 1963, 2. His New York File No. was 100-26437.

92. He became assistant professor in August 1926 and associate professor in August 1931.

93. See Diana Trilling's scathing review in the *New York Times*, 1 June 1947 and the *Daily Worker's* eulogistic review, 20 July 1947.

94. One issue of *Antioch Review*, for example, contains Burgum's fascinating discussion of "Virginia Wolf and the Empty Room" (Winter 1943: 596–611).

95. See, for example, "Out of Nazi Poland," *New York Times*, 22 July 1945; "Wings from America," *New York Times*, 21 January 1945.

96. Its 1942 report proclaimed that it "exposed" 69 instructors as communists and another potential 434 faculty and staff. Stephen Leberstein, "Purging the Profs: The Rapp Coudert Committee in New York, 1940–1942," in Michael E. Brown, Randy Martin, Frank Rosengarten, and George Snedeker, *New Studies in the Politics and Culture of U.S. Communism* (New York: Monthly Review Press, 1993), 100.

97. Schrecker, *No Ivory Tower*, 76, 83.

98. *New York Times*, 15 January 1938. Burgum had been a member of the College Teachers Section of Local 5 since October 1935. In 1939 the American Federation of Labor suspended the Local's affiliation with the AFL after it "took part in Communist activities." *New York Times*, 20 January 1939; Clarence Taylor, *Reds at the Blackboard: Communism, Civil Rights, and the New York City Teachers Union* (New York: Columbia University Press, 2011).

99. New York City Board of Higher Education Archives, New York, Transcript, Rapp-Courdet Legislative Committee Public Hearing, 8 April 1941, 961–63 (henceforth Transcript, Rapp-Courdet Hearing). This photo is reproduced in Frusciano and Pettit, *New York University and the City*, 199.

100. Because he was employed by a private university, unlike the other witnesses from City College of New York and Brooklyn College, Burgum was not subject to Section 903 of the New York City Charter, which empowered the Board of Education to summarily dismiss any public employee who took the Fifth—that is, refused to answer self-incriminating questions.

101. *New York Times*, 12 January 1935.

102. *New York Times*, 21 April 1935.

103. Transcript, Rapp-Courdet Hearing, 8 April 1941, 958–59.

104. This does, of course, include the organized actions of the various NYU student groups, from the American Youth for Democracy to the Spartacus Club, which appeared before the Student Council, visited all active NYU clubs, and distributed thousands of mimeographed leaflets in support of Burgum.

105. Letter to Heald, signed by eight students, 29 October 1952, Burgum Papers, Box 5, Folder 17.

106. See letters in ibid. A total of only four current students wrote to Heald supporting the suspension (Box 5, Folder 11).

107. "Transcript of Hearing on Charges Against Associate Professor Edwin Berry Burgum, New York University," 683, Burgum Papers, Box 1, Folder 10.

108. "Statement by Professor Riggs," 20–21, attached to memorandum to Charles Hodges, 12 March 1953, Burgum Papers, Box 5, Folder 4.

109. The FBI received an anonymous letter, dated February 4, 1947, alleging that Burgum "openly dispenses Communist propaganda in his classrooms." FBI Burgum File, Report, "Edwin Berry Burgum, Security Matter—C," 16 January 1951, 19. However, there is no indication that this letter was forwarded to a third party.

110. Peter N. Carroll and James D. Fernandez (eds.), *Facing Fascism: New York and the Spanish Civil War* (New York: Museum of the City of New York and New York University Press, 2007), 182, n.7.

111. The Internal Security Act (also known as the Subversive Activities Control Act) was passed in September 1950 over Harry Truman's trenchant opposition and presidential veto; its draconian centerpiece was the establishment of a five-person Subversive Activities Control Board.

112. Both HUAC and the FBI relied heavily on Budenz's testimony; see his *Men Without Faces*.

113. FBI Burgum File, Correspondence to SAC (Special Agent in Charge), New York and Director, Washington, 13 June 1950.

114. FBI Burgum File, Memorandum, SAC, New York to J. Edgar Hoover, 16 January 1951; Report, "Edwin Berry Burgum, Security Matter—C," 16 January 1951, 1. On the other hand, Burgum was "unknown" to confidential informants T-23, T-24, and T-25 (Report, "Edwin Berry Burgum, Security Matter—C," 16 January 1951, 12).

115. Kenneth O'Reilly, *Hoover and the Un-Americans: The FBI, HUAC, and the Red Menace* (Philadelphia: Temple University Press, 1983), 76, 98; Athan Theoharis, *Chasing Spies* (Chicago: Ivan R. Dee, 2002), 161; Schrecker, *Many Are the Crimes*, 214–15.

116. "The FBI Responsibilities Program File and the Dissemination of Information File [1951–55]," microfilm copy (#9703: 8 reels), New York University.

117. *Square Bulletin*, 24 October 1952.

118. Karl E. Mundt to Frank L. Howley, 4 June 1953, Burgum Papers, Box 5, Folder 14.

119. Testimony of Edward [*sic*] Burgum, *Hearings before the Subcommittee to Investigate the Administration of the Internal Security Act and Other Internal Security Laws, 82nd Congress, 2nd Session, on Subversive Influence in the Educational Process* (Washington: U.S. Government Printing Office, 1952), 13 October 1952 (henceforth *Hearings*, McCarran committee), 276.

120. FBI Burgum File, Correspondence, A. H. Belmont to D. M. Ladd, 19 February 1953, "Testimony Before McCarran Committee September 25, 1952, Volume #6, Pages 63–89," 5. Rhodri Jeffries-Jones, *The FBI: A History* (New Haven, Conn.: Yale University Press, 2007), 159, confirms the assistance Hoover gave to the McCarran committee, while Tim Weiner, *Enemies: A History of the FBI* (New York: Random House, 2012), 172–73, confirms the convergence between the wishes of Hoover and the provisions of the Internal Security Act.

121. FBI Burgum File, Correspondence, A. H. Belmont to D. M. Ladd, 19 February 1953, "Testimony Before McCarran Committee September 25, 1952, Volume #6, Pages 63–89," 9.

122. Presumably he did not take the Fifth because, as indicated above, under Section 903 of the New York City Charter, academics from city public colleges who refused to answer questions suffered automatic dismissal. In this way, Ogur and dozens of others from Brooklyn, Hunter, and Queens colleges were trapped.

123. FBI Burgum File, Correspondence, A. H. Belmont to D. M. Ladd, 19 February 1953, "Testimony Before McCarran Committee September 25, 1952, Volume #6, Pages 63–89," 6.

124. Leonard B. Boudin, "The Fifth Amendment: Freedom's Bastion," *The Nation*, 29 September 1951.

125. *New York Times*, 14 October 1952.

126. See I. F. Stone, "What Are you Going to Do About School Witch Hunt?," *Daily Compass*, 8 October 1952.

127. *Square Bulletin*, 14 October 1952. Indicative of that liberalism was the high proportion of NYU faculty (more than 300) who supported Adlai Stevenson over Dwight Eisenhower in the upcoming presidential election. *The Evening News*, 27 October 1952. But as Burgum was to discover, rhetorical support behind closed office doors was one thing; taking a public stand was another. (*Square Bulletin* was published by the Day Organization of Washington Square College, *The Evening News* by the Evening Organization of Washington Square College of NYU.)

128. Reproduced in *The Evening News*, 27 October 1952.

129. For copies of this open letter, see "72 Students on the Burgum Case," in Burgum Papers, Box 6, Folders 7 and 11. By early November the group had 150 members; see *New York University Heights Daily News*, 3 November 1952.

130. One of the speakers was Michael Harrington, editor of *The Catholic Worker* (1951–53) and later author of the influential *The Other America: Poverty in the United States* (New York: Macmillan, 1962). One of the debate topics was "Should Communists Be Allowed to Teach in Our Universities?"; another was "Is Burgum Law Abiding?" Because of his suspension, Burgum was denied per-

mission to speak at any of the meetings; see *NYU Commerce Bulletin*, 26 November 1952. However, he did speak outside NYU but was closely monitored and recorded by NYU; see three-page "Transcript of remarks by Professor Burgum at Palm Garden Ballroom November 14, 1952" in Pollock's files, Burgum Papers, Box 6, Folder 27. This meeting was sponsored by the Intercollegiate Committee for Academic Freedom; see advertising leaflet, *The "Worm" Turns!*, Burgum Papers, P-FILE.

131. See assorted leaflets in Burgum Papers, Box 6, Folder 7; Box 7, Folder 3.

132. *Square Bulletin*, 29 October 1952. In fact, Washington Square College students signed an astonishing total of 102 petitions relating to Burgum. Burgum Papers, Box 5, Folder 19. One, organized by the Student Committee for Academic Freedom, condemned Heald's suspension of Burgum as a "serious threat to our education" and a "present and clear danger to our academic freedom." *Square Bulletin*, 29 October 1952. There were also handbills produced by other NYU student groups, including American Youth for Democracy and the Spartacus Club.

133. This phrase was used in a memorandum, Voorhis to Vice Chancellor David D. Henry, 15 October 1952, Burgum Papers, Box 6, Folder 12.

134. Memorandum from the Registrar's Office to Voorhis, 23 October 1952 (report of the meeting attached), Burgum Papers, Box 6, Folder 12.

135. Voorhis to E.C.K. [Elaine C. Kashman], 15 October 1952, Burgum Papers, Box 6, Folder 12.

136. Voorhis to Henry, 21 October 1952, Burgum Papers, Box 6, Folder 12.

137. They were *Education Sun*, *Evening News*, *Heights Daily News*, and *Square Bulletin*.

138. *NYU Commerce Bulletin*, 15 October 1952 ("Heald's action praised") compared with 12 November 1952.

139. *New York Times*, 23 July 1952. This issue, however, continued to be an irritant; see "President Conant Meets a Senate Committee," *New York Times*, 11 February 1953.

140. As a Cornell University professor asked Heald, "Is it too much to ask that New York University emulate Columbia rather than an institution that is part of a State apparatus?" John W. Bickness to Heald, 18 October 1952, Burgum Papers, Box 5, Folder 6.

141. Schrecker, *No Ivory Tower*, 167.

142. Howard Mumford Jones to Heald, 1 December 1952, Burgum Papers, Box 5, Folder 15.

143. Cited in *The Evening News*, 27 October 1952. He reiterated these sentiments in his commencement speech delivered on June 12, 1952, and spoke of the importance of NYU's remaining "free from pressures" outside the university. *The Education Sun*, 15 October 1952.

144. *The Education Sun*, 15 October 1952.

145. For the full resolution of the 38th Annual Meeting of the AAUP in 1952, which condemned the purpose, manner, and outcomes of current legislative

investigations, see letter to "Dear Colleague" from Burgum and five dismissed professors from New York City colleges, 1 November 1952, in Burgum Papers, Box 5, Folder 9. Although impotent at the time, the AAUP later placed NYU on its censure list (1959 to 1961) because of the Bradley and Burgum dismissals.

146. John J. De Boer to Heald, 12 May 1953, Burgum Papers, Box 5, Folder 6. De Boer was professor of education at the University of Chicago.

147. Bicknell (Cornell University) to Heald, 18 October 1952, Burgum Papers, Box 5, Folder 6.

148. *NYU Commerce Bulletin*, 15 October 1952.

149. *Square Bulletin*, 17 October 1952; *NYU Commerce Bulletin*, 15 October 1952.

150. *Evening News*, 26 January 1953; *New York University Heights Daily News*, 15 October 1952.

151. This was the judgment of Hollis Cooley, who also called him "old stone-face"; interview with Hollis Cooley, 4 November 1981, Tillett Files (henceforth Cooley interview, 1981). In 1948–49 Cooley was president of the AAUP chapter at NYU.

152. "Insert in speech 'A Chance to Serve,'" Burgum Papers, P-FILE (no box/folder).

153. See, for example, *New York Times*, 8 November 1952; *New York Herald Tribune*, 8 November 1952; *Commerce Bulletin*, 12 November 1952 ("Heald blasts communism before business confab"). Public relations was often considered. A note in the chancellor's files reads: "TCP [Thomas C. Pollock] called. He and Riggs [Pollock's legal counsel] are of the strong opinion that . . . we should make a bold statement as a matter of public relations." Burgum Papers, Box 5, Folder 8. The insert was, of course, sent to Pollock (Box 7, Folder 4).

154. *New York Times*, 20 January 1953 ("Academic Freedom Not for Reds").

155. See Richard Gid Powers, *Not Without Honor: The History of American Anti-communism* (New York: The Free Press, 1995), 199–212.

156. See "Academic Freedom and Tenure, Statements of Principles," *AAUP Bulletin* 38:1 (Spring 1952): 116–22.

157. "Insert in speech 'A Chance to Serve,'" 1–2, Burgum Papers, P-FILE.

158. Burgum actually alleged that Heald's views "follow[ed]" Hook's "philosophy." Letter to "Dear Colleague," 13 November 1952, Burgum Papers, Box 4, Folder 14. However, Heald's views on communist educators also echoed those of HUAC's chief investigator (1938–48), Robert Stripling; see his *Red Plot Against America* (Drexel Hill, Penn.: Bell, 1949), 191–212.

159. Alan M. Wald, *The New York Intellectuals: The Rise and Decline of the Anti-Stalinist Left from the 1930s to the 1980s* (Chapel Hill and London: University of North Carolina Press, 1987), 51.

160. *Square Bulletin*, 29 October 1952; *Education Sun*, 29 October 1952; NYU *Commerce* Bulletin, 29 October 1952; New York *University Heights Daily News*,

5 November 1952; *Evening News*, 10 November 1952. See also Edward S. Shapiro (ed.), *Letters of Sidney Hook: Democracy, Communism and the Cold War* (New York: M. E. Sharpe, 1995). Hook was also one of the founding members of the Congress for Cultural Freedom.

161. This was neither the first nor last time Hook wrote on this topic; see Sidney Hook, "What Shall We Do About Communist Teachers?," *Saturday Evening Post*, 10 September 1949: 164–68; "Academic Integrity and Academic Freedom," *Commentary*, 8 (October 1949): 329–39; "Indoctrination and Academic Freedom," *The New Leader*, 9 March 1953, 2–4.

162. "Insert in speech 'A Chance to Serve,'" 2, Burgum Papers, P-FILE.

163. As a communist lawyer later wrote, "[T]he witnesses were so many and the possible choices so few that most lawyers representing those witnesses in the early 1950s fell into habit of advising all clients to 'take the Fifth.'" Victor Rabinowitz, *Unrepentant Leftist* (Urbana: University of Illinois Press, 1996), 119–20.

164. See Herbert A. Philbrick, *I Led Three Lives: Citizen, "Communist," Counterspy* (New York: McGraw-Hill, 1952).

165. Philbrick to Heald, 10 November 1952, Burgum Papers, Box 5, Folder 14.

166. Heald to Philbrick, 14 November, ibid.

167. By then, judging by the annotations and underlining, Dean Pollock had read Philbrick's book; see his personal copy in Burgum Papers, Box 4, Folder 17.

168. Burgum to Heald, 13 November 1952, Burgum Papers, Box 5, Folder 8.

169. Theodore H. Skinner (chairman of the Board of Review) to Heald, 19 November 1952, ibid.

170. Excerpt from the minutes of NYU Council meeting, 24 November 1952, Burgum Papers, Box 5, Folder 1 (also contained in Box 2, Folder 2).

171. Burgum to Heald, 2 December 1952; Heald to Burgum, 5 December 1952, Burgum Papers, Box 3, Folder 5. He also formally appealed the decision, but on December 23, the Executive and Education Committees of the University Council unanimously rejected his appeal. Minutes of meeting, Burgum Papers, Box 5, Folder 1.

172. "Statement for the University Council, November 24, 1952," Burgum Papers, Box 5, Folder 2.

173. Excerpt from the minutes of NYU Council meeting, 24 November 1952, 2–3, Burgum Papers, Box 2, Folder 2. This was reproduced on the front page of *Square Bulletin*, 3 December 1953.

174. Burgum to Heald, 2 December 1952, Burgum Papers, Box 3, Folder 4.

175. Heald to Burgum, 5 December 1952, Burgum Papers, Box 3, Folder 5.

176. Burgum to Heald, 18 December 1952, Burgum Papers, Box 5, Folder 10. Emphasis in original.

177. Heald to Burgum, 5 January 1953, ibid.

178. He was, of course, actively assisted by the regular supply of FBI intelligence. According to Hoover, "I view [McCarthy] as a friend, and I believe he so views me." Weiner, *Enemies*, 184, and note, 481.

179. Harry B. Gould to Heald, 26 October 1952, Burgum Papers, Box 5, Folder 17. Gould was a New York architect and town planner.

180. Cooley interview, 1981.

181. Ibid.

182. *NYU Commerce Bulletin*, 25 February 1953.

183. According to one committee member, they were so preoccupied with this case that they "couldn't do other things." Cooley interview, 1981.

184. Untitled document (annotated "Pollock 3/5/53"), Burgum Papers, Box 4, Folder 21.

185. Murray Kempton, *Part of Our Time: Some Ruins and Monuments of the Thirties* (New York: Simon and Schuster, 1955), 214 (ch. 5 is devoted to Joseph Brown Matthews); Caute, *Fellow-Travellers: A Postscript to the Enlightenment* (New York: Macmillan, 1973), 141, 319.

186. Caute, *Fellow-Travellers*, 325.

187. Schrecker, *No Ivory Tower*, 72, 151. See also Robert M. Lichtman, "J. B. Matthews and the 'Counter-subversives': Names as a Political and Financial Resource in the McCarthy Era," *American Communist History* 5:1 (2006), 1–36.

188. His links with NYU continued; see J. B. Matthews Papers, 1862–1986, Special Collections Library, Duke University, Box 438, Folder 11.

189. The *Science & Society* editorship and May Day photograph were again emphasized by Riggs in his subsequent questioning of Philbrick and Johnson, whom we meet below.

190. These are now located in Burgum Papers, Box 4, Folder 13.

191. "Transcript of Hearing on Charges Against Associate Professor Edwin Berry Burgum New York University" (henceforth Transcript of hearing), 99, 105, 156.

192. Transcript of hearing, 720 (see 710–22 for this section).

193. At least one member of the Senate Faculty Committee, Professor Walter Anderson, remained highly skeptical of Riggs' methodology; Transcript of hearing, 722.

194. Ibid., 119, 179. These exhibits are located in Box 3, Folders 15–25, and Box 4, Folders 1–26. Burgum's eighteen exhibits are located in Box 3, Folders 2–14. HUAC also forwarded Pollock a copy of its extraordinary *Guide to Subversive Organizations and Publications (and Appendix)*, House Document No. 137, 82nd Congress, 1st Session, 14 April 1951.

195. Committee on Un-American Activities, U.S. House of Representatives, *Review of the Scientific and Cultural Conference for World Peace* (Washington, 1949), 18. For Pollock's use of this booklet, see Transcript of hearing, 78–81.

196. A comparison of the activities listed in Burgum's FBI file with Pollock's exhibits reveals striking similarities. The fact that Burgum had never appeared

before HUAC seems to confirm that it did not generate the original documents. See twenty-two-page report attached to Memorandum, SAC, New York to Hoover, 16 January 1951, "Edwin Berry Burgum Security Matter—C."

197. Transcript of hearing, 126.

198. Before the hearings formally commenced, Cooley had sought clarification of the charges but was overruled by the chair. Cooley interview, 1981.

199. As Heald's former Chicago colleague remarked (and his words were echoed less eloquently by Popper):

> If it could be shown that Burgum used his position as a teacher to advance a political cause, or to recruit members for a political party; if it could be shown that he neglected his academic responsibilities in order to engage in political activity; if it could be shown that he distorted what he knew to be true in order to conform to an arbitrary political directive, there would be every justification for dismissing him.

De Boer to Heald, 12 May 1953, Burgum Papers, Box 5, Folder 6.

200. The phrase is Cooley's (interview, 1981).

201. Pollock's copy is located in Burgum Papers, Box 4, Folder 17. Unlike (it would appear) Pollock, the U.S. Attorney General at the time, Tom Clark, commented in 1975: "I thought Philbrick's book was a bunch of trash." Cited in Peter Steinberg, *The Great "Red Menace": United States Prosecution of American Communists, 1947–1952* (Westport, Conn.: Greenwood Press, 1984), 165. Nevertheless, a highly popular television series of the same name was spawned by Philbrick's book.

202. Cooley interview, 1981.

203. Steinberg, *The Great "Red Menace,"* 164.

204. Transcript of hearing, 734–89.

205. Transcript of hearing, 829–30; David Caute, *The Great Fear: The Anti-Communist Purge Under Truman and Eisenhower* (New York: Simon & Schuster, 1978), 129.

206. Transcript of hearing, 791–803. Although African American, he was later an early recruit to the John Birch Society. He died in 1959 with perjury charges pending.

207. *Square Bulletin*, 29 October 1952. Boardman joined the FBI in 1934 and was previously director of the Kansas City office. Under his directorship the New York office had expanded to 1,786 employees in 1955, of whom 1,234 were Special Agents overseeing 7,121 Security Index cases and 19,940 "Active Pending Cases." FBI New York Field File 100-80638, Domestic Intelligence Division Inspection Report by R. T. Harbo, 3 June 1955; Inspection Report summary in Memo from H. L. Edwards to John P. Mohr, 11 October 1956; see https://sites.google.com/site/ernie124102/cpusa.

208. "Statement by Professor Riggs," 54–55, attached to letter to Charles Hodges, 12 March 1953, Burgum Papers, Box 3, Folder 4 (duplicate in Box 2, Folder 3).

209. Attached to "Memorandum to the Professorial Members of the Faculty of Washington Square College," 20 May 1953, in New York University Archives, Dorothy Arnold Papers, RG 19.3, Box 2, Folder 16.

210. Carl Beck, *Contempt of Congress: A Study of the Prosecutions Initiated by the Committee on Un-American Activities, 1945–1957* (New York: Da Capo Press, 1974), 84–86.

211. See, for example, *New York Times*, 7 December 1952, 26 December 1952, 30 December 1952; Leonard B. Boudin, "The Fifth Amendment: Freedom's Bastion," *The Nation*, 29 September 1951 and "The Constitutional Privilege in Operation," *Lawyers' Guild Review* 12:3 (Summer 1952), 1–22.

212. For some of the vast literature on the Fifth, see Beck's bibliography, *Contempt of Congress*, 257; this does not include Sidney Hook, *Common Sense and the Fifth Amendment* (New York: Criterion Books, 1957); Leonard W. Levy, *Origins of the Fifth Amendment: The Right Against Self-Incrimination* (New York: Oxford University Press, 1968); Mark Berger, *Taking the Fifth: The Supreme Court and the Privilege Against Self-Incrimination* (Toronto: Lexington Books, 1980); and Alan M. Dershowitz, *Is There a Right to Remain Silent? Coercive Interrogation and the Fifth Amendment After 9/11* (New York: Oxford University Press, 2008).

213. Cooley interview, 1981. Cooley decided to write a lengthy (twelve-page) dissenting opinion. For the full text, see attachment to "Memorandum to the Professorial Members of the Faculty of Washington Square College," 20 May 1953, in New York University Archives, Dorothy Arnold Papers, RG 19.3, Box 2, Folder 16. Burgum later described Cooley's statement as "a masterpiece of reasoning, deserving to stand alongside the great opinions of jurists in our courts." Letter, Burgum to "Dear Colleague," 22 June 1953, Burgum Papers, Box 5, Folder 9.

214. "New York University Statement on the Suspension, Hearing, and Dismissal of Edwin Berry Burgum," 30 April 1953, 11, Burgum Papers, Box 6, Folder 8 (henceforth NYU Statement).

215. NYU Statement, 12–13. This jaundiced fifteen-page statement was not well crafted. But Heald obviously thought otherwise and sent it to numerous individuals and institutions in May 1953. One responded: "This report is incredible. . . . I throw up my hands." De Boer (professor of education, University of Illinois–Urbana) to Heald, 12 May 1953, Burgum Papers, Box 5, Folder 6. See also D. L. Bollinger to Heald, 12 May 1953, ibid., for a systematic but scathing analysis.

216. Cooley interview, 1981. Cooley did not identify him, but other evidence points to Professor S. Bernard Wortis, from the School of Medicine.

217. For the full transcript of both, see "Meeting of the Council of New York University," 27 April 1953, Burgum Papers, Box 5, Folder 1.

218. Ibid., 34.

219. Minutes of Special Meeting, NYU Council, 30 April 1953, Burgum Papers, Box 5, Folder 1.

220. See *New York Times, New York World-Telegram and Sun, New York Herald Tribune*, 1 May 1953.

221. *New York Times*, 16 July 1953; Caute, *The Great Fear*, 321–24.

222. "Testimony of Edwin B. Burgum," *Executive Sessions of the Senate Permanent Subcommittee on Investigations of the Committee on Government Operations. 83rd Congress 1st Session 1953.* Volume 2, 1198–1203. (Released in 2003, these documents are available at the New York Public Library.) That friend of the NYU administration Karl Mundt was a member of this subcommittee but was not present during this executive session.

223. Letter, 22 June 1953, Burgum Papers, Box 6, Folder 27.

224. *New York University Heights Daily News*, 22 March 1954.

225. Born Mildred Rabinowich on June 16, 1906, in Pittsburgh, Pennsylvania, she was also a progressive, being affiliated with the left-wing National Council of the Arts, Sciences and Professions. In February 1954, she contributed some poignant poetry ("Four Poems") to *Contemporary Reader* (1, no. 3, 1954: 33–37), the short-lived literary journal (it lasted four issues) founded and edited by her husband.

226. "Edwin Berry Burgum," ch. 4, Burgum Family History Society, http://www.burgumfamily.com/.

227. Confidential Report, New York, "Edwin Berry Burgum," 8 April 1957, FBI Burgum files.

228. Questionnaire completed by Burgum [n.d.] in Tillett Files.

229. Report, with attachments, to SAC, New York, Director, Washington, 22 March 1962, FBI Burgum file.

230. *New York Times*, 17 September 1964.

231. *New York Times*, 31 March 1965.

232. "I do not intend to renounce anything that I have publicly stood for during this quarter century." As outlined above, a copy was sent by an NYU informant to the FBI in Washington.

233. Hoover to SAC, New York, 5 March 1968.

234. Report, New York office, 11 March 1966.

235. In March 1960, no fewer than fifteen informants were contacted. "Pretext interviews" involved an FBI agent's using subterfuge when visiting or telephoning Burgum's residence in order, presumably, to confirm that he continued to live at 175 Riverside Drive, #3F, New York City, to which he and his wife moved in March 1955. On November 3, 1965, a "suitable" photograph was taken and affixed to his Security Index card. His subscriptions included *The American Socialist* and *Science & Society*.

236. Belfrage co-founded in 1948 and co-edited throughout the 1950s the radical weekly paper the *National Guardian* and wrote, among other works, *The American Inquisition, 1945–1960: A Profile of the "McCarthy Era"* (New York: Thunder's Mouth Press, 1989).

237. By 1969 the ACGM had become less nefarious, being described as a "loose association of a predominantly social nature" of former members, friends,

and associates of the American Communist Party. Memorandum, Legat [U.S. Legal Attaché], Mexico City to Hoover, 18 September 1969, FBI Burgum file. Certainly, a great many American communists, mainly from the West Coast, fled to Mexico in the 1950s, but it became a place of refuge, not a center for conspiracy. One who visited Cuernavaca, as we have seen, was Howard Fast; see his *Being Red*, 331–42.

238. In 2013 he is still listed under the "Editorial Honor Roll" of *Science & Society*.

239. *New York Times*, 3 July 1979. (There was no obituary, merely a death notice placed, presumably, by his New York–based daughter, Naomi Smith).

4. The Composer: Dimitri Shostakovich

1. Shostakovich, interview with Kurt Sanderling, cited in Wendy Lesser, *Music for Silenced Voices: Shostakovich and His Fifteen Quartets* (New Haven, Conn.: Yale University Press, 2011), 97. The German-born Sanderling (1912–2011) was an eminent conductor and close friend of Shostakovich's since 1943.

2. They were Igor Stravinsky, Paul Hindemith, and Arnold Schoenberg.

3. Arthur Miller, *Timebends: A Life* (London: Minerva, 1990), 239.

4. William Barrett, "Culture Conference at the Waldorf," *Commentary* 7 (May 1949), 489.

5. Nicolas Nabokov, *Old Friends and New Music* (London: Hamish Hamilton, 1951).

6. "Notes on the Writing & Publishing Panel–Discussion, Cultural & Scientific Conference for World Peace; Starlight Roof Hotel Waldorf-Astoria, Saturday March 26," p. 2, Dwight Macdonald Papers, Yale University Library, MS 730, Box 80, Folder 199. Macdonald echoed this in a published account; Shostakovich "looked tense, withdrawn, unsmiling—a tragic and heart-rending figure." Dwight Macdonald, "The Waldorf Conference," *Politics*, May 1949, 32-B.

7. Dimitri Shostakovich, *Testimony: The Memoirs of Dimitri Shostakovich as Related to and Edited by Solomon Volkov* (London: Hamish Hamilton, 1979), 152.

8. Cited in Howard Fast, "Cultural Forces Rally Against the Warmakers," *Political Affairs* 28 (May 1949), 31.

9. Shapley was also a strong supporter of the Joint Anti-Fascist Refugee Committee and, earlier, the Spanish Republican cause; this was exemplified by his attempt to meet with and persuade President Roosevelt to support the Republican government during the civil war.

10. Those writers who support the first interpretation include Alice Kessler-Harris, *A Difficult Woman: The Challenging Life and Times of Lillian Hellman* (New York: Bloomsbury, 2012), 245; Robbie Lieberman, "'Does that make peace a bad word?': American Responses to the Communist Peace Offensive, 1949–1950," *Peace & Change* 17:2 (April 1992), 203–11; Robbie Lieberman, *The Strangest Dream: Communism, Anticommunism, and the U.S. Peace Movement, 1945–1963* (Syracuse,

N.Y.: Syracuse University Press, 2000), 58–61; Scott Lucas, *Freedom's War: The American Crusade Against the Soviet Union* (New York: New York University Press, 1999), 95–96; Giles Scott-Smith, *The Politics of Apolitical Culture: The Congress for Cultural Freedom, the CIA and Post-war American Hegemony* (London: Routledge, 2002), 94. A close reading of Shapley's correspondence suggests that the Waldorf conference had domestic origins and was not Soviet-inspired; see Papers of Harlow Shapley, 1906–1966, Harvard University Archives, HUG 4773.10, Box 10c. For the alternative view, that it was essentially a Cominform propaganda initiative and part of its "peace offensive," see Carol Brightman, *Writing Dangerously: Mary McCarthy and Her World* (London: Lime Tree, 1993), 322–25; Sidney Hook, *Out of Step: An Unquiet Life in the 20th Century* (New York: Harper & Row, 1987), 382–96; Hilton Kramer, *The Twilight of the Intellectual: Culture and Politics in the Era of the Cold War* (Chicago: Ivan R. Dee, 1999), 134, 308; Michael Wreszin, *A Rebel in Defense of Tradition: The Life and Politics of Dwight Macdonald* (New York: Basic Books, 1994), 213.

11. Neal to Thompson, 12 April 1949, National Archives, Department of State, Lot 53 D 47, Records Relating to International Information Activities, Box 27, Shapley Meeting.

12. Oral History Transcripts, 16 April 1968, 12, Box 8, Folder 14, Frank Campenni Papers, UWM MSS 213 University of Wisconsin–Milwaukee Archives, Milwaukee (henceforth Campenni Papers); Fast, *Being Red: A Memoir* (Boston: Houghton Mifflin, 1990), 199. This was not a hubristic slip; he said twice more that he "originated the idea" (Fast, *Being Red*, 200, 202).

13. Fast, *Being Red*, 202.

14. In August 1948 a World Congress of Intellectuals was held in Wrocław, Poland. It was Soviet-inspired and Harlow Shapley attended—hence the allegation that the Waldorf conference had foreign origins.

15. FBI file 100-23044, National Council for the Arts, Sciences and Professions, Bureau File No. 100-356137, 22 March 1949, 3–5, 7. Dorner was assisted by Maxine Wood, also a party member

16. "Peace: Everybody Wars Over It," *Newsweek*, 4 April 1949, 20.

17. Private correspondence, Mary McCarthy to John Rossi, 1 June 1982. (My thanks to Professor Rossi for making this available to me.) Hook also claimed that Shapley was "either a captive of Communist fellow-travelers or their willing tool." *New York Times*, 20 March 1949.

18. Guenter Lewy, *The Cause That Failed: Communism in American Political Life* (New York: Oxford University Press, 1990), 181; John Patrick Diggins, "The -Ism that Failed," *American Prospect*, December 2003, 78.

19. See Records, American Committee for Cultural Freedom, Tamiment Library, New York University (henceforth Tamiment), TAM 023, Box 2, Folders 7–8.

20. Donald Jameson, interview, 1994, cited in Frances Stoner Saunders, *Who Paid the Piper? The CIA and the Cultural Cold War* (London: Granta, 1999), 56.

21. Miller, *Timebends*, 234.

22. Arthur Schlesinger Jr., *The Vital Center: The Politics of Freedom* (Boston: Houghton Mifflin, 1962 ed.), ix. On the Waldorf meeting's providing the genesis of the Congress for Cultural Freedom, see Nathan Abrams, "'A Profoundly Hegemonic Moment': De-Mythologizing the Cold War New York Jewish Intellectuals," *SHOFAR* 21:3 (2003), 76–77; Peter Coleman, *The Liberal Conspiracy: The Congress for Cultural Freedom and the Struggle for the Mind of Postwar Europe* (New York: Free Press, 1989), 5–7; Stoner Saunders, *Who Paid the Piper?*, 53–6; Michael Warner, "Origins of the Congress for Cultural Freedom, 1949–50," *Studies in Intelligence* 38:5 (1995), 89–98.

23. Lieberman, "'Does that make peace a bad word?'" 210.

24. Wreszin, *Rebel*, 222.

25. Hugh Wilford, *The Mighty Wurlitzer: How the CIA Played America* (Cambridge, Mass.: Harvard University Press, 2008), 70–71.

26. Solomon Volkov, *Shostakovich and Stalin: The Extraordinary Relationship between the Great Composer and the Brutal Dictator* (London: Little, Brown, 2004), 286.

27. Garry Wills, commentary, in Lillian Hellman, *Scoundrel Time* (London: Macmillan, 1976), 165.

28. See note 7; Neil Jumonville, *Critical Crossings: The New York Intellectuals in Postwar America* (Berkeley: University of California Press, 1991), 1–2; William L. O'Neill, *A Better World. The Great Schism: Stalinism and the Intellectuals* (New York: Simon & Schuster, 1983), 163–69; Henry A. Singer, "An analysis of the New York press treatment of the Peace Conference at the Waldorf-Astoria," *Journal of Educational Sociology* 23:5 (1950), 258–70.

29. A. J. Liebling, "The Wayward Press: 100,000—Count 'em—1,000," *The New Yorker*, 9 April 1949, 86–92; Fast, "Cultural Forces Rally Against the Warmakers," 29–38; "Foreign Relations: Tumult at the Waldorf," *Time*, 4 April 1949; "Peace: Everybody Wars Over It," *Newsweek*, 4 April 1949, 19–22; Dwight Macdonald, "The Waldorf Conference," *Politics*, May 1949, 32A–32D ("special insert") and reprinted in *Horizon* 19:113 (May 1949), 313–26; "America Afraid," *The Progressive* 13 (May 1949), 4; Barrett, "Culture Conference," 487–93; Joseph P. Lash, "Weekend at the Waldorf," *New Republic*, 18 April 1949, 10–14; "Red Visitors Cause Rumpus," *Life* 26:14 (4 April 1949), 39–43; Freda Kirchwey, "Battle of the Waldorf," *Nation*, 2 April 1949, 377–78; George S. Counts, "Kulturefest at the Waldorf: Soapbox for Red Propaganda," *The New Leader* 22:12 (19 March 1949), 1, 4. For subsequent assessments, see Arthur Miller, "The Year It Came Apart," *New York*, 30 December 1974–6 January 1975, 30–44; Daniel S. Gillmor, *Speaking of Peace* (New York: National Council of the Arts, Sciences and Professions, 1949); Committee on Un-American Activities, *Review of the Scientific and Cultural Conference for World Peace* (Washington: U.S. Government Printing Office, 1949); Committee on Un-American Activities, *Report on the Communist "Peace" Offensive: A Campaign to Disarm and Defeat the United States* (Washington: U.S. Govern-

ment Printing Office, 1951), 11–15; [Karl Baarslag], "Report on the Scientific and Cultural Conference for World Peace," seventeen-page report distributed by the American Legion and attached to memo, L. R. Pennington to D. Milton Ladd, 7 April 1949, National Council of the Arts, Sciences and Professions File No. 100-HQ-356137 (henceforth FBI file, NCASP).

30. "Red Visitors Cause Rumpus," 42–43. In contrast, Howard Fast asserted that the Waldorf conference's sponsors "read like a rollcall of American honor and dignity and achievement." Fast, "Cultural Forces Rally Against the Warmakers," 30.

31. Saunders, *Who Paid the Piper?*, 52.

32. Michael Wreszin, "Arthur Schlesinger, Jr., Scholar-Activist in Cold War America: 1946–1956," *Salmagundi* 63/64 (1984), 269.

33. The following is based on *Shostakovich v vospominaniakh syn Maksima, docheri Gallnu i protoiereia Mikhaila Ardora* (Moscow: 2003), 63–65, cited in Volkov, *Shostakovich and Stalin*, 279–80; Shostakovich, *Testimony*, 111–12; Yuri Levitin, "The Year 1948," unpublished article, in Elizabeth Wilson, *Shostakovich: A Life Remembered* (London: Faber & Faber, 1994), 212–13.

34. There were other reasons for his reluctance: Shostakovich's daughter: "First of all because he wasn't able or at liberty to express his true thoughts and feelings. Also because he knew that persistent and unscrupulous journalists would ask him provocative questions." Michael Ardov, *Memories of Shostakovich: Interviews with the Composer's Children* (London: Short Books, 2004), 125.

35. Stalin, of course, wished to use Shostakovich to enhance the prestige of the party and the Soviet Union. Or, as one scholar put it, "The composer was to represent a live example of Stalin's fatherly care of Soviet artists"; Sofia Moshevich, *Dmitri Shostakovich, Pianist* (Montreal and Kingston: McGill-Queen's University Press, 2004), 129.

36. *Sovetskaia muzyka* 4 (1991), 17, in Volkov, *Shostakovich and Stalin*, 281.

37. Shostakovich, *Testimony*, 112, 152. According to Nabokov, Shostakovich told him in 1967 that he had been "ordered" to attend; Nicolas Nabokov, *Bagázh: Memoirs of a Russian Cosmopolitan* (New York: Atheneum, 1975), 235–36. The fact that the American embassy in Moscow received a formal request from the Kremlin for a visa for Shostakovich and others on March 10—six days earlier—suggests that Shostakovich had few options. *Chicago Daily Tribune*, 11 March 1949. Harlow Shapley's announcement on February 20 that Shostakovich would be attending (*Los Angeles Times*, 21 February 1949, 14) also indicates it was a *fait accompli*. Shostakovich's remark that "it's over for me" was not atypical. According to his son, Maxim, "There were many times when Father felt he was a hair's brea[d]th away from destruction." Ardov, *Memories of Shostakovich*, 159.

38. For Zhdanov's views on Lysenko, a controversial Soviet geneticist supported by Stalin, see Kees Boterbloem, *The Life and Times of Andrei Zhdanov* (Montreal: McGill-Queen's University Press, 2004), 325–27. By the time of the Waldorf conference, Lysenko's views were being authoritatively challenged; see

Julian Huxley, *Soviet Genetics and World Science* (London: Chatto & Windus, 1949), esp. 151–95.

39. Laurel E. Fay, *Shostakovich: A Life* (Oxford: Oxford University Press, 2000), 156.

40. "Gas-wagon" most likely refers to the extermination method used in Poland by the Einsatzgruppen (Nazi mobile killing units) before the crematoria were built.

41. According to an unidentified Moscow source, Shostakovich failed to produce music "to which workers can beat time and hum as they try to accelerate production"; cited in Committee on Un-American Activities, *Report on the Communist "Peace" Offensive*, 13.

42. The foregoing quotations are taken from a fascinating little book, Alexander Werth, *Musical Uproar in Moscow* (London: Turnstile Press, 1949), which contains the verbatim report of the three-day conference.

43. Ibid., 86. Vasily Grossman believed that such subservience predated Stalin; he referred to Lenin's "central role in reducing to the status of lackeys—State lackeys—such outstanding figures of Russian culture as . . . the composer Dmitry Shostakovich." Vasily Grossman, *Everything Flows* (London: Vintage Books 2011), 195.

44. It was subsequently revealed that the murder was carried out on Stalin's orders in an early expression of the anti-Semitic campaign against "rootless cosmopolitans" that later blossomed into the Doctors' Plot. See Timothy Snyder, *Bloodlands: Europe Between Hitler and Stalin* (New York: Basic Books, 2010), 339–41; Arkady Vaksberg, *Stalin Against the Jews* (New York: Knopf, 1994), 166. For the "anti-cosmopolitan" campaign in 1948–49, see Benjamin Pinkus and Jonathan Frankel, *The Soviet Government and the Jews, 1948–1967: A Documented Study* (New York: Cambridge University Press, 1984), 154–65. The pretext for the Doctors' Plot was the death of Andrei Zhdanov in August 1948, ostensibly poisoned by his Jewish physicians. Indicative of his apparent repentance, Shostakovich, in an obituary, felt obliged to praise Zhdanov as a man of "extraordinary erudition" whose death was a "grievous, bitter loss." Cited in Brian Morton, *Shostakovich: His Life and Music* (London: Haus Books, 2006), 5.

45. Interview with Nataliya Vovsi-Mikhoels, 1991, cited in Fay, *Shostakovich*, 157.

46. Cited in Edward Rothstein, "A labour of love," *Independent Magazine*, 12 November 1988, 50.

47. For a summary of the decree, see Werth, *Musical Uproar*, 28–34.

48. For some of the devastating consequences of this campaign, recalled through first-hand personal accounts, see Wilson, *Shostakovich*, 215–26.

49. Reminiscence of M. Kozhunova, cited in Fay, *Shostakovich*, 164. According to Werth, Shostakovich, against whom Zhdanov had "a particular spite," was "too subtle, too delicate a personality to tolerate in Moscow in 1948"; Werth, *Musical Uproar*, 34.

50. D. M. Ladd to J. Edgar Hoover, 14 March 1949, FBI File, NCASP. Clark (who became a Supreme Court justice in August 1949) also recommended that the Russians be "restricted to certain areas" and that their baggage and belongings be thoroughly searched when they left the United States. The FBI also maintained surveillance on all foreign delegates. "Notice to all Agents from Director Hoover," 31 March 1949, FBI File, NCASP. There is abundant evidence in this FBI file that from 1948 both Shapley's phone and those in the NCASP offices were wiretapped, and that the NCASP was infiltrated by FBI informants. See, for example, Memo, "Personal and Confidential," Peyton Ford, Assistant to the Attorney General, to Director, FBI, 30 September 1948, FBI File, NCASP. A FOIPA request (1169530-000) in 2011 resulted in 1,801 pages of this file being released.

51. Lenhart to Hoover, 15 March 1949 and 21 March 1949. See also letters from Ursula M. Williams (March 13), Dorothy A. Kania (March 16), and Mrs. Harold C. Davis (March 29) expressing similarly strident sentiments. FBI file, NCASP. The White House and the State Department also received scores of protest letters; *New York Times*, 24 March 1949, 4.

52. *Chicago Daily Tribune*, 16 March 1949, citing letter from Brown to Acheson.

53. The governor of New York, Thomas E. Dewey, received "hundreds" of letters asking him to stop the conference; *New York Times*, 23 March 1949.

54. *New York Times*, 17 March 1949.

55. Ibid. The British writer and philosopher Professor William Olaf Stapledon was denied but then given a visa; none of the other British (or western European, South American, or African "unofficial" delegates) was so fortunate. No explanation for the reversal in Stapledon's case was given, but the Home Secretary, Chuter Ede, later denied rumors that Scotland Yard was involved. *New York Times*, 8 April 1949, 16. According to Stapledon himself, "I suppose they let me in because they think I'm harmless. Well, I am harmless." *New York Times*, 26 March 1949, 3. For an indignant letter from Stapledon's publisher to Dwight Macdonald repudiating the latter's implication that Stapledon was a fellow-traveler, see James D. Staver to Macdonald, 12 June 1949, Dwight Macdonald Papers, Yale University Library, MS 730, Box 80, Folder 199.

56. *Daily Telegraph and Morning Post*, 23 March 1949, 1,6. This is confirmed by a memo from the assistant Attorney General, Criminal Division, A. M. Campbell, to Hoover, 17 March 1949, FBI file, NCASP. Campbell later recommended that the FBI confer with the CIA regarding the delegates' status "as officers of foreign political parties." Campbell to Hoover, 28 March 1949, FBI file, NCASP.

57. *New York Times*, 17 March 1949. Editorials in east coast newspapers supported the government's decision; see *New York Times*, 18 March 1949; *Washington Post*, 19 March 1949 ("The Open Door") and 31 March 1949; *Christian Science Monitor*, 19 March 1949 ("Democracy Can Take It"); *Wall Street Journal*, 18 March 1949. For the restrictions and limitation imposed by the INS on these foreign

visitors, see memo, J. S. Ammarell to V. P. Keay, 23 March 1949, 1–2, FBI file, NCASP.

58. *Washington Post*, 23 March 1949.

59. *New York Times*, 23 March 1949. Equally disingenuously, he added, "We are going to the conference to speak freely as free individuals, we are not restricted in any way." For Shostakovich, these words would soon assume a hollow ring. Fadeyev, however, did possess a detailed knowledge of aspects of nineteenth-century American history; *New York Times*, 28 March 1949.

60. [British Foreign Office], "Peace and Soviet Policy," April 1951, p. 2, National Archives (UK), FO 975/50. This speech was later reported in, *inter alia*, *Chicago Daily Tribune* (6 March 1949) and *The New Leader* (19 March 1949).

61. *Washington Post*, 22 March 1949; *New York Times*, 22 March 1949.

62. Andrei Vishinskyi was Stalin's state prosecutor during the show trials of the 1930s and Soviet Foreign Minister from 1949 to 1953.

63. Another disembarking Russian was A. I. Oparin, secretary of the biological sciences section of the Academy of Sciences of the Soviet Union, which purged all scientists who subscribed to the "heretical" Mendelian theories of heredity, denounced by Trofim Lysenko in 1948.

64. This echoed an incident in Berlin, en route to New York: "[A]n unknown man comes up to me, slaps me on the shoulder, and shouts at me: 'Hello Shosty. What d'you like best, blondes or brunettes?'" Shostakovich added, "I simply cannot stand this familiarity." *Travel Notes*, cited in David Caute, *The Dancer Defects: The Struggle for Cultural Supremacy during the Cold War* (Oxford: Oxford University Press, 2003), 424. According to the composer Edison Denisov, Shostakovich told him, "I don't like relations between people to be too friendly. . . . [They] should be kept simple." Unpublished diary, 1 December 1953, cited in Wilson, *Shostakovich*, 243.

65. Shostakovich, *Testimony*, 196. His daughter, Galina, corroborated this sentiment: "Not without reason, he [Shostakovich] considered [journalists] rude and uneducated, capable of asking the most tactless and provocative questions." Ardov, *Memories of Shostakovich*, 143.

66. *New York Times*, 24 March 1949. The headline was "7 Russians Silent on 'Peace Mission.'"

67. Ibid., 24 March 1949. These groups were described as "a choice sample of the Christian Front Lumpenproletariat." Kirchwey, "Battle of the Waldorf," 378.

68. Kirchwey, "Battle of the Waldorf," 378. For a more general discussion of Catholic anticommunism, see Patrick McNamara, *A Catholic Cold War: Edmund Walsh, S.J., and the Politics of American Anticommunism* (New York: Fordham University Press, 2005). The new but increasingly better-known anticommunist group the AIF was also planning its activities: a counterconference at Freedom House on West 40th Street on March 26. Sidney Hook, "The Communist Peace Offensive," *Partisan Review* 51 (1984), 694–96.

69. *New York Times*, 26 March 1949. These pickets were described as a "choice example of the Christian Front Lumpenproletariat." Kirchwey, "Battle of the Waldorf," 377. Another group, also formed in direct response to the Waldorf conference, was the Russian League for People's Freedom, in which Alexander Kerensky, the leader of the Provisional Government in Russia in 1917, played a leading role.

70. See Stephen J. Whitfield, *The Culture of the Cold War* (Baltimore: Johns Hopkins University Press), 92–96, for a discussion of Catholicism and McCarthyism.

71. The hotel itself had come under "considerable pressure" to deny the booking. It had been booked by the NCASP in August 1948 only after the hotel cross-checked the NCASP against the Attorney General's List of Subversive Organizations. A spokesman felt obliged to declare the "patriotism of the hotel and its management." *Chicago Daily Tribune*, 25 March 1949, 6 March 1949; *Christian Science Monitor*, 25 March 1949; *New York Times*, 25 March 1949; Horace Sutton, *Confessions of a Grand Hotel: The Waldorf-Astoria* (New York: Henry Holt, 1951).

72. Liebling, "The Wayward Press," 86; Singer, "An analysis of the New York press treatment," 263–65.

73. The following reports are taken from the *New York Times*, 26 March 1949, and the *Chicago Daily Tribune*, 26 March 1949.

74. Several placards referred to the imprisoned Primate of Hungary, Cardinal József Mindszenty, and one banner depicted him nailed to a cross fashioned as a hammer and sickle; *Los Angeles Times*, 26 March 1949, 5.

75. *Life*, 26:14 (4 April 1949), 39; *The New Yorker*, 2 April 1949. Although badly injured, Kasenkina defected and became an icon for anticommunists. With Alexander Kerensky, she attended the rival AIF conference as well as a rally the next day of the Russian League for People's Freedom. *New York Times*, 27 March 1949, 1; *Los Angeles Times*, 28 March 1949. See also Lawrence Preuss, "Consular Immunities: The Kasenkina Case." *American Journal of International Law* 43:1 (1949), 37–56.

76. Miller, "The Year It Came Apart," 36. On this incident, see also Stefan Kanfer, *A Journal of the Plague Years* (New York: Atheneum, 1973), 109. Most newspapers carried dramatic photographs of the praying nuns.

77. *New York Times*, 27 March 1949.

78. In an editorial, the *Wall Street Journal* (29 March 1949) opposed the picketing as "bad tactics; bad morals." The *New York Herald-Tribune* was also concerned that such street demonstrations were "favorite Communist techniques." Cited in *Christian Science Monitor*, 4 April 1949.

79. *Life* 26:14 (4 April 1949), 14. Similarly, *Newsweek* (4 April 1949, 20) called him the "magnet" and "draw card" that evening. Shostakovich's celebrity status was indicated by a sign placed in a New York drugstore window, "Shostakovich Shops Here" after he bought some aspirin. Several admirers also wrote to Shapley seeking Shostakovich's autograph; see, for example, Kenneth E. Crouch to Shap-

ley, 26 February 1949, Papers of Harlow Shapley, 1906–1966, Harvard University Archives, HUG 4773.10, Box 10c.

80. *New York Times*, 26 March 1949; *Christian Science Monitor*, 26 March 1949.

81. Fast, "Cultural Forces Rally Against the Warmakers," 33. However, Fast called Cousins' manners "abominable" and caricatured his address as "a shrill and savage call to war and slaughter."

82. Daniel S. Gillmor (ed.), *Speaking of Peace* [transcripts of addresses], 1949, 15–17 ("A Dissenting Opinion").

83. *New York Times*, 26 March 1949; *Newsweek*, 4 April 1949. Although his speech received widespread publicity in New York papers, it is an overstatement by Dudley that it shook the conference "to its very roots." E. Samuel Dudley, "Warfare at the Waldorf," *Today's Speech* 11:4 (November 1963), 2. Dudley alleged that two New York detectives remained "nearby but off to the side" of the ballroom in case of trouble.

84. *Chicago Daily Tribune*, 26 March 1949.

85. Private correspondence, Norman Cousins to John Rossi, 9 March 1982. According to Hellman's most recent biographer, the Waldorf conference became "an important part of the indictment of Lillian Hellman." Kessler-Harris, *A Difficult Woman*, 249.

86. See, for example, Dudley, "Warfare at the Waldorf"; Frank A. Ninkovich, *The Diplomacy of Ideas: U.S. Foreign Policy and Cultural Relations, 1938–1950* (Cambridge: Cambridge University Press, 1981), 163. Implausibly, Ninkovich claimed Cousins took the floor "at the behest of the State Department."

87. Cousins to Rossi, 9 March 1982.

88. Transcript of Interview, 3 February 1988, with Andrew D. Basiago (Oral History Program: University of California, 1992), pp. 324–25 (tape no. 11, side 1).

89. *Los Angeles Times*, 27 March 1949. Barker Fairley was taken into custody but permitted to remain because he was a visiting professor at Columbia University. His wife, Margaret, and John Goss, an actor and theater director, were deported. For a detailed FBI report on this opening evening (supplied by an informant), see four-page memo from Hoover to Peyton Ford (Assistant Attorney General), 31 March 1949, FBI file, NCASP.

90. [Baarslag], "Report on the Scientific and Cultural Conference for World Peace," 6.

91. For a full transcript of Fadeyev's address, see American Russian Institute, *Americans, Russians and Peace* (San Francisco, 1949), 3–8.

92. After the Waldorf conference, Untermeyer was no longer invited to appear as a guest on panel shows; Kanfer, *Journal*, 109.

93. "Statement by Dwight Macdonald"; "Notes on the Writing & Publishing Panel–Discussion," 2, 26 March 1949, Dwight Macdonald Papers, Yale University Library, MS 730, Box 80, Folder 199; Macdonald, "The Waldorf Conference," 32-C; *New York Times*, 27 March 1949; Wreszin, *A Rebel*, 217.

94. Macdonald, "Notes," 3; *Washington Post*, 27 March 1949, 2. In contrast, Macdonald noted, Fadeyev had "responded with polemical ardor to my questions." At the same time in uptown Manhattan, Rabbi William Rosenblum was sermonizing that the Soviet government had taken Shostakovich, this "mild sheep," and dressed him in "the wolves' clothing of red propaganda." *New York Times*, 27 March 1949.

95. *New York Times*, 26 March 1949, 46.

96. O. John Rogge, "The Cold War at Home," in Gillmor, *Speaking of Peace*, 24.

97. *New York Times*, 29 March 1949, 1 April 1949; *Washington Post*, 1 April 1949.

98. O. John Rogge, "The Cold War at Home," 23–25.

99. Barrett, "Culture Conference at the Waldorf," 488.

100. FBI Report, NY 100-93553, 68–78.

101. His 461-page file commenced in 1947; see Tony Ortega, "Red Scare at Harvard," *Astronomy* 30:1 (January 2002), 42.

102. Downes was neither a communist nor a fellow-traveler but opposed to Franco and the Truman Doctrine, and a supporter of Henry A. Wallace. He stated in his opening address to the Fine Arts Panel, "I am neither fascist nor communist, nor politician, but an American citizen who detests iron curtains, whenever, wherever or by whomsoever, lowered." For a heavily slanted biographical sketch, see *Counterattack*, 18 March 1949 (Special Supplement), 1–2, American Business Consultants, Inc., Counterattack: Research Files, TAM 148, Box 28, Folder 14–156, Tamiment.

103. *Washington Post*, 28 March 1949; *New York Times*, 28 March 1949. The latter's front-page article was headlined "Shostakovich Bids All Artists Lead War on New 'Fascists'" and noted that the language was as bitter as the diatribes of Foreign Minister Vyshinsky. As one biographer noted, "[W]e can be sure that the politically deficient Shostakovich was not entrusted with writing the speech that was delivered in his name." Fay, *Shostakovich*, 173. For a full transcript, see American Russian Institute, *Americans, Russians and Peace*, 9–17.

104. See his "Russian Music after the Purge," *Partisan Review* 19 (1949), 842–51.

105. Nabokov, *Bagázh*, 237.

106. Nicolas Nabokov, *Old Friends and New Music* (London: Hamish Hamilton, 1951).

107. Ibid., 204–5.

108. Ibid., 238; *New York Times*, 28 March 1949. According to Volkov, it was Stravinsky, who "just hated Shostakovich," considered him a rival, and treated him ruthlessly, who was behind Nabokov's confronting Shostakovich in an open forum. In short, Nabokov was "Stravinsky's man." Solomon Volkov, interview with Galia Drubachevskaya, in Allan B. Ho and Dmitry Feofanov (eds.), *Shosta-*

kovich Reconsidered (London:Toccata Press, 1998), 338–39; 395–96. See also "Stravinsky Snubs Composer," *New York Times*, 18 March 1949.

109.Volkov, *Shostakovich and Stalin*, 286.

110. Miller, *Timebends*, 239.

111. Shostakovich, *Testimony*, 112.

112. See, for example, Edward Rothstein, "What Shostakovich Was Really Expressing," *New York Times Sunday Book Review*, 8 May 2011, 16–17. However, controversy still exists over the extent to which *Testimony* was the legitimate voice of Shostakovich.

113. Private correspondence, Schlesinger to Rossi, 22 September 1982.

114. In this he overstated his role (see Nabokov, *Bagázh*, 233; Hook, *Out of Step*, 382–96), but he was financially assisted by the CIA. In 1951 he was elected Secretary General of the Congress for Cultural Freedom.

115. Hook to Rossi, 11 March 1982. For a more detailed account of the motivating factors, see Hook, *Out of Step*, 382–85. Nevertheless, one writer claimed that the State Department, which "contacted Sidney Hook," was the guiding influence. Abrams, "A Profoundly Hegemonic Moment," 76. This is debatable, but the State Department certainly supported a more broad-based anti-Soviet cultural organization in the immediate aftermath of the Waldorf conference.

116. Papers of Harlow Shapley, 1906–1966, Harvard University Archives, HUG 4773.10, Box 10c, Shapley to Dorothy Fisher, 15 March 1949 (see also correspondence dated 7, 10, 13, 14 March 1949).

117. *Washington Post*, 26 March 1949; *New York Times*, 27 March 1949. See also *New York Times*, 20 March 1949. The hotel incident is described in Jumonville, *Critical Crossings*, 1–2, and Hook, *Out of Step*, 390–92. The correspondence from Hook pertaining to the conference, and with which he confronted Shapley, is contained in both the Shapley papers and Hook, "The Communist Peace Offensive," 708–11.

118. *Christian Science Monitor*, 26 March 1949.

119. McCarthy to Rossi, 1 June 1982.

120. See his "Kulturfest at the Waldorf: Soapbox for Red Propaganda," *The New Leader*, 19 March 1949. Counts intervened at one panel session. Despite shouts of "shut up" from many of the 700-strong audience, he was permitted to speak. *Los Angeles Times*, 27 March 1949.

121. Farrell's famous character Studs Lonigan inspired Louis Terkel, who was a delegate at Waldorf, to adopt the moniker "Studs."

122. *New York Times*, 27 March 1949, 46.

123. Brightman, *Writing Dangerously*, 324–25; William Phillips, *A Partisan View* (New York: Stein & Day, 1983), 149.

124. Hook, *Out of Step*, 394.

125. *Christian Science Monitor*, 28 March 1949. In such a statement, we can see the genesis of the Congress for Cultural Freedom, in which Hook was to play a major role. See Records, American Committee for Cultural Freedom, Tamiment,

TAM 023, Box 2, Folders 7–8; Wilford, *The Mighty Wurlitzer*, 71; Stoner Saunders, *Who Paid the Piper?*, 54–55.

126. Margaret Marshall, "Notes by the Way," *The Nation*, 168: 9 April 1949, 419.

127. *New York Times*, 27 March 1949.

128. Brightman, *Writing Dangerously*, 324.

129. Fast, *Being Red*, 202. Matthiessen, a Harvard University professor, committed suicide in the spring of 1950. It was alleged that HUAC's investigation of his political beliefs contributed to his death, but his deep depression after the death of his homosexual partner was a more probable cause. Eric Jacobsen, *Translation: A Traditional Craft* (Copenhagen: Gyldendalske Boghandel, 1958), 9–10; Harry Levin, "The Private Life of F. O. Matthiessen," *New York Review of Books*, 20 July 1978, 42–46.

130. Hook, *Out of Step*, 395.

131. *New York Times*, 28 March 1949; *Los Angeles Times*, 28 March 1949. Eighty uniformed police were stationed inside the Garden, where 3 arrests were made, and a reserve force of 300 was stationed in the basement.

132. *Christian Science Monitor*, 28 March 1949.

133. *Washington Post*, 29 March 1949.

134. Shostakovich, *Testimony*, 112.

135. *Los Angeles Times*, 28 March 1949. Harlow Shapley excused this refusal by announcing, "A very tired artist says 'No more, please'"; *Christian Science Monitor*, 28 March 1949.

136. [Baarslag], "Report," 14.

137. *New York Times*, 29 March 1949.

138. *Washington Post*, 30 March 1949; *New York Times*, 30 March 1949. According to a non-communist left-wing paper, the government "cracked down in a style to which the visitors have become accustomed in their own countries" and was "an exhibition of weakness and fear." "America Afraid," *The Progressive* 13 (May 1949), 4. For Henry A. Wallace's denunciation of the decision ("the hysterical action of a fearful state"), see *New York Times*, 30 March 1949; for the Soviet response, see *Christian Science Monitor*, 1 April 1949.

139. *Washington Post*, 30 March 1949; *Chicago Daily Tribune*, 30 March 1949; *New York Times*, 30 March 1949. Yale University had already refused permission for Shostakovich to play in Woolsey Hall; Professor John Marsalka, who invited him, was sacked soon after. *New York Times*, 12 April 1949.

140. *New York Times*, 4 April 1949; *Christian Science Monitor*, 4 April 1949.

141. *Christian Science Monitor*, 4 April 1949.

142. Shostakovich, *Testimony*, 198.

143. Termed "The Great Stalinist Plan for Remaking Nature," it was a grandiose fifteen-year tree-planting project to protect southern central Asia from drought; it commenced in October 1948 and ceased immediately upon Stalin's death.

144. L. Kovnatskaya, *D. D. Shostakovich: sbornik statey Khrushchev 90-leyiyu so dnya rozhdeniya* (St. Petersburg, 1996), 242, in Fay, *Shostakovich*, 175.

145. S. Khentova, *Udivitel"niy Shostakovich* (St. Petersburg, 1996), 153, in Fay, *Shostakovich*, 175.

146. See, for example, Joshua Rubenstein, *Tangled Loyalties: The Life and Times of Ilya Ehrenburg* (New York: New Press, 1996), 253–76.

147. Memorandum, British Embassy, Vienna, to Foreign Office, London, 31 December 1952, NA: FO 1110/550.

148. Cited in Fay, *Shostakovich*, 181. Ehrenburg noted that "his face was very gloomy" until he learned the trick of surreptitiously unplugging the headphones.

149. Comment to Edison Denisov, cited in Fay, *Shostakovich*, 184.

150. Cited in Wilson, *Shostakovich*, 335.

151. Grossman, *Everything Flows*, 195.

152. Nevertheless, Shostakovich remained a deeply troubled man. When he received an honorary degree of Doctor of Music from Oxford University in June 1958, his host, Isaiah Berlin, wrote to a friend that when Shostakovich was accompanied by two "diplomats" from the Soviet Embassy, he was "terribly nervous . . . I have never seen anyone so frightened and crushed in all my life." Berlin concluded: "S.'s face will always haunt me somewhat, it is terrible to see a man of genius victimized by a regime, crushed by it into accepting his fate as something normal, terrified of being plunged into some other life, with all powers of indignation, resistance, protest removed. . . ." Isaiah Berlin, "Shostakovich at Oxford," *New York Review of Books*, 16 July 2009.

5. The Lawyer: O. John Rogge

1. W. E. B. Du Bois, *In Battle for Peace: The Story of My 83rd Birthday* (New York: Masses & Mainstream, 1952), 110.

2. Ronald Radosh and Joyce Milton, *The Rosenberg File* (New Haven, Conn.: Yale University Press, 1997, 2nd ed.), 82.

3. See O. John Rogge, *Why Men Confess* (New York: Thomas Nelson & Sons, 1959), 146–47.

4. *Current Biography* (New York: H. W. Wilson, 1948), 534; Alan Schaffer, *Vito Marcantonio, Radical in Congress* (Syracuse, N.Y.: Syracuse University Press, 1966), 186.

5. This quest failed mainly because he was too little-known outside New York and Washington.

6. *Current Biography*, 534; Richard J. Walton, *Wallace, Harry Truman and the Cold War* (New York: Viking, 1976), 42, 193. Rogge strongly endorsed Wallace's call for rapprochement with the Soviet Union, which attracted strong support from the CPUSA. They spoke together at the Waldorf conference in March 1949.

7. Karl M. Schmidt, *Henry A. Wallace: Quixotic Crusade 1948* (Syracuse, N.Y.: Syracuse University Press, 1960), 278.

8. See Robbie Lieberman, *The Strangest Dream: Communism, Anti-Communism, and the United States Peace Movement, 1945–1963* (Syracuse, N.Y.: Syracuse University Press, 2000), ch. 2.

9. *New Leader*, 29 January 1951, 2.

10. *New York Times*, 4 February 1946, 14 October 1946, 4 April 1947, 5 December 1947. For an extended discussion of the "Brown Scare" and Rogge's role in prosecuting thirty pro-Nazi conspirators in 1944, see Leo P. Ribuffo, *The Old Christian Right: The Protestant Far Right from the Great Depression to the Cold War* (Philadelphia: Temple University Press, 1983), 198–213; Brett Gray, *The Nervous Liberals: Propaganda Anxieties from World War 1 to the Cold War* (New York: Columbia University Press, 1999), ch. 6, esp. 224–27 and 236–41. See also O. John Rogge, *The Official German Report: Nazi Penetration, 1924–1942* (New York: Thomas Yoseloff, 1961).

11. *In Fact*, vol. XIV, no. 19 (10 February 1947), 1–4.

12. *New York Times*, 7 October 1947, 53.

13. *Lawyers' Guild Review*, 9:1 (Winter 1949), 15. This was part of a vitriolic "Report on Civil Liberties" (13–17) written by Rogge.

14. *New York Times*, 8 November 1947. The purpose of this maneuver, he stated (in language that would have been at home in the *Daily Worker*), was to "whip up a new wave of anti-Soviet hysteria to divert public attention from the wave of reaction into which the Truman administration had plunged because of Wall Street influence." Ibid.

15. Joseph R. Starobin, *American Communism in Crisis, 1943–1957* (Cambridge: Mass.: Harvard University Press, 1972), 173, 292n32.

16. See Bureau of the Committee of the World Congress of Peace, *In Defence of Peace*, no. 2, March 1950.

17. For the National Lawyers' Guild see John A. Salmond, *The Conscience of a Lawyer: Clifford J. Durr and American Civil Liberties, 1899–1975* (Tuscaloosa: University of Alabama Press, 1990), 136–39 (Durr was president of the Guild in 1948–49). For the Civil Rights Congress, see *Liberator*, 1:1 (January 1949), 2. The rhetoric of this inaugural issue is identical to that of Communist Party publications in this period.

18. Like the infamous rape trials of the Scottsboro Boys (1931–37), the Trenton Six trials (1948–52) involved race more than justice. Initially, Rogge and Emmanuel ("Manny") Block represented the six black defendants but, controversially, were barred from the case by the presiding judge; see *New York Times*, 18 December 1949.

19. O. John Rogge, *Our Vanishing Civil Liberties* (New York: Gaer Associates, 1949), 37. For the text of one of his many attacks on HUAC, see *New York Times*, 31 October 1947.

20. *New York Times*, 17 April 1947.

21. Rogge, *Our Vanishing Civil Liberties*, 274–75.

22. FBI Rogge file, letter [identity redacted] to Hoover, 2 February 1947.

23. Roy M. Cohn and Sidney Zion, *The Autobiography of Roy Cohn* (Secaucus, N.J.: Lyle Stuart, 1988), 71

24. Du Bois, *In Battle for Peace*, 115, 118.

25. See Albert E. Kahn, *Treason in Congress: The Record of the House Un-American Activities Committee* (New York: Publications Committee, 1948).

26. Albert E. Kahn, "The Case of O. John Rogge," *Masses & Mainstream*, Vol. 5, No. 1, January 1952, 15–16.

27. Ibid., 21.

28. Gus Hall, *Basics for Peace, Democracy and Social Progress* (New York: International Publishers, 1980), 164–65.

29. *Daily Worker*, 21 November 1951.

30. MI5 paper PR87/98, classified "Secret," entitled "Developments in the World Peace Campaign," 21 August 1950, 8. National Archives, Kew, London (henceforth NA): FO 1110/347.

31. *Daily Worker*, 14 November 1951, 6; 15 November 1951, 1. Others, on the left, were no less damning: The radical journalist I. F. Stone accused him of "betrayal." *Daily Compass* (New York), cited in *National Guardian*, 21 November 1951, 5.

32. Sam Roberts, *The Brother: The Untold Story of Atomic Spy David Greenglass and How He Sent His Sister, Ethel Rosenberg, to the Electric Chair* (New York: Random House, 2001), 257.

33. See *New York Times*, 11 January 1951; Bureau of the Committee of the World Congress of the Defenders of Peace, *In Defense of Peace*, No. 8, March 1950.

34. The following is drawn from *World Biography* (New York: Institute for Research in Biography, 1948), 4058; *Current Biography* (New York: H. W. Wilson Co. [1948]), 533–35; *The Annual Obituary 1981* (New York: St. Martin's Press [1981]), 197–98; *New York Times*, 22 March 1981, obituary.

35. Harnett T. Kane, *Louisiana Hayride: The American Rehearsal for Dictatorship, 1928–1940* (New York: Morrow, 1941), 315.

36. O. John Rogge, "Witch Hunting," transcript of address delivered at City Club, Boston, Massachusetts, 27 January 1940, 16–17.

37. O. John Rogge, "Criminal Law Enforcement and Civil Liberties," transcript of address delivered at YWCA, Newark, New Jersey, 11 June 1940, 5.

38. O. John Rogge, "Witch Hunting," 16–17.

39. Personal conversation with Leo Ribuffo, New York; Ribuffo interviewed Rogge for his *Old Christian Right* (1983).

40. Kane, *Louisiana Hayride*, 314.

41. David Shannon, *Decline of American Communism: A History of the Communist Party of the United States since 1945* (New York: Harcourt, Brace, 1959), 205.

42. Committee on Un-American Activities, U.S. House of Representatives, *Report on the Communist "Peace" Offensive. A Campaign to Disarm and Defeat the United States*, Report 378, 1 April 1951 (Library of Congress, Washington), 37.

43. FBI file, Rogge, Octje [*sic*] John, 62-54144-101 (henceforth FBI Rogge file), handwritten comment on memo, 9 December 1950.

44. NA: FO 1110/346, Annex "A" to Secret memorandum, C. F. A. Warner to Sir William Strang, 25 May 1950. The IRD was a clandestine anti-Soviet propaganda unit established in 1948. It was the brainchild of Christopher Mayhew, then Parliamentary Under-Secretary to Ernest Bevin. In 1950, as an executive committee member of the United Nations Association, he wrote a long article for the *Sheffield Telegraph* (13 November 1950), "Democratic Solution Exists Already If You Really Want Peace"; the timing (the opening day of the congress) was deliberate. For one of the first analyses of the IRD, see W. Scott Lucas and C. J. Morris, "A Very British Crusade: The Information Research Department and the Beginning of the Cold War," in Richard J. Aldrich, *British Intelligence, Strategy and the Cold War, 1945–51* (London: Routledge, 1992), 84–109.

45. The "two-camp" thesis, first enunciated by the Soviet theorist Andrei Zhdanov (whom we met in Chapter 4) at the inaugural meeting of the Communist Information Bureau (Cominform) in September 1947, refers to the division of the world into, and the inevitability of conflict between, two power blocs: the democratic and peace-loving led by the Soviet Union and the imperialist and warmongering led by the United States.

46. *New York Herald Tribune*, 25 April 1949. See also *New York Times*, 24 April 1949.

47. See Howard Fast, *Peekskill: USA* (New York: Civil Rights Congress, 1951).

48. *New York Times*, 10 September 1949.

49. *Bulletin of the Atomic Scientists*, 6:4 (April 1950), 128.

50. *New York Times*, 9 March 1950, 9. On the other hand, Rogge subsequently noted that "Ever since my Kremlin speech I have received requests from all over the [United] States to address meetings. . . . I will accept these invitations." Committee of the World Peace Congress, *In Defence of Peace*, No. 9, April 1950, 57.

51. The Secretary of State, Dean Acheson, judged the Stockholm Appeal as a "propaganda trick in the spurious 'peace offensive' of the Soviet Union." *New York Times*, 13 July 1950.

52. See Allan Taylor, "Story of the Stockholm Petition," *New York Times*, 13 August 1950, 6E; NA: FO 975/54, "The Record of the World Peace Council," November 1951, 3–4; National Archives of Australia (henceforth NAA): A1838/1, 851/19/1 Pt. 1A, "Stockholm Appeal," Memorandum from A. H. Tange to Secretary, Prime Minister's Department, 17 July 1951.

53. According to Julius Rosenberg's KGB "handler," in 1950 a leading Soviet member of the Partisans of Peace, the writer Ilya Ehrenburg, had been "very

much concerned" by Rogge who, allegedly, was "constantly obstructing every decision made by the [peace] movement." Alexander Feklisov and Sergei Kostin, *The Man Behind the Rosenbergs* (New York: Enigma Books, 2001), 296.

54. *In Defence of Peace*, No. 9, April 1950, 55–58. This publication contained all the addresses given to the Stockholm Congress; none echoed Rogge's.

55. From January 1946 until April 29, 1950, when he was dismissed, Joliot-Curie was the French High Commissioner for Atomic Energy; he was also a prominent member of the French Communist Party and president of the World Federation of Scientific Workers. Within the communist-dominated peace movement he was revered, and to attack him from "within," as Rogge did, was a major transgression.

56. *New York Times*, 17 August 1950.

57. For an explanation of the dispute, see Anne Applebaum, *Iron Curtain: The Crushing of Eastern Europe 1944–1956* (New York: Doubleday, 2012), 254–55.

58. *For a Lasting Peace, for a People's Democracy!*, No. 6 (66), 10 February 1950, 4; No. 5 (65), 3 February 1950, 1; No. 47 (107), 19 November 1950, 2.

59. On Zilliacus, see Archie Potts, *Zilliacus: A Life for Peace and Socialism* (London: Merlin, 2002). His pro-Tito leftism shaped the alliance with Rogge, who stayed with Zilliacus when he visited London. Memo, 15 August 1950, Rogge FBI File.

60. O. John Rogge, Jean Cassou, and K. Zilliacus, "Korea, Yugoslavia and World Peace: Where We Stand," August 1950, 5. This joint statement was never published, but a copy was sent by Rogge to Jesse M. MacKnight at the U.S. State Department. See National Archives and Records Administration, Washington (henceforth NARA) RG: 59, Misc. Records of the Bureau of Public Affairs, Lot File 61D53, Stack 252/62/14/05/03, Box 72.

61. Ibid., 4, 6, 7–8, 10.

62. See editorial, *Daily Worker*, 21 November 1950; transcript of speeches by Charles Howard and Pero Popivoda to the Warsaw Congress, Second World Congress, Warsaw, 16–22 November 1950 [n.p. 1951], 58, 67; Du Bois, *In Battle for Peace*, 112; Kahn, "The Case of O. John Rogge," 19–20; *For a Lasting Peace, for a People's Democracy!*, No. 47 (107), 19 November 1950, 2. Two other prominent American leftists, William Gailmor and Louis Adamic, were also both castigated and marginalized for writing sympathetically about the Yugoslavs; see Starobin, *American Communism in Crisis*, 299, n. 7.

63. NA: FO 1110/347, "Developments in the World Peace Campaign," paper sent to P. A. Wilkinson, Information Research Department, 21 August 1950, 8.

64. FBI Rogge file, memo, J. Edgar Hoover to Jack D. Neal, Division of Security, Department of State, 14 March 1950. According to Hoover, it was possible that Rogge, who visited Moscow in March, was engaged by the Yugoslav government as an "intermediary" between it and the Soviet government.

65. Steven Casey, "Selling NSC-68: The Truman Administration, Public Opinion, and the Politics of Mobilization, 1950–51," *Diplomatic History*, Vol. 29, No. 4 (September 2005), 658.

66. *New York Times*, 17 April 1950.

67. FBI Rogge file, Summary, Yugoslav Home Service, 25 November 1950 (FBI memo dated 12 December 1950).

68. "Korea, Yugoslavia and World Peace," 2.

69. NARA RG: 59, Misc. Records of the Bureau of Public Affairs, Lot File 61D53, Stack 252/62/14/05/03, Box 72, O. John Rogge, "An Appeal to Moderates," [n.d.].

70. Indicative of this interest are the voluminous notes and clippings on this subject in his papers; see O. John Rogge papers, 1945–56, Library of Congress archives, Washington, MMC 3504.

71. NARA RG: 59, Misc. Records of the Bureau of Public Affairs, Lot File 61D53, Stack 252/62/14/05/03, Box 72, O. John Rogge, Memorandum, Mac-Knight to Phillips, 19 June 1951.

72. Ibid., Memorandum of Conversation, 1 November 1950.

73. According to MI5, the British Peace Committee had attempted to obtain the Empress Hall in Earl's Court, London but that the request had been refused on political grounds. NA: FO 1110/375, MI5 paper "Second World Peace Congress Sheffield/Warsaw 1950," 3 attached to correspondence from MI5 to J. H. Peck (IRD), 30 January 1951.

74. In 1950–51 a range of lengthy papers was prepared; see NA: FO 975/50, "Peace and Soviet Foreign Policy"; FO 975/54, "The Record of the World Peace Council," FO 975/64, "Aspects of Peace. A Study in Soviet Tactics"; FO 371/84825, "Russian Strategic Intentions and the Threat to Peace"; PREM 8/1150, "Disarmament and the Soviet Peace Campaign" (ten-page brief for the UK delegation to the UN General Assembly). Briefer documents on communist-organized peace congresses can also be found in PREM 8/966 and 8/1103. All these testify strongly to the importance placed by the British government on this activity.

75. NA: FO 1110/371, K. G. Younger to J. Chuter Ede, 5 June 1951. This view was shared by Vincent Tewson, the General Secretary of the powerful Trades Union Congress, who alleged the peace campaign was "fraudulent" and a "tactic in the strategy of international communism." *Manchester Guardian*, 7 September 1950, 6.

76. NA: PREM 8/1150, Bevin to Attlee, 26 November 1950, Annex, "Aims of the World Peace Movement," 1.

77. See Lawrence S. Wittner, *One World or None: A History of the World Nuclear Disarmament Movement Through 1953* (Stanford, Calif.: Stanford University Press, 1993), 177–86.

78. Denis Healey, "The Trojan Dove" in NA: FO 1110/349. See also Denis Healey, *The Time of My Life* (London: Michael Joseph, 1989), 106–7.

79. NA: FO 1110/349, Information Research Department minute, 7 December 1950.

80. NA: FO 1110/370, Appreciation, "Secret," "Second World Peace Congress" [p. 1].

81. NA: PREM 8/1150, A. N. Noble to Bevin, 13 November 1950.

82. NA: FO 1110/349, J. Nicholls (British Embassy, Moscow) to Bevin, 4 December 1950; FO 1110/370, Nicholls to Murray, 27 December 1950.

83. *The Times* (London), 13 November 1950; Phillip Deery, "The Dove Flies East: Whitehall, Warsaw and the 1950 World Peace Congress," *Australian Journal of Politics & History* 48:4 (December 2002), 449–68; Wes Ullrich, "Preventing 'Peace': The British Government and the Second World Peace Congress," *Cold War History* 11.3 (August 2011), 341–62.

84. Rogge was questioned for nearly one hour at Heathrow. Presumably his non-communist credentials were established. The British Foreign Office had already decided that "it would be inadvisable to exclude him." NA: FO 1110/346, Annex "A" to Secret memorandum, C. F. A. Warner to Sir William Strang, 25 May 1950.

85. *Sheffield Telegraph*, 14 November 1950, 1.

86. NARA RG: 59, Misc. Records of the Bureau of Public Affairs, Lot File 61D53, Stack 252/62/14/05/03, Box 72, undated cable, USIS London to VOA Kaufman New York.

87. *Sheffield Telegraph*, 14 November 1950.

88. *Sheffield Telegraph*, 19 November 1950.

89. *Daily Worker*, 16 November 1950.

90. *New York Times*, 17 November 1950, extracted in NAA: A1838/283, Item 69/1/1/16/1 Pt. 2.

91. NA FO 1110/349, J. H. Peck to P. Jordan (PM's office), 1 December 1950.

92. Ian Turner, "My Long March," *Overland*, 59 (Spring 1974), 36. In 1950 I. A. H. Turner was secretary of the Australian Peace Council and was expelled from the Australian Communist Party in 1958 over Hungary.

93. The following is based on reports in *Daily Worker, Challenge, Manchester Guardian, The Times*, and an interview with one Australian delegate present, Roger Wilson.

94. Stakhanovite-like propaganda was evident: According to the Polish press, the congress was "inspiring the Polish workers to a spontaneous increase of output." *The Times*, 17 November 1950. Similarly: "Polish factory workers joined 'Peace Shifts' in honour of the Congress and ran their machines at a still faster pace." *Congress of Peace, Warsaw 1950* (Listopad, 1950), 14.

95. J. D. Bernal, "The Way to Peace," *Labour Monthly* 23:1 (January 1950), 13.

96. *Daily Worker* (UK), 21 November 1950.

97. NA: FO 1110/347, "Developments in the World Peace Campaign," paper sent from MI6 to P. A. Wilkinson, Information Research Department, 21 August 1950, 2.

98. See *We Can Save Peace: The Story of the Second World Peace Congress Warsaw 1950*, London [1951], 46pp; *Peace: A World Review*, No. 21, Special Number: Second World Peace Congress, 16–22 November 1950 (144pp); *Congress of Peace, Warsaw 1950*, Listopad, 1950 (160pp); *New Times* (Special Supplement, Reports

and Documents), no. 49, 6 December 1950. All are located in the J. D. Bernal papers, Marx Memorial Library, London.

99. Elinor Burns, "The Warsaw Peace Congress," *World News and Views*, 30:48 (2 December 1950), 567.

100. See *The Times*, 20 November 1950; *New York Times*, 20 November 1950; *National Guardian*, 22 November 1950; NA: FO1110/349, C. H. Bateman to Ernest Bevin, "Second World Peace Congress at Warsaw, 16th November, 1950," PR 87/454, 3; *Peace: A World Review*, no.21, "Special Number of the Second World Peace Congress, November 16–22 1950," 99; NAA: A1838/283, Item 69/1/1/16/12, extracts from Polish Home Service broadcast, 19 November 1950.

101. *New York Times*, 20 November 1950.

102. Ibid.; NAA: A1838/283, Item 69/1/1/16/1 Pt. 2, Department of External Affairs Press Cuttings.

103. *New York Times*, 20 November 1950.

104. NA: FO1110/349, C. H. Bateman to Ernest Bevin, "Second World Peace Congress at Warsaw, 16th November, 1950," PR 87/454, 3.

105. Ibid., 2. ("The American delegate, John Rogge, told members of my staff . . .")

106. NARA RG 59, Misc. Records of the Bureau of Public Affairs, Lot File 61D53, Stack 252/62/14/05/03, Box 72, correspondence, "Personal," MacKnight to Rogge, 3 November 1950. Again suggestive of the close working, if not personal, relationship between the two, Rogge visited MacKnight on November 1 "to do some thinking out loud." He also promised to inform MacKnight of the names of the American delegates who "might be expected to take an independent point of view" at Sheffield; as it turned out, there were none. Ibid., Memorandum of Conversation, Confidential, 1 November 1950.

107. *New York Times*, 20 November 1950.

108. NARA RG 59, Misc. Records of the Bureau of Public Affairs, Lot File 61D53, Stack 252/62/14/05/03, Box 72, Memorandum of Conversation, Restricted, 12 December 1950.

109. *National Guardian*, 29 November 1950.

110. *New York Times*, 23 November 1950. He stated that at Warsaw the two things he found were "hate and violence. They want peace by force."

111. NARA RG 59, Misc. Records of the Bureau of Public Affairs, Lot File 61D53, Stack 252/62/14/05/03, Box 72, Memorandum of Conversation, Restricted, 12 December 1950. The following day, December 13, he sent to Rogge's New York office the State Department's so-called White Book on China, entitled *U.S. Relations with China*, and referred him to particular sections.

112. NARA RG 59, Misc. Records of the Bureau of Public Affairs, Lot File 61D53, Stack 252/62/14/05/03, Box 72, Memorandum of Conversation with O. John Rogge, January 19, 1951.

113. *The New Leader*, 29 January 1951. An accompanying editorial, "What Does Mr. Rogge Offer?," explained *The New Leader*'s decision to publish Rogge's "ex-

clusive statement"—because the editors "welcome[d] any cleavage in the Soviet front," and because the article may "encourage others to follow [Rogge] out of the pro-Communist movement." Ibid., 4–5.

114. Mari Jo Buhle et al., *Encyclopedia of the American Left* (New York: Oxford University Press, 1998), 771–72.

115. *Masses & Mainstream*, 5:1 (January 1952), 20.

116. NARA RG 59, Misc. Records of the Bureau of Public Affairs, Lot File 61D53, Stack 252/62/14/05/03, Box 72, handwritten statements on memo from MacKnight requesting review and comments, 24 April 1951 ("WRS says he has already told JMM [MacKnight] he does not think this is good" and "PHB doesn't like it at all").

117. FBI Rogge file, memo, L. B. Nichols to C. Tolson, 14 June 1950; memo, 5 January 1951. On these individuals, see Ted Morgan, *A Covert Life. Jay Lovestone: Communist, Anti-Communist, and Spymaster* (New York: Random House, 1999); Robert D. Parmet, *The Master of Seventh Avenue: David Dubinsky and the American Labor Movement* (New York: New York University Press, 2005); Nelson Lichtenstein, *The Most Dangerous Man in Detroit: Walter Reuther and the Fate of American Labor* (Champaign: University of Illinois Press, 1997).

118. Raymond Wolters, *Du Bois and His Rivals* (Columbia: University of Missouri Press, 2002), 250. They married one week later, on February 14.

119. According to an overheated *New York Herald Tribune* editorial (11 February 1950), the PIC represented "an attempt to disarm America and yet ignore every from of Communist aggression."

120. *Daily Worker*, 14 November 1951.

121. NARA RG 59, Misc. Records of the Bureau of Public Affairs, Lot File 61D53, Stack 252/62/14/05/03, Box 72, Memorandum, MacKnight to Phillips, 19 June 1951.

122. Unknown to anyone in the United States, in 1951 Noel, an unusual casualty of the Stalinist show trials in Prague and Budapest, was incarcerated in a Hungarian jail, while Hermann spent five years in a secret Polish prison cell for political prisoners. See Applebaum, *Iron Curtain*, 286–88; and Hermann Field and Kate Field's remarkable *Trapped in the Cold War: The Ordeal of an American Family* (Stanford, Calif.: Stanford University Press, 1999).

123. Papers of O. John Rogge, Library of Congress archives, Washington, MMC 3504.

124. NARA RG 59, Misc. Records of the Bureau of Public Affairs, Lot File 61D53, Stack 252/62/14/05/03, Box 72, attachment to correspondence, Rogge to MacKnight, 19 December 1951; correspondence, MacKnight to Rogge, 5 January 1952.

125. See, for example, *New York Times*, 22 February 1951, 37 ("Rally Backs Du Bois").

126. Gerald Meyer, *Vito Marcantonio: Radical Politician, 1902–1954* (Albany: State University of New York Press, 1989), 84–85. Marcantonio represented the

ALP in Congress from 1938 to 1950, when he lost his seat. As we have seen, Howard Fast later stood for his seat in the 1952 congressional elections.

127. For accounts of the trial, on which the above is based, see *Daily Worker*, 14–15 November 1951; *New York Times*, 14 November 1951; *National Guardian*, 21 November 1951; Gerald Horne, *Black and Red: W. E. B. Du Bois and the Afro-American Response to the Cold War, 1944–1963* (Albany: State University of New York Press, 1986), 176–79.

128. *Daily Compass*, 22 November 1951.

129. *National Guardian*, 28 November 1951.

130. FBI Rogge file, memo, Director's Reception Room, 28 July 1950; memo, D. M. Ladd to Hoover, 31 July 1950.

131. Ibid., memo, Director's Reception Room, 14 June 1951. It is difficult to discern what underlay these approaches. The two men had known each other since the late 1930s (see ibid., letter, Rogge to Hoover, 22 May 1939: "I am sure our future association will prove to be a mutually pleasant and helpful one"), but that alone seems insufficient. There is a remote possibility that Rogge wished to work with the FBI in intelligence-gathering; Feklisov, Julius Rosenberg's handler, claimed that Rogge was "probably working with the FBI." Feklisov and Kostin, *Man Behind the Rosenbergs*, 296. Rogge's cooperation with the State Department was encouraged: As Macknight commented, Rogge "might be extremely useful, for propaganda purposes, if he gets some help to operate at Berlin." NARA RG 59, Misc. Records of the Bureau of Public Affairs, Lot File 61D53, Stack 252/62/14/05/03, Box 72, Memorandum, MacKnight to Phillips, 19 June 1951.

132. Ibid., letter, Hoover to Rogge, 6 June 1951. Similarly, Rogge addressed Hoover as "Dear Edgar."

133. Roberts, *The Brother*, 257 (no source given); FBI Rogge file, memo, 17 May 1954; memo, A. H. Belmont to L. V. Boardman, 1 September 1955. The last-mentioned instruction was issued on March 3, 1950, and was still in force when his FBI file ceased at the end of 1957.

134. FBI Rogge file, memo, A. H. Belmont to L. V. Boardman, 1 September 1955. See also note attached to letter from Hoover to Rogge, 12 June 1957, 1–2.

135. FBI Rogge file, memo, SAC, New York to Hoover, 19 April 1957, 6–7.

Conclusion

1. Peter Y. Sussman (ed.), *Decca: The Letters of Jessica Mitford* (London: Weidenfeld & Nicholson, 2006), 146–47.

2. Ellen Schrecker, *Many Are the Crimes: McCarthyism in America* (Boston: Little Brown, 1998), 369. Her final chapter (359–418) provides a comprehensive discussion of the consequences and legacies of McCarthyism.

Bibliography

Archives

American Business Consultants, Inc., Counterattack Papers, Tamiment Library & Robert F. Wagner Archives, New York University, New York (hereafter Tamiment Library)

American Committee for Cultural Freedom Papers, Tamiment Library

American Library Association Archives, University Archives, University of Illinois at Urbana–Champaign

Dorothy Arnold Papers, New York University Archives

Edward K. Barsky Papers, Abraham Lincoln Brigade Archives, Tamiment Library

J. D. Bernal Papers, Marx Memorial Library, London

Board of Education Records, Municipal Archives, City of New York

Lyman Bradley Papers, New York University Archives

Edwin Berry Burgum Papers, New York University Archives

Kenneth Cameron Papers, Tamiment Library

Frank Campenni Papers, University Manuscript Archives, University of Wisconsin–Milwaukee

Harry W. Chase Papers, New York University Archives

Department of External Affairs files, National Archives of Australia, Canberra

Fales Manuscript Collection, Fales Library, New York University

Howard Fast Papers, Manuscript Library, University of Pennsylvania

Foreign Office files, National Archives, Kew

James Jackson Papers, Tamiment Library

Dwight Macdonald Papers, Manuscripts and Archives, Yale University Library, New Haven

James Marshall Papers, Municipal Archives, City of New York

Carl Aldo Marzani Papers, Tamiment Library
Steve Nelson Papers, Tamiment Library
Office of President/Chancellor Papers, NYU, New York University Archives
Rapp-Courdet Legislative Committee Public Hearing, New York City Board of
    Higher Education Archives
Records of the Bureau of Public Affairs, National Archives and Records Admin-
    istration, College Park
O. John Rogge Papers, Library of Congress Archives, Washington
Morris Schappes Papers, Tamiment Library
Harlow Shapley Papers, Harvard University
Charlotte Todes Stern Papers, Tamiment Library
Paul Tillett Files, Seeley G. Mudd Library, Princeton University, Princeton
Unitarian Service Committee, Administrative Records, Andover–Harvard Theo-
    logical Library, Harvard Divinity School, Cambridge
VALB Records, Abraham Lincoln Brigade Archives, Tamiment Library

FBI Files

Edward Barsky
Lyman Richard Bradley
Helen Reid Bryan
Edwin Berry Burgum
COINTELPRO, Communist Party of the United States of America
Domestic Intelligence Division Inspection Reports
Howard Fast
Joint Anti-Fascist Refugee Committee
Felix Kusman
National Committee for the Arts, Sciences and Professions
Responsibilities Program File and the Dissemination of Information File
O. John Rogge

Official Records

Barsky v. Board of Regents, 347 U.S. 442 (1954)
Barsky v. United States, 167 F. 2d 241 (1948)
Barsky v. United States, 334 U.S. 843 (1948)
Brown v. Board of Education, 347 U.S. 483 (1954)
Bryan v. United States, 174 F. 2d 525 (1949)
Bryan v. United States, 340 U.S. 866 (1950)
Joint Anti-Fascist Refugee Committee v. McGrath, 341 U.S. 123 (1951)
U.S. Congress. Congressional Record. Proceedings and Debates,1946–47, Washington
U.S. Congress, House. Committee on Un-American Activities. Guide to Subver-
    sive Organizations and Publications (and Appendix) 85th Congress, 1st sess., 1957,
    Washington

———. Committee on Un-American Activities. *Hearings on Gerhardt Eisler: Investigation of Un-American Propaganda Activities in the United States*, 1947, Washington

———. Committee on Un-American Activities. *Report on the Communist "Peace" Offensive: A Campaign to Disarm and Defeat the United States*, 1951, Washington

———. Committee on Un-American Activities. *Review of the Scientific and Cultural Conference for World Peace*, 1949, Washington

———. *Executive Hearings, House Committee on Un-American Activities*, 79th Congress, 2nd sess., 1946, Washington

———. *Hearings, House Committee on Un-American Activities*, 79th Congress, 2nd sess., 1946, Washington

———. *Investigation of Un-American Propaganda Activities in the United States. Executive Board Joint Anti-Fascist Refugee Committee*, Washington

———. *Report No. 1936—Proceedings Against the Joint Anti-Fascist Refugee Committee*, Washington

U.S. Congress, Senate. *Executive Sessions of the Senate before the Permanent Subcommittee on Investigations of the Committee on Government Operations*, 83rd Congress, 1st sess., 1953, Washington

———. *Hearings before the Permanent Subcommittee on Investigations of the Committee on Government Operations*, 83rd Congress, 1st sess., 1953, Washington

———. *Hearings before the Subcommittee to Investigate the Administration of the Internal Security Act and Other Internal Security Laws. Subversive Influence in the Educational Process*, 82nd Congress, 2nd sess., 1952, Washington

United States v. Barsky, 72 F. Supp. 165 (1947)

United States v. Bryan, 339 U.S. 323 (1950)

Newspapers and Periodicals

ALA Bulletin
American Prospect
Catholic News
Chicago Daily Tribune
Christian Science Monitor
Commentary
Commonweal
Counterattack
Daily Compass
Daily Telegraph and Morning Post
Daily Worker (London)
Daily Worker (New York)
Education Sun
Evening News
For a Lasting Peace, for a People's Democracy!
Fortune

Forward
Harper's Magazine
Hartford Times
Heights Daily News
I. F. Stone's Weekly
Journal of the Board of Education of the City of New York
Labour Monthly
Lawyers' Guild Review
Liberator
Life
Los Angeles Times
Mainstream
Masses & Mainstream
Militant
The Nation
National Guardian
The New Leader
New Masses
New Republic
New Times
New York Daily News
New York Herald Tribune
New York Post
New York Times
New York Times-Herald
New York Times Magazine
New York World Telegram & Sun
New Yorker
Newsweek
NYU Commerce Bulletin
PM
Political Affairs
The Progressive
Publishers Weekly
Saturday Evening Post
Science & Society
Sheffield Telegraph
Square Bulletin
Tablet
The Times (London)
U.S. News and World Report
Wall Street Journal
Washington Evening Star

Washington Post
Washington Times Herald
World Telegram

Books and Articles

Aaron, Daniel. *Writers on the Left: Episodes in American Literary Communism* (New York: Harcourt, Brace & World, 1961).

Abella, Irving. "Portrait of a Jewish Professional Revolutionary: The Recollections of Joshua Gershman," *Labour / Le Travail: Journal of Canadian Labour Studies* 2 (1977).

Aldrich, Richard J. *British Intelligence, Strategy and the Cold War, 1945–51* (London: Routledge, 1992).

American Business Consultants, Inc. *Red Channels: The Report of Communist Influence in Radio and Television* (New York: Counterattack, 1950).

American Russian Institute. *Americans, Russians and Peace* (San Francisco, 1949).

America's "Thought Police": Record of the Un-American Activities Committee (New York: Civil Rights Congress, 1947).

Anthony, David H. *Max Yergan: Race Man, Internationalist, Cold Warrior* (New York: New York University Press, 2006).

Applebaum, Anne. *Iron Curtain: The Crushing of Eastern Europe 1944–1956* (New York: Doubleday, 2012).

Ardov, Michael. *Memories of Shostakovich: Interviews with the Composer's Children* (London: Short Books, 2004).

Barrett, James R. *William Z. Foster and the Tragedy of American Radicalism* (Urbana: University of Illinois Press, 1999).

Beck, Carl. *Contempt of Congress: A Study of the Prosecutions Initiated by the Committee on Un-American Activities, 1945–1957* (New York: Da Capo Press, 1974).

Belfrage, Cedric. *The American Inquisition, 1945–1960: A Profile of the "McCarthy Era"* (New York: Thunder's Mouth Press, 1989).

Belknap, Michael. *Cold War Political Justice: The Smith Act, the Communist Party, and American Civil Liberties* (Westport, Conn.: Greenwood, 1977).

Ben-Avi Fast, Rachel. "A Memoir," in Judy Kaplan and Linn Shapiro (eds.), *Red Diapers: Growing Up in the Communist Left* (Urbana and Chicago: University of Illinois Press, 1998).

Bentley, Eric. *Thirty Years of Treason: Excerpts from Hearings before the House Committee on Un-American Activities, 1938–1968* (New York: Viking, 1971).

Blauner, Bob. *Resisting McCarthyism: To Sign or Not to Sign California's Loyalty Oath* (Stanford, Calif.: Stanford University Press, 2009).

Boterbloem, Kees. *The Life and Times of Andrei Zhdanov* (Montreal: McGill-Queen's University, 2004).

Brightman, Carol. *Writing Dangerously: Mary McCarthy and Her World* (London: Lime Tree, 1993).

Brown, Deming. *Soviet Attitudes Toward American Writing* (Princeton, N.J.: Princeton University Press, 1962).

Brown, Michael E. (et al.). *New Studies in the Politics and Culture of U.S. Communism* (New York: Monthly Review Press, 1993).

Bryan, Helen. *Inside* (Boston: Houghton Mifflin, 1953).

Buckley, William F., Jr. (ed). *The Committee and Its Critics* (New York: Putnam, 1962).

Budenz, Louis Francis. *Men Without Faces: The Communist Conspiracy in the USA* (New York: Harper & Bros., 1948).

Buhle, Mari Jo (et al.). *Encyclopedia of the American Left* (New York: Oxford University Press, 1998).

Carroll, Peter N. *The Odyssey of the Abraham Lincoln Brigade: Americans in the Spanish Civil War* (Stanford, Calif.: Stanford University Press, 1994).

Carroll Peter N., and James D. Fernandez (eds.). *Facing Fascism: New York and the Spanish Civil War* (New York: Museum of the City of New York and New York University Press, 2007).

Caute, David. *The Dancer Defects: The Struggle for Cultural Supremacy during the Cold War* (Oxford: Oxford University Press, 2003).

———. *Fellow-Travellers: A Postscript to the Enlightenment* (New York: Macmillan, 1973).

———. *The Great Fear: The Anti-Communist Purge Under Truman and Eisenhower* (New York: Simon & Schuster, 1978).

Charney, George. *A Long Journey* (Chicago: Quadrangle, 1968).

Cohn, Roy M., and Sidney Zion. *The Autobiography of Roy Cohn* (Secaucus, N.J.: Lyle Stuart, 1988).

Coleman, Peter. *The Liberal Conspiracy: The Congress for Cultural Freedom and the Struggle for the Mind of Postwar Europe* (New York: Free Press, 1989).

Commager, Henry Steele. "Who Is Loyal to America?," *Harper's Magazine*, 9 September 1947.

Crossman, Richard (ed.). *The God That Failed: Six Studies in Communism* (London: Hamilton, 1949).

Deery, Phillip. "The Dove Flies East: Whitehall, Warsaw and the 1950 World Peace Congress," *Australian Journal of Politics & History* 48:4 (December 2002), 449–68.

Dennis, Peggy. *The Autobiography of an American Communist* (Westport/Berkeley: L. Hill, 1977).

Dittmer, John. *The Good Doctors: The Medical Committee for Human Rights and the Struggle for Social Justice in Health Care* (London: Bloomsbury, 2009).

Djagalov, Rossen. "'I Don't Boast About It, but I'm the Most Widely Read Author of This Century': Howard Fast and International Leftist Literary Culture, ca. Mid–Twentieth Century," *Anthropology of East Europe Review* 27:2 (Fall 2009).

Djilas, Milovan. *The New Class: An Analysis of the Communist System* (New York: Praeger, 1957).

Du Bois, W. E. B. *In Battle for Peace: The Story of My 83rd Birthday* (New York: Masses & Mainstream, 1952).

Duberman, Martin. *Paul Robeson: A Biography* (New York: Knopf, 1998).

Dudley, E. Samuel. "Warfare at the Waldorf," *Today's Speech* 11:4 (1963).

Estraikh, Gennady, and Mikhail Krutikov (eds.). *Yiddish and the Left* (Oxford: Legenda, 2001).

Faber, Sebastiaan. *Exile and Cultural Hegemony: Spanish Intellectuals in Mexico, 1939–1975* (Nashville: Vanderbilt University Press, 2002).

Fariello, Griffen. *Red Scare. Memories of the American Inquisition: An Oral History* (New York: Norton, 1995).

Fast, Howard. *Being Red: A Memoir* (Boston: Houghton Mifflin, 1990).

———. *Citizen Tom Paine* (New York: Duell, Sloan & Pearce, 1943).

———. *Literature and Reality* (New York: International Publishers, 1950).

———. *The Naked God: The Writer and the Communist Party* (New York: Praeger, 1957).

———. "On Leaving the Communist Party," *The Saturday Review*, 16 November 1957.

———. *Peekskill: USA* (New York: Civil Rights Congress, 1951).

———. "The Writer and the Commissar," *Prospectus* 1:1 (1957).

Fay, Laurel E. *Shostakovich: A Life* (Oxford: Oxford University Press, 2000).

Feklisov, Alexander, and Sergei Kostin. *The Man Behind the Rosenbergs* (New York: Enigma Books, 2001).

Field, Hermann and Kate. *Trapped in the Cold War. The Ordeal of an American Family* (Stanford, Calif.: Stanford University Press, 1999).

Frusciano, Thomas T., and Marilyn H. Pettit. *New York University and the City* (New Brunswick, N.J.: Rutgers University Press, 1997).

Gates, John. *The Story of an American Communist* (New York: Nelson, 1958).

Gillmor, Daniel S. *Speaking of Peace* (New York: National Council of the Arts, Sciences and Professions, 1949).

Gilmore, Glenda Elizabeth. *Defying Dixie: The Radical Roots of Civil Rights, 1919–1950* (New York: Norton, 2008).

Goldstein, Robert Justin. *American Blacklist: The Attorney General's List of Subversive Organizations* (Lawrence: University Press of Kansas, 2008).

———. *Political Repression in Modern America* (Cambridge, Mass.: Schenkman, 1978).

Gornick, Vivian. *The Romance of American Communism* (New York: Basic Books, 1977).

Grossman, Vasily. *Everything Flows* (London: Vintage Books, 2011).

Haight, Lyon. *Banned Books: Informal Notes on Some Books Banned for Various Reasons at Various Times and in Various Places* (New York: Bowker, 1955).

Haynes, John E. *Red Scare or Red Menace? American Communism and Anticommunism in the Cold War Era* (Chicago: Ivan R. Dee, 1996).

Healey, Denis. *The Time of My Life* (London: Michael Joseph, 1989).

Healey, Dorothy, and Maurice Isserman. *Dorothy Healey Remembers* (New York: Oxford University Press, 1990).

Hellman, Lillian. *Scoundrel Time* (London: Macmillan, 1976).

Ho, Allan B., and Dmitry Feofanov (eds.). *Shostakovich Reconsidered* (London: Toccata Press, 1998).

Hoberman, J. *The Dream Life: Movies, Media, and the Mythology of the Sixties* (New York: New Press, 2003).

Hofstadter, Samuel H. *The Fifth Amendment and the Immunity Act of 1954: Aspects of the American Way* (New York, 1955).

Hook, Sidney. *Out of Step: An Unquiet Life in the 20th Century* (New York: Harper & Row, 1987).

Horne, Gerald. *Black and Red: W. E. B. Du Bois and the Afro-American Response to the Cold War, 1944–1963* (Albany: State University of New York Press, 1986).

Howe, Irving. *A Margin of Hope: An Intellectual Autobiography* (San Diego: Harcourt Brace Jovanovich, 1982).

Huxley, Julian. *Soviet Genetics and World Science* (London: Chatto & Windus, 1949).

Isserman, Maurice. *Which Side Were You On? The American Communist Party During the Second World War* (Middletown, Conn.: Wesleyan University Press, 1982).

Jacobsen, Eric. *Translation: A Traditional Craft* (Copenhagen: Gyldendalske Boghandel, 1958).

Jeffries-Jones, Rhodri. *The FBI: A History* (New Haven, Conn.: Yale University Press, 2007).

Johanningsmeier, Edward. *Forging American Communism: The Life of William Z. Foster* (Princeton, N.J.: Princeton University Press, 1994).

Jumonville, Neil. *Critical Crossings: The New York Intellectuals in Postwar America* (Berkeley: University of California Press, 1991).

Kane, Harnett T. *Louisiana Hayride: The American Rehearsal for Dictatorship, 1928–1940* (New York: Morrow, 1941).

Kanfer, Stefan. *A Journal of the Plague Years* (New York: Atheneum, 1973).

Kempton, Murray. *Part of Our Time: Some Ruins and Monuments of the Thirties* (New York: Simon & Schuster, 1955).

Kessler-Harris, Alice. *A Difficult Woman: The Challenging Life and Times of Lillian Hellman* (New York: Bloomsbury, 2012).

Kramer, Hilton. *The Twilight of the Intellectual: Culture and Politics in the Era of the Cold War* (Chicago: Ivan R. Dee, 1999).

Krugler, David F. *The Voice of America and the Domestic Propaganda Battles, 1945–1953* (Columbia: University of Missouri Press, 2000).

Larner, Jeremy. "Remembering Irving Howe," *Dissent* 40 (Fall 1993).

Laski, Harold J. *The Secret Battalion: An Examination of the Communist Attitude to the Labour Party* (London: 1946).

Leab, Daniel J. *I Was a Communist for the FBI: The Unhappy Life and Times of Matt Cvetic* (University Park: Pennsylvania State University Press, 2000).

Lesser, Wendy. *Music for Silenced Voices: Shostakovich and His Fifteen Quartets* (New Haven, Conn.: Yale University Press, 2011).

Levin, Harry. "The Private Life of F. O. Matthiessen," *New York Review of Books*, 20 July 1978.

Lewy, Guenter. *The Cause That Failed: Communism in American Political Life* (New York: Oxford University Press, 1990).

Lichtman, Robert M., and Ronald D. Cohen. *Deadly Farce: Harvey Matusow and the Informer System in the McCarthy Era* (Urbana and Chicago: University of Illinois Press, 2004).

Lieberman, Robbie. "'Does that make peace a bad word?': American Responses to the Communist Peace Offensive, 1949–1950," *Peace & Change* 17:2 (April 1992).

———. *The Strangest Dream: Communism, Anti-Communism, and the United States Peace Movement, 1945–1963* (Syracuse, N.Y.: Syracuse University Press, 2000).

Lucas, Scott. *Freedom's War: The American Crusade Against the Soviet Union* (New York: New York University Press, 1999).

Macdonald, Andrew. *Howard Fast: A Critical Companion* (Westport, Conn.: Greenwood Press, 1996).

Macdonald, Dwight. "The Waldorf Conference," *Horizon* 19:113 (May 1949).

McNamara, Patrick. *A Catholic Cold War: Edmund Walsh, S.J., and the Politics of American Anticommunism* (New York: Fordham University Press, 2005).

Medvedev, Zhores A., and Roy A. Medvedev. *The Unknown Stalin* (London: J. B. Tauris, 2006).

Meyer, Gerald. *Vito Marcantonio: Radical Politician, 1902–1954* (Albany: State University of New York Press, 1989).

Meyer, Hershel D. *History and Conscience: The Case of Howard Fast* (New York: Anvil-Atlas, 1958).

Miller, Arthur. *Timebends: A Life* (London: Minerva, 1990).

———. "The Year It Came Apart," *New York* 30 December 1974–6 January 1975.

Morton, Brian. *Shostakovich: His Life and Music* (London: Haus Books, 2006).

Moshevich, Sofia. *Dmitri Shostakovich, Pianist* (Montreal and Kingston: McGill-Queen's University Press, 2004).

Nabokov, Nicolas. *Bagázh: Memoirs of a Russian Cosmopolitan* (New York: Atheneum, 1975).

———. *Old Friends and New Music* (London: Hamish Hamilton, 1951).

Nelson, Steve, James R. Barrett, and Rob Ruck. *Steve Nelson: American Radical* (Pittsburgh: University of Pittsburgh Press, 1981).

Neugass, James. *War Is Beautiful: An American Ambulance Driver in the Spanish Civil War* (New York: New Press, 2008).

Ninkovich, Frank A. *The Diplomacy of Ideas: U.S. Foreign Policy and Cultural Relations, 1938–1950* (Cambridge: Cambridge University Press, 1981).

O'Neill, William L. *A Better World. The Great Schism: Stalinism and the Intellectuals* (New York: Simon & Schuster, 1983).

O'Reilly, Kenneth. *Hoover and the Un-Americans: The FBI, HUAC, and the Red Menace* (Philadelphia: Temple University Press, 1983).

Ortega, Tony. "Red Scare at Harvard," *Astronomy* 30:1 (2002).

Philbrick, Herbert Arthur. *I Led Three Lives: Citizen, "Communist," Counterspy* (New York: McGraw-Hill, 1952).

Phillips, William. *A Partisan View* (New York: Stein & Day, 1983).

Pinkus, Benjamin, and Jonathan Frankel. *The Soviet Government and the Jews, 1948–1967: A Documented Study* (New York: Cambridge University Press, 1984).

Potts, Archie. *Zilliacus: A Life for Peace and Socialism* (London: Merlin, 2002).

Powers, Richard Gid. *Not Without Honor: The History of American Anticommunism* (New York: The Free Press, 1995).

Preston, Paul. *The Spanish Civil War, 1936–39* (London: Weidenfeld & Nicolson, 1986).

Preston, William. *Aliens and Dissenters: Federal Suppression of Radicals, 1903–1933* (Chicago: University of Illinois Press, 1995).

Preuss, Lawrence. "Consular Immunities: The Kasenkina Case." *American Journal of International Law* 43:1 (1949).

Rabinowitz, Victor. *Unrepentant Leftist: A Lawyer's Memoir* (Urbana: University of Illinois Press, 1996).

Radosh, Ronald, and Joyce Milton. *The Rosenberg File* (New Haven, Conn.: Yale University Press, 1997, 2nd ed.).

Richmond, Al. *A Long View from the Left: Memoirs of an American Revolutionary* (Boston: Houghton Mifflin, 1973).

Roberts, Sam. *The Brother. The Untold Story of Atomic Spy David Greenglass and How He Sent His Sister, Ethel Rosenberg, to the Electric Chair* (New York: Random House, 2001).

Robins, Natalie. *Alien Ink: The FBI's War on Freedom of Expression* (New York: Morrow, 1992).

Rodden, John, and Ethan Goffman (eds.). *Politics and the Intellectual: Conversations with Irving Howe* (West Lafayette, Ind.: Purdue University Press, 2010).

Rogge, O. John. *The Official German Report: Nazi Penetration, 1924–1942* (New York: Thomas Yoseloff, 1961).

———. *Our Vanishing Civil Liberties* (New York: Gaer, 1949).

———. *Why Men Confess* (New York: Thomas Nelson & Sons, 1959).

Romerstein, Herbert, and Stanislav Levchenko. *The KGB Against the "Main Enemy": How the Soviet Intelligence Service Operates against the United States* (Lexington and Toronto: Lexington Books, 1989).

Rothstein, Edward. "What Shostakovich Was Really Expressing," *New York Times Sunday Book Review*, 8 May 2011.

Rubenstein, Joshua. *Tangled Loyalties: The Life and Times of Ilya Ehrenburg* (New York: New Press, 1996).

Salmond, John A. *The Conscience of a Lawyer: Clifford J. Durr and American Civil Liberties, 1899–1975* (Tuscaloosa: University of Alabama Press, 1990).

Salzman, Jack. *Albert Maltz* (Boston: Twayne, 1978).

Schaffer, Alan. *Vito Marcantonio, Radical in Congress* (Syracuse, N.Y.: Syracuse University Press, 1966).

Schlesinger, Arthur, Jr. *The Vital Center: The Politics of Freedom* (Boston: Houghton Mifflin, 1962 ed.).

Schmidt, Karl M. *Henry A. Wallace: Quixotic Crusade 1948* (Syracuse, N.Y.: Syracuse University Press, 1960).

Schrecker, Ellen. "Immigration and Internal Security: Political Deportations During the McCarthy Era," *Science & Society* 60: 393 (1997).

———. *Many Are the Crimes: McCarthyism in America* (Boston: Little, Brown, 1998).

———. *No Ivory Tower: McCarthyism and the Universities* (New York: Oxford University Press, 1986).

Scott-Smith, Giles. *The Politics of Apolitical Culture: The Congress for Cultural Freedom, the CIA and Post-war American Hegemony* (London: Routledge, 2002).

Shannon, David. *The Decline of American Communism: A History of the Communist Party of the United States since 1945* (New York: Harcourt, Brace, 1959).

Shapiro, Edward S. (ed). *Letters of Sidney Hook: Democracy, Communism and the Cold War* (New York: M. E. Sharpe, 1995).

Shields, Art. *On the Battle Lines, 1919–1939* (New York: International Publishers, 1986).

Shostakovich, Dimitri. *Testimony: The Memoirs of Dimitri Shostakovich as Related to and edited by Solomon Volkov* (London: Hamish Hamilton, 1979).

Singer, Henry A. "An analysis of the New York press treatment of the Peace Conference at the Waldorf-Astoria," *Journal of Educational Sociology* 23:5 (1950).

Snyder, Timothy. *Bloodlands: Europe Between Hitler and Stalin* (New York: Basic Books, 2010).

Sorin, Gerald. *Howard Fast: Life and Literature in the Left Lane* (Bloomington: Indiana University Press, 2012).

Spalding, Elizabeth Edwards. *The First Cold Warrior: Harry Truman, Containment, and the Remaking of Liberal Internationalism* (Lexington: University Press of Kentucky, 2006).

Starobin, Joseph R. *American Communism in Crisis, 1943–1957* (Cambridge, Mass.: Harvard University Press, 1972).

Steinberg, Peter. *The Great "Red Menace": United States Prosecution of American Communists, 1947–1952* (Westport, Conn.: Greenwood Press, 1984).

Stoner Saunders, Frances. *Who Paid the Piper? The CIA and the Cultural Cold War* (London: Granta, 1999).

Stripling, Robert. *The Red Plot Against America* (Drexel Hill, Pa.: Bell, 1949).

Sussman, Peter Y. (ed). *Decca: The Letters of Jessica Mitford* (London: Weidenfeld & Nicholson, 2006).

Taylor, Clarence. *Reds at the Blackboard: Communism, Civil Rights, and the New York City Teachers Union* (New York: Columbia University Press, 2011).

Theoharis, Athan. *Chasing Spies* (Chicago: Ivan R. Dee, 2002).

Traister, Daniel. "Noticing Howard Fast," *Prospects: An Annual of American Cultural Studies* 20 (1995).

Vaksberg, Arkady. *Stalin Against the Jews* (New York: Knopf, 1994).

Volkov, Solomon. *Shostakovich and Stalin: The Extraordinary Relationship between the Great Composer and the Brutal Dictator* (London: Little, Brown, 2004).

Wald, Alan M. *Exiles from a Future Time: The Forging of the Mid-Twentieth-Century Literary Left* (Chapel Hill: University of North Carolina Press, 2002).

———. *The New York Intellectuals: The Rise and Decline of the Anti-Stalinist Left from the 1930s to the 1980s* (Chapel Hill and London: University of North Carolina Press, 1987).

Wald, Alan, and Alan Filreis. "A Conversation with Howard Fast, March 23, 1994," *Prospects: An Annual of American Cultural Studies* 20 (1995).

Walker, Samuel. *In Defense of American Liberties: A History of the ACLU* (New York: Oxford University Press, 1990).

Walton, Richard J. *Wallace, Harry Truman, and the Cold War* (New York: Viking, 1976).

Walzer, Michael. "The Travail of the U.S. Communists," *Dissent* 3:4 (Fall 1956).

Warner, Michael. "Origins of the Congress for Cultural Freedom, 1949–50," *Studies in Intelligence* 38:5 (1995).

Weiner, Tim. *Enemies: A History of the FBI* (New York: Random House, 2012).

Werth, Alexander. *Musical Uproar in Moscow* (London: Turnstile Press, 1949).

Whitfield, Stephen J. *The Culture of the Cold War* (Baltimore: Johns Hopkins University Press, 1996).

Wilford, Hugh. *The Mighty Wurlitzer: How the CIA Played America* (Cambridge, Mass.: Harvard University Press, 2008).

Wilson, Elizabeth. *Shostakovich: A Life Remembered* (London: Faber & Faber, 1994).

Wittner, Lawrence S. *One World or None: A History of the World Nuclear Disarmament Movement Through 1953* (Stanford, Calif.: Stanford University Press, 1993).

Wolters, Raymond. *Du Bois and His Rivals* (Columbia: University of Missouri Press, 2002).

Wreszin, Michael. "Arthur Schlesinger, Jr., Scholar-Activist in Cold War America: 1946–1956," *Salmagundi* 63/64 (Spring/Summer 1984).

———. *A Rebel in Defense of Tradition: The Life and Politics of Dwight Macdonald* (New York: Basic Books, 1994).

Index